The Digital God

ALSO BY WILLIAM INDICK
AND MCFARLAND

*Ancient Symbology in Fantasy Literature:
A Psychological Study* (2012)

*The Psychology of the Western: How the
American Psyche Plays Out on Screen* (2008)

*Psycho Thrillers: Cinematic Explorations of the
Mysteries of the Mind* (2006)

*Movies and the Mind: Theories of the
Great Psychoanalysts Applied to Film* (2004)

The Digital God

How Technology Will Reshape Spirituality

WILLIAM INDICK

McFarland & Company, Inc., Publishers
Jefferson, North Carolina

LIBRARY OF CONGRESS CATALOGUING-IN-PUBLICATION DATA

Indick, William, 1971–
 The digital God : how technology will reshape spirituality / William Indick.
     p. cm.
 Includes bibliographical references and index.

 ISBN 978-0-7864-9892-5 (softcover : acid free paper) ∞
 ISBN 978-1-4766-2012-1 (ebook)

 1. Technology—Religious aspects. 2. Spirituality. I. Title.
BL265.T4I53 2015
204.0285—dc23   2015003858

BRITISH LIBRARY CATALOGUING DATA ARE AVAILABLE

© 2015 William Indick. All rights reserved

No part of this book may be reproduced or transmitted in any form or by any means, electronic or mechanical, including photocopying or recording, or by any information storage and retrieval system, without permission in writing from the publisher.

Cover image © 2015 Blend Images

Printed in the United States of America

*McFarland & Company, Inc., Publishers
   Box 611, Jefferson, North Carolina 28640
       www.mcfarlandpub.com*

For my mother with love

Table of Contents

Introduction   1

One: The Digital Dream   9

Two: The Neuropsychology of Spiritual Perception and Digital Zen   37

Three: The Stages of Spiritual Perception and Digital Nirvana   79

Four: The History of Spiritual Perception and the Digital Idol   111

Five: The Psychology of Spiritual Perception and the Digital Peak   159

Six: The Philosophy of Spiritual Perception and Spiritual Networking   178

Conclusion: The God Machine   214

Chapter Notes   219

Bibliography   241

Index   245

Introduction

> There are more things in heaven and earth, Horatio, than are dreamt of in your philosophy.—*Hamlet* (Act I, Scene 5)

On the rainy evening of August 21, 1879, in County Mayo, Ireland, Mary McLoughlin and Mary Beine, from the village of Knock, walked by the town church on their way home. To their surprise, they saw a vision on the church wall of the Virgin Mary, St. Joseph, and St. John. They were standing beside an altar. A lamb and a cross were on the altar, and several angels hovered above the lamb. As they gazed at the vision for about two hours, standing in the pouring rain, 13 other villagers joined them, and they all claimed to see the vision as well. In time, the Marian Apparition at Knock received official acknowledgment from the Catholic Church. A shrine was built on the site of the apparition, which has been visited by millions of pilgrims.

What exactly happened in Knock? We will never know. However, we can be fairly certain that the two women named Mary and their fellow villagers saw *something*, and what they believed they saw was, in fact, the Virgin Mary, two saints, angels, an altar, a lamb, and a cross. Whether or not this vision was objective or subjective will never be known. However, if we ask the question—"Was the vision real?"—the answer, incontrovertibly, is "Yes." People see what they see, and their visions are always real to them, because at the neurological level, all perception is a combination of belief, expectation, memory, imagination, intuition, and also a bit of visual sensory input. If I happened to be walking by the church in Knock on that very night, and if I looked at the wall and saw only shadows and reflections, the images that I beheld in my mind would be no more or less real than the image of Mary and the angels and saints beheld in the minds of the Knock villagers. At the electrochemical level of neurons firing in the brain, there would be no difference between a perception based primarily on visual sensory input, or a perception based primarily on expectation and belief.

At the neuronal level, both perceptions are equally real, although only one of the perceptions would be considered "spiritual." This book will explore the phenomenon of spiritual perception—the experience of perceiving with one's senses something that is believed to be otherworldly, supernatural, or divine. The experience of spiritual perception is completely real, at least within the mind of the beholder, which is where all reality is perceived anyway. However, there is an extremely important rub. If perception is largely shaped by belief, how can someone perceive spirits, or angels, or Mary, or God, if he doesn't believe in their existence? Belief appears to be a prerequisite for spiritual perception. Religion, unfortunately, forces us to confront a paradox....

The "paradox of faith" is the dilemma that any reasonable individual faces when he thinks about God. Why should I believe in God, when there is absolutely no objective empirical evidence to prove his existence? Whereas faith is belief without the presence of proof, the contemporary educated individual has been taught to seek for objective evidence before he believes in the existence of anything. This is the paradox: Faith requires belief without proof, while rational thought requires proof before belief. So what are we to do? The problem of faith has been with me my entire life. I attended a very traditional parochial school from preschool through high school. When I was very young, before the age when I could reasonably question what was taught to me by my elders, I believed completely in God. But at a relatively early age, around 6 or 7 years old, I began to question the validity of my own faith and the existence of God. I have vivid memories of standing in my place of worship during prayer time, closing my eyes and praying fervently ... hoping, begging, pleading to hear something, see something, feel something—*anything*—that could establish and affirm a true and undoubting belief in the existence of God. Others around me seemed to have it. Why couldn't I? What was *wrong* with me? Why was God avoiding me? Or was it that there was no God in the first place? There had to be a solution to my nascent sense of spiritual envy ... a cure for my religious anxiety.

As I grew into adolescence, the question of my religious identity gnawed away inside of me. Some atheists I spoke to seemed to think that true believers in God were stupid. After all, why would an intelligent, rational, discerning individual believe in the existence of a being in the light of no objective evidence? Such a person would have to be either naïve, gullible, or ignorant! This opinion seems to be behind Freud's opinion of religion—that it is an "illusion"—and Richard Dawkins' similar attitude—that it is a "delusion." While I felt myself veering towards atheism, I was disinclined towards a derisive opinion of believers from a very early age. My best friend, for example, was not only the smartest kid in my class, but the smartest person I ever met, and he was a true believer. When we were very young—we couldn't have been more than 10 years old—I admitted to him that I was struggling with my faith, and I asked him about his. He told me without hesitating that faith was not something that could be taught, nor was it something that you could force yourself or anyone to have, nor could someone convince himself intellectually to acquire it. You either had it or you didn't, and it had nothing to do with how clever you were. My friend's thoughts on the matter seemed very true to me then, and they have stayed with me until this day. For one thing, what he said was extremely different from what my teachers were preaching. They insisted that the key to faith was to be found in a devout dedication to the rituals, prayers, and orthodox studies of religion. Any omission of these rituals, prayers, and studies displayed a lack of dedication to one's faith, and therefore a personal lacking in one's own spiritual identity. Essentially, what they were saying was that my lack of spiritual feeling was my own fault—I was spiritually lazy—I wasn't trying hard enough. My friend's explanation of faith made more sense to me, and it also helped to relieve me of the tremendous burden of guilt that I had been carrying on my narrow shoulders. If faith came from within and couldn't be forced through ritual, study, and prayer, then it wasn't my fault that I didn't have faith. I wasn't a heathen or a bad person, I simply lacked the attribute of faith that some people have and some people don't.

Furthermore, since my friend was far smarter than me or anyone else I knew, faith, clearly, had nothing to do with intelligence. One benefit to attending a religious school for 14 years was that I was exposed to the literary works of some of the most brilliant scholars who ever lived. By means of a thorough and deliberate study of Torah and Talmud scholars such as Rabbi Shlomo Titzchaki (Rashi), Rabbi Moshe ben Maimon (Maimonides), and Rabbi Hillel, I realized that these men were so brilliant that I could never, in my entire life, accomplish even a fraction of the intellectual greatness that they achieved. I had similar experiences as I grew older and read the works of great philosophers such as Søren Kierkegaard, Thomas Aquinas, and Martin Buber. All of these scholars were light-years ahead of me in their intellectual capacities, yet they were all true believers, each and every one. Even Albert Einstein believed in God! So while the true nature and origin of faith remained a mystery to me, there was one thing I did know for sure.... Belief and intelligence were not intrinsically linked to one another. Yet, the solution to the mystery of faith must lay *somewhere* in the mind. In retrospect, I see that my fascination with this subject guided me into the field of psychology, which I've been studying for nearly 25 years, as a student at New York University and Cornell University, and as a professor of psychology at Dowling College.[1]

Anthropologists who have studied preliterate societies have noted that these people generally do not have a word in their vocabulary that is equivalent to the word "faith." Though they have names for all the spirits around them, they have no word that indicates the belief or disbelief in these spirits, because such a word is not only unnecessary, it's incomprehensible. To have the word "faith" presupposes the notion that one could either have faith or not have faith. To the preliterate people living amongst the spirits, faith as a concept is not needed, because the existence of the spirits is self-evident. They are perceived constantly and continuously. They are a part of life just as the wind and the rain and other people are a part of life. The existence of spirits would not be called into question, just as you wouldn't call into question the existence of the wind or the rain or other people. True spiritual perception, experiencing spirits or gods or God on a sensory-emotional level, negates the need for faith. The only people who need faith in God are the people who need a *reason* to believe in God, because they do not perceive God. Religion based on faith, however, is on shaky ground, because a person can always lose his faith. Religion based on perception, on the other hand, is grounded in much firmer soil. My focus in this book will not be on the abstract concept of faith, but on the sensory-emotional experience of spiritual perception—a religious phenomenon that is exponentially more powerful than faith.

Spiritual perception has always been an elusive topic, because it is a qualia—a subjective experience that can be felt but not properly described. For example, if you were colorblind, I could try to explain to you the experience of the color blue, and I could use scientific descriptions of light spectrums to demonstrate my point; but in the end, the essential quality of blueness—the essence of what it means to experience the color blue—would be lost on you. Blueness cannot be explained rationally, nor could it be experienced in any qualitatively similar way by someone who is colorblind. However, while some people cannot see blue, there are few people who would deny the existence of blue, just because they cannot see it. Perhaps God is akin to a qualia. In the end, the god experienced by the believer is always a subjective, personal god, a sensed presence of an "other" being who is felt viscerally, but never completely understood. While I do not believe, I believe that other people believe, and I believe that their belief is not just an illusion or a delusion, but a belief based on real experience ... real perception. If you have experienced God and felt him, then faith is unnecessary for you. But for those of us, like me, who have not or cannot, despite their greatest efforts, perceive God—for the spiritually blind—their only recourses are faith, or hope.

We live in a technological society that is perpetually advancing. We're always at the crest of this wave of advancing technology, always experiencing new inventions that provide new and unique ways of perceiving our environment. At the moment, technology is advancing at an unprecedented rate. We literally cannot tell what will happen at any given moment, given the rate and velocity of technological innovation in the Digital Age. In the past, we've seen immense leaps forward in our technological capability of improving vision for the visually impaired and hearing for the hearing impaired. Digital media, with its ability to engage multiple modes of perception with instantaneous, interactive, and individualized streams of high density stimulation, has the power to enhance and create direct sensory perceptual experiences. In the near future, we will be able to make virtual spectacles for the spiritually blind. In effect, these spectacles will make faith or belief unnecessary, as you do not need to have faith in what you can directly perceive.

In my life, I have developed from a true believer as a child, to an atheist as an adolescent, and now, as an adult, to an agnostic. I gave up my atheism because I didn't have the intellectual confidence to state quite decisively: "I know that there is nothing." It seemed to me to be as definitive a statement as the true believer's: "I know that there is something." Both statements declare knowledge, and both are based on a sort of faith: the latter based on a faith in God, the former based on a faith in Science and Reason. I'm comfortable in my agnosticism. I'm ok with admitting that in terms of the nature of the universe, and even in terms of the nature of my own existence, I know very little—almost nothing. I embrace the mystery. Yet, at the same time, I am searching—just as I was searching when I was a little child—when I would say my prayers, close my eyes, and reach out into the darkness for something that I hoped would be there. Maybe, one day, something *will* be there. Who knows? If, as I suggest in this book, spiritual perception is a way of seeing that exists, potentially, in all of us, then being an agnostic means that I'm leaving the door of spiritual perception open, or at least ajar. After all, it's quite likely that there are dimensions that exist in our universe that we are not aware of, because our minds are simply not equipped to do so. Cognitive psychologists call this inability "cognitive constraint." A classic example of this constraint is found in Edwin Abbot's 19th-century satire, *Flatland*, about a world in which everybody and everything is purely two-dimensional. In Flatland, there is width and depth, but no height. Everybody and everything is perfectly flat. One day, an inhabitant of Flatland named Square is visited by a traveler named Sphere, who comes from the three-dimensional world of Spaceland. Square visits Spaceland and is astounded to see a world with three dimensions. However, when he returns to Flatland, nobody believes him, because nobody *can* believe him. They simply cannot conceive of a dimension of existence that goes beyond anything they've ever experienced or perceived. Only Square can understand the third dimension, because he had a transcendent experience within that dimension. And so we're left wondering if there's a fourth dimension to our existence. If so, what would it be like? Is it possible that spiritual perception is not just an illusion or a delusion, but a glimpse of a dimension of existence that is for the most part invisible to us, because of our cognitive constraints? This underlying question is a thread of inquiry that will run throughout this book.

Beginning in the late 1950s, linguists such as Noam Chomsky began to prove that the human mind is "hardwired" to acquire and process verbal language. While their theories were at first considered radical, they are now accepted as fact, and can be demonstrated using neurological tools that can actually observe the brain as it functions. Today, some neurologists argue that the brain is hardwired to acquire and process sensory experiences of a spiritual nature. This radical new field is called "neurotheology," and it can help explain why some people's brains are more open to spiritual experiences than other people's brains. When we speak of the direct sensory experience of a god or spirit, we enter the realm of "mysticism," an area that is not as peculiar or esoteric as one might think. Recent survey data shows that more than ⅓ of the people polled in America and Britain have experienced "mystical phenomena," such as having the "feeling of being close to a powerful, spiritual force that seemed to lift you out of yourself?"[2] When religious people are polled, the vast majority believe that when they are praying, God actually hears their prayers. A smaller proportion report that they have at one point or another heard or sensed the presence of God in response to their prayers.[3] Studies conducted all over the world indicate clearly that spiritual perception is a normative phenomenon. But if this is the case, why are there so many people who never experience spiritual perception?

Although we are hard-wired for language, not every human being speaks. Babies don't speak because they haven't developed language skills yet. If that baby is never exposed to language, it will grow up to be an adult who will never speak. Some monks choose not to speak. Mute people cannot speak because of a physical disability, selectively mute people cannot speak because of a psychological disability, and many autistics cannot speak because of a neuropsychological disability. So, people who cannot experience spiritual perception may, in a sense, be "spiritually disabled." Indeed, many spiritually disabled people may want to believe, but their brains are inhibited from perceiving the spiritual realm. Without this sense, they cannot accomplish the leap of faith that is required to believe. And, without belief, perceptions that could be spiritual are not perceived as being spiritual, because belief is what frames and molds our perceptions.

Shortly after my father died of cancer, I spoke with him ... in a dream. My father had a stroke a few weeks before he died, so he was unable to speak during his last days alive, but he spoke to me in my dream. Was this dream a form of spiritual perception? The answer, truly, is a matter of subjective interpretation. If I believe that I spoke with my father's spirit, then the dream would be my own subjective experience of spiritual perception. However, if I believe that the dream is just a mélange of memory, hallucination, and imagination, then it would not be spiritual perception. In the end, it is belief that gives form and being to any potentially spiritual experience. It is this ontological concern that afflicts many agnostics who want to believe, but who cannot take the leap of faith to will themselves to believe, and who cannot experience the spiritual perception that would give them the inspiration to believe. Thus, the inability to believe becomes a wall to both spirituality and religion. However, digital technology may be the gateway through this wall, because it can provide a virtual experience of real spiritual perception.

We already have the digital technology as well as the neurological knowledge and hardware to create a direct sensory experience of a spiritual nature, by stimulating the parts of the brain that are associated with spiritual perception, and also by creating a virtual reality experience in which spiritual perceptions are evoked and enhanced. This technology can provide an experience of spiritual perception for anyone, even for those people who consider themselves unspiritual or atheistic. Because the technology provides a direct sensory experience of the divine, the problem of spiritual perception inhibition can be bypassed, as well as the problem of non-belief. The digital spiritualist does not have to believe in God in order to perceive God. He only has to believe that there is some part of his own mind that perceives experiences of a spiritual nature, and that the technology and methodology being employed can help him get in touch with the spiritual aspect of his own mind. Some belief is required, but not much. The main barrier for the individual would not be belief in the existence of spiritual perception, because that truth, even at the purely psychological and neurological levels, is manifest. The main barrier would be volition. The digital spiritualist must be willing to take the leap, to venture within to discover something new about himself and his existence, to swallow the "Drink Me" potion that enables Alice to enter Wonderland. For certain, a leap of faith will be required—but just a small one—and it is a leap that can be taken from one's own living room, into a virtual world that exists entirely within one's own mind.

Chapter One

The Digital Dream

> Senseless as beasts I gave men sense, possessed them of Mind....
> In the beginning, seeing they saw amiss, and hearing heard not,
>   but, like phantoms huddled.
> In *dreams*, the perplexed story of their days; Confounded.
> —Aeschylus, *Prometheus Bound*

> Very old are we men;
> Our *dreams* are tales
> Told in dim Eden
> By Eve's nightingales.
> —Walter De La Mare, "All That's Past," 1921

It's Sunday morning, some day in the foreseeable future. You wake up late and, after a light breakfast, hop into the living room and power up your interactive virtual reality multimedia system. Suiting up with all the cords and cables hooked up to the virtual reality suit and digitalized helmet is a bit of a chore, but you're excited to get started. The last time you were engaged, you felt that you were really getting the hang of exploring the digital dream. Your system scores recorded that you were in the dream for nearly 50 minutes, and that the spiritual perception stimulator was self-activated for about 10 of those minutes. You remember encountering something very powerful in those minutes, something deeply personal and emotionally intense, but it's hard for you to remember exactly what it was. If you keep on improving your performance, you'll probably make the steep investment of upgrading your system with the latest hardware, which can digitally record and playback your dreams. That's really the only way to recall and integrate the spiritual content of the dream encounters. Unless you really know and can control your own spiritual dream imagery, you can't expect to plug in to one of the online interactive networks, where you can share your spiritual dreams with other people, and experience the unconscious spiritual images of other users as well. Right now, your spiritual perception scores are still in the "Beginners" range on your system, but you're already light years ahead of where you were before you started using the system. It's hard for you to imagine that just a couple of weeks ago, you didn't even believe that there was such a thing as a "soul"—but now, you're getting in touch with aspects of your spiritual self that you never knew existed—and each time you explore your spiritual dreams, you discover even more. Now, the limits of your spiritual perception seem to be infinite!

No, this is not a science fiction book. This is a book about the psychology of spirituality, and how it is molded by media. However, if our perception is heavily influenced by the media we use to perceive the world, then looking even a little bit into the future will seem like science fiction. A few decades ago, most people couldn't imagine that we'd be spending a significant portion of our lives engaging in a virtual world of digital media. Now, most people couldn't imagine living without digital media. The idea that a digital media system could be used to elicit a dream state that would evoke a spiritual experience may seem like science fiction to you right now, but it won't seem too far-fetched by the time you finish this book.

My opening premise, that spiritual perception—the sensory experience of a spiritual presence—exists as a real phenomenon, could be accepted prima facie, as long as we consider the phenomenon as a subjective experience that is perceived by the individual. The subjective experience is real to the perceiver and can have immense psychological significance, even if another person dismisses it as just a delusion, an illusion, a hallucination, or a dream. If you've ever wondered: "Does God exist?" The answer just happens to be: "Yes! God does exist." God is "psychologically real." He exists as an incredibly powerful social force in the cultures and societies of all peoples, and also as a concept of varying influence in the minds of all people. As a cultural phenomenon, belief in the existence of God is one of the few psychological universals. In every society everywhere in the world, people believe in the existence of immortal souls, in miracles, in spirits, ghosts, demons, angels, and gods. People everywhere believe that spiritual forces can be influenced by rituals and prayers in order to intervene in the course of the physical world. In America, a quarter of the population believes in witches, half of the population believes in ghosts and the Devil, nearly three-quarters of the population believes in angels, a third of the population claim that they have personally seen an angel, 87 percent of the population believes that Jesus was literally raised from the dead, and 99 percent of the American population believes in God.[1] So, psychologically speaking, the existence of God is beyond debate. Even the most devout atheist would have to admit that God is psychologically real.

Furthermore, God is *neurologically* real. God is perceived by many people as a physical sensation in the brain, resulting in a psycho-emotional spiritual experience that is the phenomenological basis of all religion and all religious beliefs. For those who experience God at this level, he is as real as anything or anyone perceived in the physical world. He is not just a concept that people believe in. God is a sensed force—a sentient other—who is felt, heard, and seen by millions, even billions of people. A survey taken in the 1990s revealed that 53 percent of Americans had experienced a "moment of sudden religious awakening or insight," in which they actually sensed, felt, heard, or saw the divine presence of God or a spiritual being.[2] All perception, whether it is objective or subjective, is processed in the brain as an existent perception. So, as a perceptual experience, God is as psychologically real as any other phenomenon perceived by humans. He is just as real as this book that you perceive through the senses of touch and sight that are processed in your brain. Since, as far as we can tell, perception is reality ... when God is perceived, he is as real as any other perception.

My second premise is that spiritual perception is inhibited in the minds of most people most of the time, in modern literate societies. The central focus of the majority of this book is to explain how this inhibition of spiritual perception developed. My third premise is that perception and cognition in general—and spiritual perception in particular—are changing rapidly as our society leaps headfirst into the Digital Age. These changes will precipitate a drastic revolution in the way that spirituality will be experienced in the not-so-distant future. To explain the last premise, I will need to provide a model for how perception and cognition evolved as a function of our interaction with our environment; and I will also need to provide a model that can predict how perception and cognition will change in the future, as a function of the changes in our environment that are happening right now. Fortunately, I do not have to invent these models. Two brilliant theorists—Merlin Donald and Marshall McLuhan—have provided them already.

Merlin Donald's Model of Cognitive Evolution

> We act in cognitive collectivities, in symbiosis with external memory systems.—Merlin Donald

In his book, *Origins of the Modern Mind: Three Stages in the Evolution of Culture and Cognition*, Merlin Donald delineates three great cognitive leaps that changed the way we perceive, communicate, and think. Before the beginning of humanity, there was "episodic culture," which is the cognitive state of higher mammals and primates, who simply respond instinctively to whatever is going on around them, and develop behavior and response patterns through repetition and association. Memory and thought at this stage is "episodic," the being lives and thinks from moment to moment, without any deliberate forethought about the future, or any constructive afterthoughts about the past. He has no way to deliberately store and retrieve specific bits of memories, and no way to communicate any specific bit of information that is not contextual, because his mind has no symbols with which to label, store, and communicate information. Imagine trying to tell someone that you wanted an apple, if you did not have a word for "apple," nor any other way to describe an apple, nor an apple in your surroundings to refer to. The image of an apple would be clear to you in your head, but there'd be no precise way to share that image with someone else, since you couldn't speak or write a word, nor draw a picture, nor point to the specific object. What was cognition like for someone like this? Aeschylus, in *Prometheus Bound,* assumed that human beings, prior to their Promethean gifts of symbolic words and numbers, were "senseless as beasts." Before Prometheus "gave men sense, possessed them of Mind," human thought was as scattered and irrational as a dream: "In dreams, the perplexed story of their days; Confounded..." If we think of our cognition while dreaming, it seems "perplexed" and "confounded," because the thought process is episodic rather than logical or sequential. Images and episodes leap from one to another, without logic or reason, but with a rhythm and rhyme that make their own sense, as each image in each episode, and each episode itself, is linked to the previous one through some sort of emotional or intuitive association. This is why the dream makes sense to us while we're dreaming it, but when we try to describe or explain the dream to someone else, or even to ourselves, it suddenly makes no sense at all. The dreamscape is imagistic and episodic, rather than conceptual, verbal, or literal. It's not a far stretch to imagine that the mental lives of our primordial ancestors were like the flashes of episodes seen in the dreams of modern humans, the surreal "tales told in dim Eden."

As hominids, we developed "mimetic culture," in which pre-linguistic gestures were used to communicate basic concrete objects and actions to others, such as the way to light a fire, or the way to make a tool. The mimetic culture depends on the transference of "extra-genetic knowledge," information that is not bred as instinct within the genes of an individual animal. For the first time, our ancestors could invent a new skill, such as fire making, and pass that new skill on from one generation to the next, without having to rely on genetic inheritance. Humans invented a cultural inheritance of knowledge and skills, shared them, and passed them down through mimetic communication from person to person. Because mimed gestures represent specific objects and actions, they set the stage for the next huge cognitive leap, the acquisition of language.

In the Paleolithic Age, humans progressed into "mythic culture," the stage in which symbols representing thoughts are expressed in words. Language multiplies cognition and communication exponentially, because it allows our thoughts to be expressed directly and clearly, in such a streamlined way that it seems that our words themselves are our actual thoughts, rather than just symbols that represent our thoughts. Furthermore, language is abstract, rather than context-dependent. While it is difficult to describe an act or an object that is not right there in front of you using only physical gestures, we do exactly that all the time with words. I can say the word "apple," and the image of an apple pops right into your head, even though there's no apple anywhere in sight. Words are essentially unbound by the limitations of time, space, and the physical world. With the cognitive abstraction of language, we can even create and share "myths" to solve the mysteries that were previously unsolvable: the origin of the universe, the origin of humans, the meaning of life, and the purpose of death.

And then, finally, humans proceeded into "theoretic culture," which expands exponentially upon mythic culture, because it is unbound by the mouth, memory, and imagination of the individual human being. Theoretic culture unbinds itself from the individual by transmitting "extra-somatic"[3] knowledge—information not contained in an individual person. This feat is achieved through the use of an "external memory system" with which humans can store and communicate ideas. External memory began with "graphic inventions" such as the Paleolithic cave paintings. These images stored memories such as a successful hunt, or knowledge such as the spiritual secret to a successful hunt, in a compartment outside of the body and mind. In doing so, the memories and knowledge are unbound by the confines of one person's or even one group's mind, so that the memories and knowledge can be seen and appreciated by people generations later—even for generations living 30,000 years later! The Paleolithic graphic inventions, however, used very broad symbols that must be interpreted. We could look at the Paleolithic cave paintings and understand them on a visual level and make our own interpretations of the symbols, but the original meanings of the symbols were undoubtedly part of the oral mythos of the people that created them, that is now lost. Similarly, subsequent graphic inventions were image-based—such as the hieroglyphs and pictographs of archaic societies in the Near East. These symbols were very broad, as they represented entire ideas that had to be interpreted. One must know what a certain hieroglyph or pictograph means *before* you see it, in order to understand it. Therefore, graphic messages can only transmit previously known concepts, they cannot convey a totally new concept.[4] Only when oral language is represented almost exactly by written language—letters forming written words—do we get to the point where graphic symbols can provide their own interpretations. This stage, literacy using a phonetic alphabet, brings us to a breakthrough in extra-somatic knowledge, as it transmits thought directly from the mind of the thinker to the eyes of the reader, without the need of a third party interpreter or a shared dictionary of meanings for symbolic images. The delivery system for this breakthrough form of media has changed and will continue to change—from tablets to parchment to papyrus to print to digitalized information and beyond—but the basic technology itself, contained within the infinite potential combinations of the alphabetic code, is the media that changed and continues to change the human mind.[5]

Marshall McLuhan's Tetrad

> We look at the present through a rear-view mirror. We march backwards into the future.—Marshall McLuhan[6]

McLuhan's "Tetrad" model of media innovation[7] demonstrates how new media always creates an advantage in one mode of perception—"Enhancement"—while simultaneously resulting in a disadvantage in another mode of perception—"Obsolescence." New media is enticing because it enhances a way of perceiving, thinking, or communicating. Iphones are popular because they make communicating and accessing information faster and more convenient. Similarly, the advent of oral language back in the Paleolithic Age enhanced our ability to communicate specific ideas. However, as a direct result, our previous ability to express ourselves using only mimetic gestures was obsolesced.[8] Though we still talk with our hands to a certain extent, the main content of our communication is expressed in words. Thousands of years later, the advent of theoretic written language enhanced our ability to store information in documents, making our previous ability to memorize massive amounts of oral information obsolete. Bards no longer needed to memorize and retell the myth of the Trojan War, once Homer wrote it all down in *The Iliad*. And now, in the Digital Age, our Iphones provide instantaneous access to limitless information, making our previous ability to document unoriginal information more-and-more obsolete. Why write information, if you can just retrieve, copy, and paste the information?

The second half of McLuhan's Tetrad is "Retrieval" and "Reversal." The advent of a new media causes a retrieval of an old faculty, which then reverses a cognitive trend caused by the existing media. The advent of oral language in Donald's mythic stage, for example, retrieved an older reliance on oral communication through grunts and growls—the language of apes and primates—that was supplanted by the mimetic system of complex gestures. Apes transmitted thoughts by making noises with their mouths that other apes heard with their ears. Hominids, in Donald's mimetic stage, transmitted thoughts by making signs with their hands that were seen by other hominids with their eyes. So, an oral/auditory mode of communication of grunts and growls was obsolesced by a tactile/visual mode of communication of signed gestures. But then in the mythic stage, humans retrieved the oral/auditory mode of communication by transmitting thoughts with their mouths and ears again, using words. The retrieval of oral communication through language, therefore, marked a cognitive reversal—from tactile/visual communication using hands and eyes—to oral/auditory communication using mouths and ears. But with the graphic inventions of the theoretic stage, the tactile/visual modes of the mimetic system were retrieved—first as images and icons, then as pictograms, hieroglyphs, ideograms, and logograms—and eventually, as phonetic writing.[9] Literacy in particular pushed our perception of ideas away from the oral/auditory modes of speaking and listening, and retrieved the tactile/visual modes of communication that had been previously obsolesced, as writing is a tactile task, and reading is a visual task. Over very long periods of time, we see that the modes of perception and cognition keep reversing or "flipping," as the media for communicating thoughts keep evolving.

However, as media technology changes at breakneck speed in modern times, the process of Enhancement, Obsolescence, Retrieval, and Reversal speed up as well. In the 20th century, electronic technology such as the telephone and radio retrieved the modes of oral/auditory communication. People began to speak on the phone rather than writing letters, and people listened to the radio to hear current events, rather than reading newspapers or magazines. At the same time, photography, film, and television retrieved the mimetic/gestural faculties, as these modalities used physical gestures and visual images to communicate ideas, rather than words alone. But then, in the early 21st century, digital media retrieved the literary mode of communication, as speech is transferred from the oral/auditory mode of the telephone into the visual/tactile mode of e-mails, text messages, blogs, posts, and tweets. However, as digital media proceeds in sophistication, many people[10] believe that voice recognition technology—computers that listen—and speech synthesis technology—computers that talk—will replace keyboards, touchpads, and touchscreens. If so, then the task of literacy will once again be flipped from tactile/visual to oral/auditory; as reading will become listening, and writing will become speaking or dictating. See any futuristic science fiction movie for examples of this change.

Digital media enhances multimodal and multidirectional forms of perception. When using digital media, we tend to distribute our attention through multiple senses—seeing pictures, hearing songs, touching screens—and onto multiple foci of attention—"multitasking." As a direct result, the faculties that become gradually but increasingly more obsolete are the uni-modal and unidirectional forms of perception, such as the deep one-tracked visual focus on only the words on this page. Reading books is unfortunately becoming an obsolete mode of perception and cognition. As a college professor, I can attest to that.

However, every new form of media retrieves a mode of perception that was previously obsolesced. The image-based mode of communication found in preliterate societies—cave paintings, ideograms, pictograms, hieroglyphs—were obsolesced by the phonetic alphabet and literacy. But now, in the Digital Age, image-based communication is being retrieved via the internet and services such as Instagram, Twitter, Facebook, etc. When pushed to the limit of its potential, a new form of media will reverse itself or flip, becoming a medium for a preceding mode of perception. For example, the telephone used electronic technology to replace the written letter or telegraph with the voice. A visual mode of perception was replaced by an auditory mode. But the cell-phone, using digital media, reversed this, by quickly becoming a medium used more for sending text messages than for making phone calls. Text messages are basically like telegraphs or brief letters. Digital media caused the auditory mode of telecommunication to be flipped back into a visual mode.

McLuhan's Tetrad is an excellent complement to Donald's model, because it forces us to remember that the stages of cognitive evolution are not sequential, they are cumulative. Modes of cognition are not eliminated by successive stages, they are just subdued, "obsolesced" for awhile, but ready to be "retrieved" in a different arena of perception, when they are evoked by a new form of media. As modern humans, we all experience our world episodically, mimetically, mythically, and theoretically. Dreaming, or intensely daydreaming, or being deeply absorbed in a movie is likely to be an episodic experience. Playing a musical instrument, playing a sport, or dancing a dance is likely to be a mimetic experience. Engaging in a conversation, telling a story, or listening to a story, is likely to be a mythic experience. You reading this book, and me writing this book, are theoretic experiences. If we apply Donald's model to spirituality, we see that theoretic spirituality is theological, involving the study of scriptures, the interpretation of religious precepts, and the learning of doctrines and dogma. Mythic spirituality is mythological, focusing on the stories and symbols that give meaning to spiritual beliefs. Mimetic spirituality is ritualistic—the physical practice of spirituality—prayer, meditation, chant, dance, trance—whatever ritualistic act that elicits the sense of communion with the spiritual that the "soul" desires. And episodic spirituality is spiritual perception itself, the sensory experience of the actual presence of the spiritual other.

By combining Donald's evolutionary model with McLuhan's model for change, we see that our brains are incredibly flexible, and extremely adaptable to the media in our environment. The different modes of perception adapt themselves to whatever new media our brains become immersed in. So now that we are becoming immersed in a digital environment, our brain and our modes of cognition must adapt to this new environment by shifting around the balance of our sense perceptions. This is not a choice that we make. Our brains must adjust to our environments, otherwise we become obsolete—like your grandmother who can't use the internet—or your grandfather who can't use a cellphone. For people growing up in the digital environment, the shift in the balance of sense perceptions happens automatically and unconsciously. We all intuitively know that digital media is changing our environment and thereby changing our minds. We are stepping across the threshold of a theoretic culture into a digital culture. How will this next stage in the evolution of the mind change us?

Because digital media is so sensory inclusive, encompassing visual, auditory, oral, and tactile modalities simultaneously, reversal of any one faculty is not so clear. What is clear is a reversal in the cognitive faculty of attention and focus. Whereas literacy evoked a singular focus of attention onto specific words on a page, digital media evokes a more global attention to multiple foci that are attended to simultaneously—"multitasking"—a mode of attention that mimics the multiprocessing of computers, and is an adaptive cognitive response to media that is copious, instantaneous, multimodal, and constantly changing. With digital literacy, we enhance our ability to focus on multiple things at once, while we necessarily obsolesce the faculty of deep focus on the singular. As we retrieve a more immediate, in-the-moment, and multisensory interface with our media, we flip back into a less individual, less contemplative, less pensive state of being. In fact, the mode of perception that digitality retrieves is the oldest tool we have in the shed—the episodic mode of perception—the experience of everything in the moment. McLuhan called it the "brand-new world of allatonceness," the world of "simultaneous happening."[11] Animals without the ability to store and recall thoughts using symbols have no choice but to experience life in the moment, to live from episode to episode without being preoccupied with a lot of conscious forethought and afterthought. Modern humans experiencing a state of information overload find themselves, ironically, in the same boat. When information is coming at you very quickly in many different formats and in many different modes of perception, you cannot focus on anything in particular, and you cannot think too far ahead or look too far behind. For example, if you are playing a challenging videogame that is highly stimulating on visual, auditory, and tactile levels of engagement, you get the sensation of being so completely immersed in the game that you become a part of the game itself. You lose track of time and maybe even forget where you are. You scream and shout, gesticulate wildly, and become emotionally charged. You are completely in the moment, and the moment that you are engaged in is an experience of episodic perception. All of your attention is focused on what you are experiencing within that momentary episode of the virtual world that you are immersed in. Digital media, with its ability to engage multiple senses at high levels of engagement with high amounts of ever-changing instantaneous stimulation, has the power to retrieve the episodic mode of perception, by placing us in a virtual world of extremely realistic sounds and imagery. The experience of this virtual world is both new and ancient, for all of us and all of our ancestors have entered our own virtual worlds many thousands of times in each of our lives. The virtual world I'm referring to is our dreams. Accessing the virtual world of dreams using digital media will be the key to the next stage of spiritual perception ... the Digital Dream.

The Psychology of Dreams

> Once upon a time, I, Chuang Chou, dreamt I was a butterfly, fluttering hither and thither....
> Soon I awaked, and there I was, veritably myself again.
> Now I do not know whether I was then a man dreaming I was a butterfly,
> or whether I am now a butterfly, dreaming I am a man.
> —Master Chang Chou, 4th century BC

Why sleep? From an evolutionary standpoint it's quite maladaptive, and from an economical point of view it's quite inefficient. One obvious answer to the question is that we sleep in order to give our bodies and minds a much needed respite. Indeed, sleep researchers note that while we are sleeping, our bodies and brains are in a state of rest—*except* for a phase sometimes referred to as "paradoxical sleep"—a phase in which our limbs often move, occasionally quite frantically, and our brain waves indicate a high amount of neuronal activity. If sleep is for the purpose of rest, then it is paradoxical that we should have a distinct phase of sleep in which our brains are not resting. This phase of sleep must obviously have a purpose other than relaxation. The phase I am referring to is REM sleep ... the state of dreaming. REM sleep gets its name from the rapid eye movements that are occurring, despite the fact that our eyelids are closed. Our eyes are moving because we are perceiving images, but the images are not coming from the outside world of objective reality, they come from the inside world of the mind, the virtual world of dreams. Dreams are hallucinations, subjective perceptions of objects, beings, sounds, and voices that are not present. They are the most consistent and universal reminder that perception is in the mind, not in the senses, and that cognition is not relegated solely to consciousness. Dreams seem to recapture an earlier, preverbal, pre-conscious mode of perception. Anna Freud, a child psychiatrist who heard the recollection of innumerable dreams, noted that "when we *dream* we *see*." Freud compared dreams to "silent movies"—"only when we wake up do we connect words to the pictures that have appeared in our heads."[12]

Psychologists of every ilk would agree that dreaming is a cognitive process that is evolutionarily far older than conscious reasoning. The fact that all mammals and some birds dream supports that assumption. MacLean, in his famous neurological model of the "triune brain," suggested that dreaming is a function that takes place in the "reptilian complex"—the hindbrain and midbrain—a much older and more primitive part of the brain than the more recently evolved "neomamallian complex," i.e., the neocortex.[13] The reptilian complex is instinctive, while the neomallian complex is analytical and language based. If dreaming were a function of the reptilian complex, it would represent a more primitive state of mind—a form of perception that is much different than the neomammalian mode of perception. A similar view has been expressed by psychoanalysts and philosophers through the ages, as Erich Fromm noted:

> Must we not expect that, when deprived of the outside world, we regress temporarily to a primitive animal-like unreasonable state of mind? Much can be said in favor of such an assumption, and the view that such a regression is the essential feature of the state of sleep, and thus of dream activity, has been held by many students of dreaming from Plato to Freud.[14]

MacLean suggested that dream function was inhibited during the day, because at a certain point in evolution, making decisions based on logical analysis of our environment was more adaptive than making instinctual intuitive decisions. The preponderance of the dream state in infants, who are dreaming most of the time, would be due to the fact that the neocortex is mostly undeveloped in infants. The complete lack of dreaming in reptiles would be due to the fact that they have no neocortex at all. The conclusion would be that the dream state in adult humans retrieves the normal waking state of human infants, reptiles, and lower mammals, whose approach to life is completely episodic, intuitive, and instinctual, and for whom memory and thought appears as a flash of associated images and episodes.[15] The "perplexed story of their days" would seem, to us, like a series of dreams.

The episodic mode of perception that is expressed in dreams is far older than the mythic and theoretic modes of perception that are expressed in conscious language-based thought. While we are awake, while we are conscious, the episodic perceptions are inhibited by the part of the brain that must remain focused, rational, logical, analytical, and theoretic. They cannot pass through the inhibitory filter and enter into consciousness. The episodic perceptions are regarded as obsolete by the theoretic mind, therefore they are constrained, inhibited, labeled at a preconscious level as "nonsense"—that which is "*not sensed*"—and unceremoniously dumped into the untended dustbin of unconscious awareness. But when nighttime falls, and the flashlight of consciousness is dimmed, the glare of consciously perceived reality no longer casts the dream elements into the shadows, and then the episodic images can be retrieved and perceived ... if only in our dreams.

The Spiritual Dream

> In the long pre–Freudian centuries, before the mystery of the dream was reduced to all too human terms, when men still listened for the voice of God in the still of the night, dreams played a greater role in shaping ideas and actions and careers than it is easy for us today to believe. —Joshua Trachtenberg

In preliterate societies, reality based distinctions about perceptions—"Was that 'real,' or was that just a dream?"—are irrelevant and arbitrary. In their perspective, what happens in a dream *is* real, just as real as what happens in waking life. Dream encounters, trances, hallucinations, visions ... these experiences are real, just as the spirits they encounter in these states are real. There is no distinction made between the waking experience and the dream experience, just as there is no distinction made between consciousness and unconsciousness, or the physical and the spiritual. All of these experiences are equally real, and they all coexist, flowing into and through each other like two streams flowing into the same pond. Most preliterate peoples believe that it is dangerous to awaken a sleeper, because his soul has not yet returned to his body.[16] This is most likely the root of the modern belief that it is dangerous to awaken a sleepwalker (this is untrue). It is also probably linked to the Christian bedtime prayer: "Now I lay me down to sleep, I pray the Lord my soul to keep...." Among the Ashanti, there was a rule that if a man dreams of having sex with another man's wife, he must pay retribution to the other man as if he had actually committed adultery with his wife, because dream sex is just as real as waking sex.[17] For these preliterate people, the division between waking consciousness and dream consciousness does not exist, at least not as formally as it does for literate peoples. For them, the open communication between the different modes of consciousness—the opening wide of the doors of perception—makes spiritual perception easily accessible to everyone.[18]

The dream experience is spiritual perception in its purest form. Just as Freud declared that dreams are the "royal road to the unconscious," I believe that dreams are the royal road to the spiritual experience. Obviously, not all dreams are spiritual. Nevertheless, all of the features of a spiritual experience—the direct sensory perception of non-objective stimuli, the sense of encountering a sentient other, the feeling of exaggerated reality, the feelings of atemporality, paradoxicality, ineffability, etc.—are typically experienced in the dream state. Many dreams, however, *are* spiritual. Most spiritual people have spiritual dreams.

For many spiritual people, the dream state provides the only occurrence of pure unadulterated spiritual perception that they ever have. Furthermore, many people who are not particularly spiritual have had the experience of having what can be called a spiritual dream, even if it's only the relatively universal experience of communing with a deceased loved one within a dream. The dream I had of my father shortly after he died comes to mind. The question of whether or not that was a spiritual dream is purely a matter of interpretation. What is not a matter of interpretation is the universality and frequency of the dream experience, and its substantial overlap with the experience of spiritual perception. All people dream several times every night, and all people either have spiritual dreams, or dreams that *could be interpreted* as being spiritual, making dreams the single most commonly experienced mode of spirituality.

Unlike Freud or Jung, I do not necessarily recommend that people analyze their dreams for psychological or spiritual content. The function of psychoanalytic dream interpretation is to translate unconscious experience into conscious knowledge; to translate the episodic perception into a mythic or theoretic perception. My primary thesis, however, is that conscious rationalization *inhibits* spiritual perception. Hence dreams, especially spiritual dreams, are best off left alone, and not deconstructed by the conscious mind. The flashlight that examines becomes the intensified magnified light that incinerates that which it illuminates. I suggest that it may be beneficial for people to dream more, but this notion is in no way controversial or novel. Every medical doctor and sleep researcher would recommend that most people should get more sleep. The direct and positive relationship between sleep, especially REM sleep, and mental health, has been documented by numerous sleep researchers. In studies where subjects are allowed to sleep a normal amount of hours, but are woken up every time they enter REM sleep, so that they are not allowed to dream, it is consistently found that the subjects develop severe symptoms of anxiety and depression within just a day or two of the study. If the study is allowed to continue, the subjects begin to show psychotic symptoms, at which point the study is terminated for ethical reasons. Clearly, dreams serve a crucial if still mysterious role in the regulation of the mind.

Modern society's single-minded focus on conscious reasoning seems to be behind the modern human being's desire to minimize his time sleeping and dreaming: "There'll be time enough for sleep when I die," is a typical aphorism of a modern human. In the world dominated by consciousness, only conscious perception is valued; while unconscious perception, the perception of dreams, is considered worthless, because it is virtually nonexistent to the conscious mind. Only conscious perception distinguishes between itself and every other form of cognition, and only conscious reasoning declares that it alone is "real," while every other form of cognition is "unreal." The consciousness bias exists, despite the plethora of evidence that points to the vital importance of sleep and dreams. Is it possible that dream life is just as important, if not more important, than conscious life? Considering that the dream state is perhaps the last vestige of spiritual perception available to the modern secular human being, this may be the case. The consciousness bias that minimizes the importance of all unconscious experience leaves us all sleep deprived, dream starved, and spiritually malnourished. To let go of conscious control, to simply fall into unconscious sleep, to rest assured that our spiritual/existential needs are being addressed unconsciously in our dreams, is inconceivable to the conscious mind, which cannot comprehend the cognitive existence of anything besides itself. So as we as a society drug ourselves to sleep—the only way to overcome our conscious' resistance to letting go of itself—the significance of our dreams becomes purely a matter of faith.

A case related to Oliver Sacks by one of his colleagues is revealing of the consciousness bias. The patient, a ten-year-old boy, woke one morning "to find a woman dressed in blue hovering at the foot of his bed, surrounded by radiant light." The woman introduced herself as his "guardian angel," and spoke to him in a "soft, gentle voice." The boy ran to his parents' room. They told him it was "just a dream," but the boy "was unconvinced, unable to make sense of the event." His family was not religious, and so the notion of an actual angel was "alien" to both the boy and his parents. The boy developed "insomnia" and "a pervasive sense of dread." At school and at home, he was "agitated and distracted, and he increasingly withdrew from relationships with peers and activities." The boy saw a psychiatrist, who helped him "make sense of what had happened, coming to understand the event as a type of hallucination that commonly occurs following arousal from sleep."[19] For the boy, the experience of these perceptions—waking up within a dream state, perceiving dreamlike images in the hypnogogic state—are universal. The only abnormality within the case described above is the severity of the subject's reaction to the event, which is linked directly to the *"meaning"* applied to the perception, i.e., the conscious interpretation.

I remember distinctly a very similar experience from my own childhood. I was around five or six years old. I woke up in the middle of the night, disturbed by a sound. I climbed out of bed, half asleep, and walked to my door, looking out into the dark night kitchen. There I saw a fairy spirit in a flowing white gown. She touched the nightlight in the kitchen and it magically lit up, spreading a glowing aura of warm yellow light around her. She looked at me, but I couldn't see her face, as it was shrouded in the glow. She said, "Go back to bed sweetheart," and so I did. The next morning I recalled my vision of the fairy to my mother. She grinned knowingly at my story. "Was it really a fairy?" I asked her. She replied with a smile, "Maybe it was." Only years later did it occur to me that the vision of the "fairy" was actually my mother. Only decades later, as I write this book, do I realize that my mother's response to my question was absolutely perfect.

The case of the boy related by Dr. Sacks' colleague is a vivid example of how anxiety is manufactured in our society. A young boy has a clear perception. Like most perceptions, it is born out of fantasies, beliefs, memories, and expectations preexistent in the mind. The perception, on the surface, seems innocuous, or even potentially beneficial. The woman, after all, was portrayed as being "soft," "gentle," and a self-described "guardian angel." If properly interpreted—that is, hardly interpreted at all—her existence in the boy's fantasy life could have been useful as a protective figure who could allay his fears and anxieties, as the boy appeared to be prone to anxiety in the first place. Instead, the perception is interpreted by the boy's parents as a meaningless dream, a figment of his imagination, an interpretation that the boy intuitively knows to be false, as the perception seemed as real to him as any other thing he ever perceived. The boy is forced to doubt the veracity of his own perceptions, resulting in paranoia. Without a meaningful interpretation, and with no spiritual frame of reference with which to understand the experience, the perception becomes "alien," evoking "fear" and "dread," leading to anxiety and insomnia. The boy eventually went to therapy, where his perception was dealt with as a "hallucination," which was apparently helpful in rationalizing the fear and anxiety, but comes as an endpoint to an extended "traumatic" episode in the boy's life, that could have been avoided by a much less rational interpretation of the boy's initial perception. Perhaps if the figure that was perceived as kind, beneficent, protective, and gentle, was simply labeled by the boy's parents as a "good fairy," the boy would have been comforted rather than terrified. But of course, for the modern theoretic mind, there can be no such thing as fairies!

The virtual reality of the dream-world is a glimpse of life from the viewpoint of episodic perception, an ancient but by no means less meaningful way of perceiving the world. The coexisting virtual realm of spirituality is a dimension of existence inhabited by spirits and souls, angels and demons, gods, goddesses, and God. The spiritual imagination that created this world evolved in the mythic stage of cognitive evolution. There is an intersection between the virtual reality of dreams and the virtual reality of spiritual perception, in the common and well-known experience of the spiritual dream. This experience can be deliberately evoked, controlled, enhanced, and manipulated, by using digital media to create a virtual experience of the spiritual dream. But before the "digital dream" process can be rolled out, there's one more piece of the puzzle that needs to be explained: How the human brain is hardwired to process and experience spiritual perceptions.

Neurotheology

> Could it be that human beings have actually evolved specialized neural circuitry for the sole purpose of mediating religious experience?—V.S. Ramachandran

The temporal lobes are involved in numerous brain functions, including perception through all of the senses, language, memory, and emotion.[20] From 1934 to 1954, Wilder Penfield, a Canadian neurosurgeon, asked his patients, mostly epileptics, questions while electrically stimulating different parts of their brains. He did this while his patients' brains were exposed for brain surgery.[21] Penfield's studies suggest that spiritual perception is experienced primarily in the temporal lobes of the brain.[22] Since Penfield's pioneering research, other investigators have found similar results when electro-stimulating the temporal lobes, eliciting feelings of "God's physical presence."[23] Michael Persinger, Professor of Psychology at Laurentian University in Canada, claims that he can create spiritual experiences in his laboratory participants by stimulating the temporoparietal region of the brain, the so-called "God Spot." By placing a special helmet equipped with four sets of solenoids, the so-called "God Helmet," on the heads of his participants, he transmits transcranial magnetic waves into the temporal lobes of their brains. Persinger believes that the stimulation is temporarily halting the inhibition of communication between the hemispheres of the brain. In this moment, the participant is not just aware of his own conscious identity, but of his connection with the unconscious "other," an aspect of his own cognition that his conscious sense of self is unaware of. The experience is that of sensing a state of oneness with one's surroundings or with other people. There is a sense of the distinct "presence" of another being, but not in the outer world—in the inner world of private thoughts and emotions. This feeling of sensing a sentient other is an inherently spiritual feeling.[24] It has been labeled "self-transcendent" by some researchers. According to Persinger's research, 80 percent of the subjects who were stimulated in this way reported a "mystical-sensed presence of a sentient or emoting being, often interpreted as the presence of God."[25] When Persinger himself applied the machine to his own brain, "he found to his amazement that he experienced God for the first time."[26] But when, on a BBC television special, Persinger applied the helmet to the brain of Richard Dawkins, preeminent evolutionary biologist, author of *The Selfish Gene* (1976) and *The God Delusion* (2006), and (as I like to think of him)—the pope of atheism—Dawkins, to his own disappointment, felt "nothing."

Persinger believes that the experience of transient moments of hyperstimulation in the temporal lobes is normative, and that they play a vital role in everyday people's spiritual experiences.[27] He also posits an evolutionary explanation for the existence of a spiritual function in the brain.[28] Spiritual experiences would provide a natural counterbalance for the "mortality salience" or death anxiety that would arise in the human mind as the consequence of developing self-conscious awareness.[29] As human minds evolved into conscious self-awareness, we could look into the future and consciously foresee our own death. It would behoove the brain to adapt itself to this new problem by developing a way of dealing with the creeping sense of anxiety that would naturally arise with our knowledge of our own inevitable demise. Spiritual perceptions of a coexistent spiritual dimension to existence, when combined with a mythical system of belief in spirits and souls, would provide this counterbalance to mortality salience. Persinger also believes that certain places, "spiritual hotspots," may have the specific magnetic fields that would induce spiritual perceptions or "sensed presences" in people who have "sensitive temporal lobes"—thus explaining holy sites and holy people. Temporal lobe sensitivity, according to Persinger, is a variable trait. Some people are highly sensitive—shamans, prophets, priests, mediums—while others are insensitive—atheists like Dawkins—and therefore not prone to spiritual perceptions.

Newberg and d'Aquili found that the temporal lobes of test subjects were highly activated when practicing transcendental meditation, especially when at the peak of their meditation experiences. At the same time, the parietal lobes, which process our sense of time and space, were highly deactivated. This would explain the sense of timelessness and the sense of oneness with space and others that are associated with the spiritual experience. Newberg found similar results in the temporal and parietal lobes of Franciscan Nuns during prayer sessions.[30] In Catholic theology, the ultimate goal of prayer is the state in which one experiences dissociation or a loss of the sense of self, occurring with a simultaneous sense of unity, a feeling of melding with the divine "Other." This is called the "Unio Mystica," the mystical union, and it is the common goal of spiritual practices throughout the religions of the world.[31]

Epilepsy has been called the "sacred disease," because epileptic seizures occasionally elicit intense episodes of spiritual perception.[32] Temporal lobe epileptics are people who experience seizures of varying length and intensity due to electrical hyper-stimulation in the temporal lobes of their brains. They pose an intriguing mystery to psychologists, as these particular seizures are likely to be accompanied by spiritual experiences, even in patients who were previously indifferent to religion and had no prior spiritual experiences.[33] It is not uncommon for a lifelong atheist to assert that he had spoken directly with God, and that he was given the ultimate secret of the universe by God himself, subsequent to a temporal lobe seizure.[34] Temporal lobe epileptics might have multiple religious conversions, each precipitated by a separate seizure experience.[35] Ramachandran suggested that temporal lobe seizures "kindle" the "salience pathways" of the brain that are responsive to spiritual experiences. Neural pathways associated with spiritual perception are stimulated for the first time during the initial seizure. Afterwards, since the pathways have been "kindled" or made more accessible to electro-conduction, spiritual perceptions come more freely.

The effect of these seizures is felt well below the cerebral cortex, where abstract thought and logic are processed. The feelings come from a deeper level of cognitive experience. The seizures evoke feelings and perceptions that cannot be inhibited by the conscious left hemisphere, because the effect of the seizure itself is to disinhibit communication between the hemispheres, by overwhelming the temporal lobes with an overload of neuro-electro-stimulation. The direct connection of the temporal lobes with the limbic system (the amygdala and hippocampus), points to the intense emotionality that is associated with seizure induced spiritual perceptions, as the limbic system is the seat of emotional experience in the brain. Hence, the spiritual perceptions of temporal lobe epileptics seem hyper-real—more real than reality—because they are perceptions that are unfiltered by the senses or by the analytic parts of the brain, and they are accompanied by intense emotional reactions. This raises the question, is there a purer level of reality, a deeper level of existence, a purely spiritual level of existence, that resides in all of us, deep within the hidden recesses of the brain?[36]

Temporal lobe seizures should not be confused with grand mal seizures that affect the entire brain and are typically severe and long lasting. Temporal lobe seizures are localized only in the temporal lobe, last only a few seconds, and usually do not result in fainting, falling, or loss of consciousness. Quite typically, the epileptic is not even aware at the time that he is having a seizure.[37] Nevertheless, the spiritual perception that may accompany these seizures can permanently alter the person's life-view, making him an entirely different and much more spiritual person. Ramachandran believes that the intensity and permanence of these profound changes come about as a result of the physical changes occurring at the neural level of the brain, as a result of the seizures.[38] The term "temporal lobe personality" has been applied to temporal lobe epileptics who, subsequent to seizures, have "heightened emotions," "see cosmic significance in trivial events," and are obsessed with matters of spirituality.[39] The person with "temporal lobe personality" seems much like a Biblical prophet, a person who, after "seeing the light," feels compelled by an inner drive to pronounce his revelation and proselytize the message to others. There's little irony in the fact that many of the accounts of temporal lobe seizure begin with the sudden vision of a blinding, bright light.[40] The fact that much of the function of language is represented in the frontal lobes is also relevant.[41] Language is usually under the power of the left hemisphere, and usually focused in a logical mode of consciousness. When language is suddenly overwhelmed by right hemispheric episodes, images, and sensations, rushing in with a complete lack of hemispheric inhibition, even the logical part of the mind cannot deny the awe and wonder and realness of the experience. Sensory perception, true experience, trumps logic and creates a new level of comprehension.

Oliver Sacks reports the case of a woman who suffered a head injury. Afterwards, she experienced partial seizures that were accompanied by "an exalted state in which God, with the form and voice of an angel, told her to run for Congress." The woman actually did run for Congress, despite a complete lack of political experience, and based her campaign primarily on her spiritual revelations. The woman "lost by only a narrow margin."[42] Théophile Alajouanine, a neurologist and biographer of Dostoevsky, noted of the famous Russian novelist: "epilepsy had created in the person of Dostoevsky a 'double man' ... a rationalist and a mystic; each having the better of the other according to the moment ... more and more the mystical one seems to have prevailed."[43] In a famous scene from his novel, *The Idiot* (1869), Dostoevsky's protagonist declares: "I have really touched God. He came into me, myself; 'Yes, God exists!' I cried, and I don't remember anything else. You all, healthy people, can't imagine the happiness which we epileptics feel during the second before our attack." Readers familiar with the topic of neurotheology will be aware of the conjecture that all or most of the renowned prophets and visionaries of the past displayed symptoms of temporal lobe epilepsy. Though I don't wish to belabor the point, I would be remiss not to cover it, if only cursorily. Please refer to the endnote for this section for a summary of this topic.[44]

If spiritual perception is indeed processed or experienced in the temporal and/or parietal lobes, then any spiritual experience—whether it be an effect of epileptic seizure or an experience arising from a non-pathological cause—would evoke the same behaviors and perceptions. Is the experience itself pathology or prophecy? Is it hallucination or revelation? Illusion or vision? These dichotomies are construed as a paradox when considered from a purely theoretic perspective, in which an experience must be classified as either "real" or "unreal." Why must it necessarily be one or the other?

The Digital Dream

> I stand amid the roar
> Of a surf-tormented shore,
> And I hold within my hand
> Grains of the golden sand —
> How few! yet how they creep
> Through my fingers to the deep,
> While I weep—while I weep!

> O God! Can I not grasp
> Them with a tighter clasp?
> O God! can I not save
> One from the pitiless wave?
> Is all that we see or seem
> But a dream within a dream?
> —Edgar Allan Poe,
> "A Dream Within a Dream"

The dream is a virtual experience. When we wake up in the middle of a dream, we realize that we have been existing in a virtual realm of imagined sight and sound. Typically, we wish nothing more than to crawl back inside that virtual dimension, the dream of life that somehow seems more real than life itself. For a little while we can sway back and forth between reality and dream, remaining consciously aware of our real identity and surroundings, while also realizing that we are dreaming. For a time, we are both within and without. We are the dreamer and also the observer observing the dream of the dreamer. This transitory intermodal phase of consciousness is referred to as "lucid dreaming." It is the one moment in life in which we truly understand that the virtual experience of the dream exists as a parallel mode of imaginary consciousness, simultaneously coexisting with our wakeful mode of rational consciousness—a virtual mode of existence that we are usually completely unaware of—a dream within a dream.

The digital experience is virtual as well. We perceive sights and sounds, friends and family, stories and songs, through a screen connected to the ether of the internet via vast invisible electromagnetic fields. These perceptions are not of real objects and subjects. We perceive only the digitally interpreted projections of the objects and subjects, bounced off orbiting satellites and beamed at light speed through the ether of electromagnetic space into our digital devices. The digital experience of a virtual reality game is the most clearly virtual of all digital experiences—especially when the game creates a world unto itself, complete with interacting characters who are all the virtual avatars of other gamers, playing the game from all different points around the world—and even more especially when the gamers are equipped with virtual reality hardware, such as immersive multimedia suits and helmets, that create the physical sensation of being inside the world of the game. The virtual digital world, in this sense, recapitulates the experience of being in the virtual world of the dream.

The realm of spirituality is also a virtual world. When we pray to a God that we cannot touch, see, or hear, we are reaching out into the virtual unknown. The worshipper can feel the presence of God, but cannot directly perceive him with any of the five senses. His relation is a virtual relation with a virtual Other. Hence, the practice of spirituality in ritual, prayer, or meditation is also a virtual experience; perhaps not so much unlike the virtual experience of the lucid dream, or the immersive experience of a virtual reality videogame. The intersection of these three virtual realities can be reached with the use of digital media and neurological technology. We have already seen the beginning of virtual spirituality in the Digital Age. Dr. Persinger's "God Helmet," which transmits transcranial magnetic waves into the temporoparietal regions of the brains of subjects to elicit spiritual perceptions, is just a crude mechanism. Compared to the complexity of the virtual reality gaming systems being developed by the U.S. Army and their corporate videogame competitors, the "God Helmet" is like a Stone Age hand axe. If big corporate or government money and/or high-level research interests focused on the issue of eliciting the neurological experience of spiritual perception via digital media and neuropsychological stimulation, the results would literally be mind-blowing. We already have the technology to create extremely vivid virtual experiences, and we have a substantial amount of knowledge about the location and existence of spiritual experiences in the brain. If these fields were to converge, this is how I would imagine it would work....

If the dream state is perpetually present but constantly inhibited, we could find a way to tap into this dream state using a combination of various methods. The process of consciously entering a dream state is referred to as "Wake Initiated Lucid Dreaming" (W.I.L.D.). This sometimes happens when we wake up in the middle of a dream, and then consciously re-enter the dream. Lucid dreams are hard to maintain, because it is a transitory state, in which we have one foot in the unconscious dream world and one foot in the conscious world. After a little while, we either fall back asleep into unconsciousness, or we rise up awake into full consciousness. However, there are methods that can be used to extend lucid dreaming and stabilize the experience. Spiritual rituals across cultures and throughout the ages have used manifold methods of achieving this sort of altered state of consciousness. Spinning, chanting, meditating, dancing, drumming, swaying, praying ... are all common methods. The use of powerful psychoactive substances, such as alcohol, marijuana, peyote, mescaline, LSD, mushrooms, etc.—are also quite effective—though not necessarily advisable, for various psychological reasons. Psychiatrists have also developed techniques for hypnosis and auto-hypnosis that can achieve a trance-like state. All of these methods, however, are Stone Age, compared to the power of digital media. A digital helmet can project a combination of coordinated sights and sounds to construct a guided imagery trip into a virtual space within the mind. The process is somewhat similar to hypnosis; however, the goal is to gradually lull the function of consciousness into a state of submission, not to completely shut down conscious awareness. The objective of the initiation phase would be to attain a semi-conscious state of awareness in which a lucid dream is evoked and sustained. This is generally hard to do—a very tricky mental balancing act—but digital media and neuropsychological hardware can provide the structure and support to achieve this with ease. Neuro-sensors in the helmet and in the virtual reality suit will gauge the individual's level of central nervous system arousal and his brain waves, which then automatically regulate the pace and intensity of the guided imagery and sounds being played. Based on his own physical and neurological feedback, the individual is gently drawn inwards, with the infinite patience, subtlety, and intricate interactivity that only a well-trained digital media system could provide. Ray Kurzweil was involved in developing a technology called "Brain Generated Music" (BGM), which elicits a state of semi-conscious awareness. The technology uses neurosensors to generate digital music in accordance to algorithms derived from the user's own brain waves. For the listener, the music feels like it's coming from inside his own mind. Because the music is synched to the user's brain waves, it gently slows down the brain waves to the point where the user is in a trancelike semiconscious state, and then maintains that state indefinitely.[45] Since ambient sound and music can still be heard when we are unconscious, Kurzweil's BGM may be extremely useful in initiating the lucid dream. BGM, in addition to guided imagery from the digital helmet and a responsive virtual reality suit providing tactile sensations, both in coordination with neurological feedback from neurosensors, will provide an easy and facile transition from the conscious state into a state of semi-consciousness. For some people, a psychoactive substance may be necessary or preferable in order to initiate, enhance, or facilitate the process. Once the sensors indicate that a lucid dream state has been entered, the ritual will commence....

Transcrannial magnetic waves emitted directly from the digital helmet into the temporal lobes of the individual will stimulate the areas of the brain that elicit spiritual perceptions. These perceptions will arise in the lucid dream state, and will be perceived as part of the dream. In addition, pre-recorded images and sounds could be played by the media system. These images and sounds will also be perceived as part of the dream. The content of these images and messages, obviously, are selected by the user. Neural imaging using MRI technology embedded in the helmet will monitor the amount of auditory and visual stimulation being processed in the brain, allowing the system to regulate and balance the amount of imagery and sound being projected by the media device, with the amount of imagery and sound that is originating internally from the mind of the individual himself. In the digital dream, the neural feedback system maintains the lucid dream state, the neural imaging system balances the amount of sensation being perceived, the neural stimulation system elicits spiritual perception, and the digital media system projects spiritual imagery and messages into the dream. The digital dream would be a state of psychological interaction between the mind and media; a state of psychological interaction between the conscious and unconscious modes of awareness; a state of unobstructed communication between the left and right hemispheres of the brain; and a state of disinhibition of spiritual perception. Because perception is experienced as reality, the virtual spiritual experience would feel as real—and possibly even *more real*—as any naturally occurring spiritual experience. In essence, the digital dream is a deliberate dimming of the flashlight of consciousness, allowing for the stars of the spiritual dream to shine through the darkness.

Spiritual Perception in the Digital Age

> Moreover, something is or seems
> That touches me with mystic gleams,
> Like glimpses of forgotten dreams—
> Of something felt, like something here;
> Of something done, I know not where;
> *Such as no language may declare.*
> —Alfred Tennyson, 1842,
> "The Two Voices"

The digital dream process will represent a great leap forward in spiritual perception, by allowing us to take a great step backwards in terms of our cognitive and spiritual evolution. A significant portion of this book is dedicated to explaining how modern consciousness inhibits spiritual perception in the waking state. Specifically, the transition from the mimetic stage to the mythic stage—the advent of thinking in words—and then the transition from the mythic stage to the theoretic stage—the advent of thinking literally and logically—have resulted in the main inhibitory effects on spiritual perception. Thinking in words, and then applying literal and logical standards to the words that represent our thoughts, creates a sense of abstract detachment in our minds. We must step away from something, we must detach ourselves from that thing, in order to analyze something. For example, figuring out a maze is usually quite easy when you are looking at the maze as an image on a page. From your detached perspective, it is quite easy to see how the maze is constructed, and by focusing in and out of specific parts of the maze, you can see which paths are dead ends and which ones lead to the exit. However, if you are *inside* the maze, such as one of the big corn mazes that farms often make around Halloween time, it is much harder to figure the way out, because you cannot detach yourself from the environment of the maze. Inside the corn maze, you are a part of the maze, and you must experience every twist and turn of the maze as a distinct episode. You are integrally connected to your environment. Some people like this experience as a change of pace, others get paranoid and claustrophobic, because they're not used to being immersed in their environment, they're used to controlling their environment. The experience of being inside the corn maze is analogical to an episodic experience, while the experience of completing a paper maze is analogical to a theoretic experience. In the latter experience, there is a disconnection from the immediate and visceral relationship with the environment, the individual is a detached observer of the maze. In the former experience, there is a direct and visceral experience of the environment, the individual is an immersed part of the corn maze. In a sense, the individual and the corn maze are in a state of unity. They are as one.

Clearly, the ability to detach, abstract, and analyze our environment as a disconnected observer is a great evolutionary advantage. If the goal is to master the maze, it's better to perceive it from the detached perspective of the observer, than from the immersed perspective of the person inside of it. However, for every perception enhanced, there is also a perception that is obsolesced. Rather than living within our environment as an integral part of it, we have become detached and aloof. While the ability to focus and analyze is enhanced, the feeling of a state of unity is obsolesced. The state of unity—the sense of deep integral connection with something bigger than yourself, the sense of oneness with the world, the sense of connection between what is felt within and what is felt without of yourself—is the essential feeling of spiritual perception. The state of spiritual unity is the perception that is symbolized in the archetypal images and ideas of God and the divine. This state of unity was intuitively felt by our primordial ancestors who experienced the world episodically rather than theoretically. This state of unity was also felt by each and every one of us during the preconscious stages of cognitive development, when we were babies and while we were in the womb. This state of unity—the "Unio Mystica"—is also the ultimate goal of every spiritual practice, every mystical ritual, and every act of worship or prayer. The digital dream, by returning us to the episodic mindset, retrieves a mode of perception that has hitherto been lost to human cognition for hundreds of thousands of years. The digital dream returns us to the state of unity within ourselves.

Dream perception, when not being filtered and constrained by the theoretic mindset of modern consciousness, is purely imagistic and episodic. In it, anything can exist, and does exist, as long as it can be imagined. There is a return to the animistic mode of perception, in which spirit potentially exists in everything. In the episodic mindset, in the dream world, and in the virtual world created by digital media, ideas come to us directly and instantaneously in sensory form, not as abstract concepts or logical words. The digital dream retrieves this multisensory, instantaneous, multimodal, and multi-focused mode of awareness. It brings us back to the primordial feelings we experienced before we were separated from beasts and nature by Prometheus' gift of consciousness, which was also, in its own way, a burden and a curse. In the cave paintings in Lascaux, France, which date back nearly 20,000 years, we see a repeated image of a man with the head of a bird and an erect penis. Anthropologists such as David Lewis-Williams argue that these paintings represent a shaman in the throes of a spiritual trance. Their arguments are based on their observations of contemporary shamans practicing in preliterate cultures, who enter a dreamlike trance state when performing spiritual rituals, typically by ingesting a powerful psychotropic drug, although other methods are used. The shamans oftentimes don animal costumes and headdresses. I would like to point out a well-known medical fact—during the REM state, most males experience nocturnal penile tumescence—men's penises are usually erect while dreaming. Perhaps the man in the painting is not necessarily a shaman, but an average Paleolithic male, engaging in a typical spiritual act of that age—a waking dream—in which his soul flies out of his body to commune with the spirits, hence, he has the head of a bird. The digital dream will retrieve this primordial waking dream state. It will allow our spirits to fly out of ourselves once again.

As human cognition progressed from episodic culture to mimetic culture, thoughts could be expressed and remembered through complex gestures and mimes. This type of communication would have been key in the transmission of skills related to hunting, gathering, tool production, and tool use. The cognitive shift from a focus on episodic images towards a focus on mimetic replication would have necessarily corresponded to a neurological shift from the right hemisphere of the brain, which is intuitive and holistic, towards the left hemisphere—the hemisphere that controls the right hand—the hemisphere that is logical, linguistic, and analytical. The digital dream, once it is entered, requires no tool use, as digital tools are smart enough to operate themselves. The digital dream experience retrieves the right hemispheric approach to the world, which is more intuitive and holistic, rather than focused, analytic, and controlling. The right hemisphere is more adept at seeing itself as an immersed part of its environment—as a person *inside* the maze rather than above it—as a player *inside* the game, rather than an observer analyzing it. This mode of perception is more open to embracing spiritual feelings that are unifying, as the dissecting and constricting mode of perception is no longer dominant. The digital dream will also retrieve the mimetic aspects of the tactile and kinesthetic modes of perception—touch and physical movement—which were the primary forms of spiritual perception in tribal rituals. By bringing the physical body and senses back into the realm of spirituality, the digital dream will revive the primary visceral qualities of spiritual experience, which have been seriously lacking in the theoretically oriented religious services of the modern West.

In Donald's mythic stage, thoughts and ideas are given their distinctness and form when they are molded into the shape of words. Like physical objects, such as the stone tools humans were using, words could now be grasped, manipulated, stored, and controlled. The older imagistic way of thinking was obsolesced, exiled to the netherworld of cognition, the world of dreams. But the thought or experience that is molded into the specific shape of a word loses much of its original vitality and spirit in the process. The original feeling may be lost in the translation from thought to word. The original spirit may be suffocated in the process of constricting the episodic image into a series of sounds. The digital dream retrieves the episodic image, the original unfiltered and un-constricted thought or experience, by bypassing the word. Spiritual perception in the digital dream will be like the experience of God before there was God ... because God is the figment of Myth. God is the mythical, verbal explanation of a spiritual truth that is ultimately ineffable and indefinable by words. That's why a million books have been written about God, but none of them can explain him adequately. The digital dream, in bypassing the word, gets past the three-letter barrier to God—the word "G-O-D," the symbol "God," the specific concept "God"—allowing us to truly experience and perceive the spiritual nature of ourselves; which is hinted to but never truly revealed in the fumbling words used to point towards God.

At the peak of Donald's theoretic stage, humans transform oral words into written words, creating a network of literary documents that extends the human mind ad infinitum.[46] Literacy transforms spirituality from a primary sensory experience into a secondary theoretic experience, as the literalization of God objectifies God, reducing the irreducible into a concrete concept, a word in a book. In the process, primal rituals become doctrines and dogma. Episodic images and visions become scriptures, blessings, and prayers. Spiritual perception becomes lost in the maze of scriptural passages and theological precepts that aim towards God, but wind up just going around in circles, attempting to wrap up in words that which cannot be grasped in words. The digital dream will reverse the spiritual perception of the previous age, the perception of theoretic culture. The unimodal, literal, doctrinal, and dogmatic approach to spirituality will be flipped into an experience of spirituality that is multimodal, intuitive, episodic, imagistic, sensory, and completely open to the personal perspective of the individual dreamer. The "Digital God" is a term that refers to a spiritual experience that cannot be truly defined, because the digital dream will be completely different for every single person.

Spiritual perception in the Digital Age will reflect the changes in perception and cognition that are reshaping the human mind. The Digital God cannot be distinctly imagined or conceived, because he lies beyond the crest of the vertical slope of technology. Nevertheless, we could predict some of the aspects of the Digital God, by observing what aspects of ourselves the medium of digitality will Enhance, Obsolesce, Retrieve, and Reverse. Because digitality enhances media communication by making it more immediate and multisensory, the Digital God will be experienced instantaneously and in multiple senses. Like much of our lives, we can expect spirituality to move online. We can expect online churches and temples to offer instantaneous connection with spiritual stimuli that appeal simultaneously to multiple senses, and are based more on sensory experience than the written word. As a result, the traditional religious practices of Bible study and church attendance—where sermons and Bible passages are read aloud and there are long phases of silent reading in study or prayer—will obsolesce. We have already seen this process begin. Personally, as someone who grew up watching television, that mode of spirituality was inaccessible to me when I was exposed to it as a child. I could not imagine how more inaccessible it would be to my children, who are growing up interacting with the internet. The God of the Book will be obsolesced. The God who is present in the moment and on Earth will be retrieved.

The rituals of the Paleolithic and Mesolithic Ages were designed to evoke a direct, personal, and sensory experience of the divine. The rituals in the forthcoming Digital Age will aspire to do the same. The idols of the Mesolithic and Bronze Ages represented the cutting edge technology of the time. So too, the cutting edge technology of the Digital Age will be employed to evoke the spiritual perception of a more personal God. We will fashion new idols out of copper and silicon, and we will use these idols to probe the deep interior spaces of our own minds.

The religious trend of the past few millennia will be flipped. The trend towards conceptualizing God as an abstract entity who is separated from humanity, cut off from nature, impersonal, detached, unknowable, and imperceptible, will obsolesce. The new digital idols will allow us to fashion our own graven images of God in any way we wish. The personalization, perceptualization, and sensualization of the experience of God may even lead a reversal back to pre-monotheistic spiritualities—polytheism, pantheism, paganism—resurgences of which have already been observed in Europe and America. As digital media, cognition, and perception continue to meld into one integrated system, the doors of perception will open wide. The virtual reality of multisensory digital simulation will give us the power to create our own spiritual perception, as vivid as any dream, and as visceral as any real world sensory experience. The power of the internet will allow us to share our spiritual images, our dreams of God, with everyone around the world, in a truly universal church, experienced as a communal dream. In due time, we will devise simulators that will bypass our conscious mode of perception, tapping directly into our unconscious awareness, the dark hidden space within, in which spiritual perception is not inhibited, and is ready to be retrieved and enhanced. The digitally fueled inward journey into the kingdom of mind will at last reveal the truth of Jesus' proverb: "The kingdom of God is within."[47]

CHAPTER TWO

The Neuropsychology of Spiritual Perception and Digital Zen

> The world is twofold for man in accordance with his twofold attitude.—Martin Buber[1]

Spiritual perception in preliterate societies typically involves encounters with the spirits of dead ancestors. Fuglesang observed that in East Africa, the Swahili word "mzimu" means spirit, an entity that is both living and dead. The spirit is "living-dead." Spiritual perception in this instance is completely paradoxical, because the spirit is both alive and dead in the same moment. This paradox is not a problem of logic to these people, however, because of their belief in the existence of a spiritual dimension that transcends the purely physical dimension of dual properties, in which something is either "alive" or "dead," "real" or "unreal," "true" or "false." This binary approach to the world is transcended in the spiritual dimension, in which there is only complete unity throughout all things.

When someone dies in this culture, they become "mzimu" for as long as there are people in the tribe who carry the "memory-picture" of the person around in their heads. Once all of the people with this memory-picture are gone, once the memory-picture has been erased, then the mzimu dies and can no longer be seen or heard by anyone. The person is now "mfu ... dead as a stone." Fuglesang observed that Mohammad Farah, a preliterate individual in the tribe he was living with, would often go to a specific tree that he associated with his recently dead father, where he saw the mzimu of his father and spoke to him. Fuglesang believes that Mohammad was seeing the "memory-picture" of his father.[2] Mohammad's perception of his father's mzimu is certainly related to Mohammad's "memory-picture" of his father, but his experience of the mzimu is not a conscious act of imagination. Mohammad is not daydreaming. He actually sees and hears his father's mzimu. Mohammad's experience is very similar to my own experience of seeing my dead father in a dream, in that we both perceived our fathers as real objects. We did not construe them as conceived subjects, as figments of our imagination. The very significant difference between the two perceptions is that I was unconscious during my experience, while Mohammad was conscious during his. My father spoke to me in my dream. What did he say? I can't remember, because I was unconscious. Was his message to me important? Did he reveal something significant about himself, or myself, or about my life? I'll never know. But Mohammad, in his conscious perception, can remember what his father said. What's more, he can think about his father's message, and then return the next day to ask follow-up questions. While my dream experience of my father was salient, it was not nearly as enlightening as Mohammad's experience, because I couldn't consciously integrate the experience in any meaningful way.

If we assume that both experiences are psychological, then both experiences denote a duality in the mind. If both Mohammad and I saw and spoke to our fathers, if there was a conversation between two conscious voices going on within each of our minds, then there must be two minds functioning within our brains: One mind that spoke for the son, and another independently thinking mind that spoke for the father. This "duality" of mind exists. The idea is by no means original, and it will be explained in depth in this chapter. The original idea that I will provide is that the phenomenon of spiritual perception is an experience of "cognitive-perceptual unity." It is a moment when the two different minds inside the brain encounter and acknowledge each other, typically in a symbolic form, such as Self and Father, Self and Mother, Self and a spirit, or Self and God. In the sections to come, I will explain how the duality of mind evolved, how the experience of duality is inhibited, and how the experience of cognitive-perceptual unity can be retrieved using digital media technology.

The Evolution of Two Minds Within One Brain

> Is it possible to think of the two hemispheres of the brain almost as two individuals, only one of which can overtly speak, while both can listen and both understand?—Julian Jaynes[3]

If we take a superficial glance at the human brain, one of the first things we might notice is that it is divided into two "hemispheres," the left and the right. Our superficial observation would reveal that the two hemispheres are roughly equal in shape and in mass. Similarly, if we took a superficial look at brain functioning by using scans that observe blood flowing through the brain and electrical activity, we would see that both hemispheres of the brain are more-or-less equally busy processing information all the time. However, neurologists and neuropsychologists tell us that the "dominant" hemisphere is the left and the "subdominant" hemisphere is the right. The dominance of the left seems counterintuitive, given the fact that the left is equal in size and is equally busy as the right. The fact is, the left side is dominant because it is almost constantly inhibiting the right side. The reason the dominant left needs to inhibit the subdominant right is because it controls the functions that are crucial to our everyday functioning in our modern world—language, logic, and analytical thinking—while the right hemisphere takes a more holistic approach to its environment.

To return to Donald's model of cognitive evolution, the primary and most fundamental mode of cognition is episodic. If we assume that the human brain evolved over the millions of years in which we functioned in the episodic mode, the most parsimonious explanation of brain evolution would be that the episodic mindset represented a brain in which both hemispheres worked conjunctively and shared a relative balance in their control of cognition. Why would we evolve brains with structurally and functionally balanced hemispheres, if their initial state was not somewhat balanced? Furthermore, why would the brain evolve a dense mass of connective tissue called the "corpus callosum," that allows for a huge amount of inter-hemispheric communication, if the original working model of the brain was not for both hemispheres to be working in tandem in a balanced way? So, if we assume an initial state of hemispheric *balance* in the episodic stage of cognition, we must also assume progressive stages of hemispheric *imbalance*, in order for us to get to where we are now—a state in which the left hemisphere is dominant and the right hemisphere is subdominant—and a state in which most of the connections in the corpus callosum have an *inhibitory* function on inter-hemispheric neural communication.[4] I will use Donald's model to illustrate this progression, in which each shift in cognitive mindset represents a shift in hemispheric dominance from the right to the left.

When we progressed from the episodic mindset of primates to the mimetic mindset of hominids, our focus turned towards manipulating, analyzing, and replicating specific movements of the hand in order to communicate or master specific tasks such as tool-making and fire-making. Imagine that you're a boy scout or girl scout, it's your first campout, and your scout leader is teaching you how to start a fire. You focus on what the scout leader is doing with his hands, and then you try to replicate his actions with your own hands. How do you hold the sticks? Most likely, you're holding one stick steady with your left hand, while you manipulate another stick with your right hand to create friction and heat. In other words, your left hand is doing very little, while your right is doing a lot. The task must be done this way. One hand must dominate, while the other hand assists by simply holding still. If both hands were busy manipulating, there'd be too many chefs, and the task would be too confusing and wouldn't get done. Neurologically, what is happening is that the part of the brain that controls the dominant hand is simultaneously inhibiting the actions of the subdominant hand, so that the dominant hand could singularly focus on the task, while the subdominant hand is cast in the supporting role. For most people, the right hand is the dominant hand, which is controlled by the left hemisphere of the brain. Hence, the shift from episodic to mimetic mindsets necessitated a shift in the balance of hemispheric control from right to left, because it was now necessary for humans to take a focused "right-handed" approach to their world. Interestingly, instrumentality—the manual manipulation of objects—is preferentially represented in the left hemisphere, even in lefties![5]

Language originally evolved in the right hemisphere of the brain. The protolanguage of primates, "emotional growls and shrieks," is located in the right hemisphere of primate brains.[6] In modern humans, from infancy through early childhood, language develops in the right hemisphere *before* it develops in the left.[7] Only in modern adult humans do we see language processed primarily in the left.[8] The leftward shift in language control that occurs during "ontogeny"—the development of the individual person—reflects a shift in "phylogeny"—the evolution of the human race. In other words, "ontogeny recapitulates phylogeny," the story of our individual development retells the story of our evolution. Specifically, what happened is that the original area in the left hemisphere used to grasp, create, and manipulate tools, was duplicated in a nearby region, sometime during the Paleolithic Age. Duplication is a naturally occurring adaptation in the brain that allows for the further development of processing areas that are crucial to survival, as tool usage surely was in primordial times. In the mythic stage of cognitive evolution, older forms of communication—the primordial grunts and growls of primates and the newer hand signs and gestures of hominids—were transformed into oral words by humans. When we shifted from communicating mimetically to communicating with words, the original area used for tool making and manipulation, rather than remaining redundant, became further specialized in the creation and manipulation of a new tool—language—which was "grasped" away from the right hemisphere and co-opted by the left.[9]

We all talk with our hands, to different degrees. The old joke—"How do you get an Italian to shut up? Tie up his hands."—actually applies to everyone. The fact that deaf and mute people can speak fluently using *only* their hands points to the close neural connection between language and hand control.[10] The evolutionary story of language begins with oral grunts and growls processed in the right hemisphere that were later complemented by mimetic gestures and hand signs processed in the left hemisphere. However, when tool use and tool creation became a significant evolutionary player in the Paleolithic Age, and when this crucial task was married with oral language, the left hemisphere "grasped" the oral function of language away from the right.[11] In order to pass down the knowledge involved in tool making and tool use, extragenetic learning—language—would be key. Thus, the evolution of tool use and language go *hand-in-hand*.

When humans progressed from mythic culture to theoretic culture, eventually culminating with the advent of literacy, language once again became a manual operation. Writing is an instrumental task that is mastered through the use of a manual tool. The history of writing recapitulates the history of language generally: originating in the right hemisphere, but translating itself into the left.[12] In Hebrew, the word for the verb, "to know"—Yad'ay'ah—, is derived from the Hebrew noun, "hand"—Yad—. To know something is similar to having something in your hand. To hold an idea in one's mind is akin to holding something in your grip. Both meanings, the figurative and the literal, are subsumed in the English verb, "to grasp."[13] Recent research in genetics has found that the genes responsible for language processing are present in both hemispheres, but that the right hemispheric genes are repressed.[14] Stroke patients who suffer neurological trauma to the left are able to relearn a lot of their language functioning, which is then processed in the right hemisphere.[15] While the ascendance of the left hemisphere occurred quite recently in our evolutionary history,[16] the emotional core of language remained in the right hemisphere, eventually becoming the seat of music and poetic thought. Though the left hemisphere is dominant, language is still processed in both hemispheres, creating a practical redundancy of language that produces an echo chamber of words in the mind ... the dialectic back and forth of verbalized thought that composes the interior dialogue of private contemplation. Conscious self-awareness, the sense of self that arises from the inner conversations we have with ourselves in our own minds, is the byproduct of a brain that has two languages, one in the left and one in the right, that constantly speak to each other, though the rational voice on the left drowns out the voice on the right.

The left hemisphere dominates the language of thought and therefore dominates cognition, because language itself has become extremely analytical and abstract, and analysis and abstraction are the modus operandi of the left hemisphere. If language begins with a gesture, such as pointing to an apple, that language is direct and concrete. Pointing to the apple means "apple." If a mimetic sign gives us the ability to make a gesture than means "apple," even when no apple is present, then we have created an "analog" for an apple, a sign that mimics the look or feel of an apple, and therefore directly represents the object apple. Oral language then translates that gestural analog into an oral analog, making it much more abstract, because unlike the gesture, the word "apple" has no physical connection with an actual apple. Literacy then represents the oral analog as a visual analog. The written word is a symbol of a symbol, a meta-abstraction, because the written word is merely a representation of the spoken word. The individual letters that compose the word apple—"a" "p" "p" "l" "e"—could in no way be construed as having any concrete, direct, sensory relationship to the thing, apple. Now, in the Digital Age, our relationship with our media is changing our mode of literacy, our balance of sense perceptions, and our styles of cognition. Dr. Iain McGilchrist, author of the masterwork, *The Master and His Emissary: The Divided Brain and the Making of the Western World,* which is cited ad infinitum in this chapter, believes that the leftward trend in cognitive dominance that has been going on for thousands if not millions of years, is speeding up in the Digital Age, as our minds evolve as extensions of the computers with which we interface. Digital language at the processing level of the computer is based on a binary code that evolved from telegraphic code. There are only two signals, "current on" and "current off," symbolized in digital code as "1" and "0." Therefore, to a computer, the written word "apple" looks like this: "01100001011100000111000001101100 01100101." Clearly, digital language is an even further abstraction than literacy. If our minds begin to process information digitally, we will move one step further away from thinking about the apple in a direct, concrete, imagistic way.

Marshall McLuhan, writing before the dawn of the Digital Age, believed that the different balance of sense perceptions fostered by electronic media is moving our cognitive balance *back* towards the right hemisphere, as the pinnacle of left-minded cognition—literacy—is being obsolesced by other modes of media that require less abstraction and less singular focus. So even though the computer thinks in complete abstraction, and even though the computer processes the word "apple" as a series of the digits "0" and "1," when *we* communicate "apple" in the digital age—if I wanted to "send" you the thought "apple" via a digital device—the appearance of the analog to the user will not be a series of digits, nor will it necessarily be a series of letters, nor a series of sounds; but a concrete image of the actual apple, recorded with the click of an iphone and communicated to a single other or to infinite others digitally at the speed of light. Hence, it may be that digital media will actually reverse or flip our perception of language back to its original episodic mindset, as McLuhan's theory predicted.

The Evolution of Cognition and Perception: From Unity to Duality

> Only the phonetic alphabet makes a break between eye and ear,
> between semantic meaning and visual code;
> and thus only phonetic writing has the power to translate man
> from the tribal to the civilized sphere, to give him an eye for an ear.
> —Marshall McLuhan[17]

When I dreamt of encountering my dead father, that phenomenon of episodic perception represented a mindset in which cognition and perception were unified in one experience. Perception is about perceiving an object from the outside world. Even though perception is accomplished within the mind, its function is to create a virtual copy—a "mental re-presentation"—of the external object. Mohammad's tribe would refer to this concept as a "memory-picture." Cognition, on the other hand, is about creating a subject, a private thought within the mind. Perception is based on our experience of the outside world of objects, cognition is based on our experience of the inside world of subjects. In the episodic mindset of animals, cognition is extremely limited, because it has no symbols with which to "grasp" or manipulate the mental representations in its head. The animal perceives an apple and it can recall or visualize the apple, but it cannot control or manipulate its mental image of the apple, because it doesn't have the cognitive tools to do so. The animal, for instance, could not imagine a blue apple, or an apple the size of an acorn, because its mental image of the subjective apple is tied concretely to its perception of the objective apple. It perceives objects but it can only conceive of subjects in the moment of perception, when the object is right there in front of it. Therefore, in the episodic mindset, cognition and perception are unified. The object and subject are one. This unified mindset is nearly impossible to describe to a modern thinker who operates in a state of mental duality, in which cognition creates subjects and perception represents objects, and the two processes typically function separately. The only example I can use is the dream state.

When I dreamt of my dead father, I experienced my father as an objective perception. He seemed as real to me as when he was alive. However, in actuality, my father was actually a subjective cognition, a figment of my imagination— my "image-in-ation"—my mind's ability to create images in absence of any external stimuli. The dream is an experience of cognitive-perceptual unity, a state in which cognition and perception, object and subject, and in this case—spirit and body—are unified into one experience. While my dream experience of cognitive-perceptual unity was unconscious, Mohammad's waking experience of cognitive-perceptual unity was conscious ... he was aware that he was perceiving his father as an external object, while he was also aware that this external object was somehow mystically connected to his subjective concept of his father, the memory-picture of his father. Hence, we could say that Mohammad's sense of spiritual perception is vastly more potent than mine, because he can consciously evoke, remember, and integrate his spiritual perceptions. The reason why Mohammad's spiritual perception is more enhanced than mine is because the cognitive skills that have enhanced my abilities to concoct complicated psychological theories and write books about them, have simultaneously inhibited and obsolesced my ability to experience a conscious state of cognitive-perceptual unity. In short, my conscious mind exists in a state of cognitive-perceptual duality, a perceptual prison from which it is nearly impossible to break free. Such is the state of most literate people.

Cognitive-perceptual duality begins when we can manipulate our mental images, truly turning perceptual objects into conceptual subjects. In the mimetic stage, hominids had to observe, memorize, and replicate complicated manual tasks, such as how to make a hand-axe or how to build a fire. In order to do this without the aid of oral language, we had to rely on an extremely vast system of visual memory that would allow us to recall at will the image of objects in motion in vivid detail. Fuglesang observed this potential for extremely vivid and detailed visual recall among a variety of preliterate tribal peoples.

> Some people have the propensity to experience mental images so intensely that they actually project the image in space in front of their eyes. In my observation, this ability appears prevalent among village people who do not have a written language but depend on strong visual memory for survival.[18]

Mimetic culture enhanced visual memory, but the succeeding mythic culture obsolesced this enhanced visual memory, and enhanced oral memory in its stead.

However, vivid and detailed visual memory is still retrievable. Small children sometimes have "eidetic memory," also referred to as "photographic memory," an ability to recall in exact detail a visual memory of objects that they have seen. This ability is usually lost as the child grows up, just as eidetic imagery of vivid "memory-pictures" among preliterate peoples is lost when these tribal people become literate. McLuhan's theory would explain that eidetic memory is lost because it is obsolesced by the more practical modes of oral memory, which recollects events by restructuring them in words, and even more so by theoretic memory, which records events extra-somatically in documents, eliminating the need for long term visual memory altogether. Autistic savants who do not completely master language often retain their eidetic memory, allowing them to perform seemingly miraculous feats of visual memory. Stephen Wiltshire, for example, is a British autistic savant who can recall an entire landscape after seeing it just once, and reproduce the landscape from memory in detailed drawings. On an episode of *60 Minutes,* Wiltshire took a single helicopter ride around Manhattan. Based on that one observation, he was able to make dozens of detailed drawings of the entire Manhattan skyline from a variety of different perspectives that were extremely vivid and precisely detailed—he even remembered which specific windows in particular apartment buildings were open or shut.[19] We could presume that eidetic memory is an obsolesced mode of memory that is dormant in all of us, but not irretrievable. The vivid and highly detailed visual imagery in dreams and hallucinations, for example, may be cognitive remnants of a vast potential for storing and recalling eidetic memories. Given the fact that there are 100 trillion potential neural connections in the human brain, it's entirely possible from a data processing perspective that we actually store in memory everything we see, but we cannot directly access this vast storehouse of visual memory. The existence of people with "total recall" of all memories for every single day of their lives gives credence to this possibility.[20] If we remember everything we see during the day, it's also quite possible that we remember everything we see during the night ... our dreams. Freud believed that all of our dreams were saved in the vast storehouse of the unconscious mind. If this is true, then the digital dream process discussed in the previous chapter may allow us to tap into this vast storehouse of forgotten dreams, to recall our dreams of childhood, of infancy, and even the dreams we had before we were born.

In the mythic stage, we translate our mental images of events into words. Words reconstruct an event, translating it from a visual memory into an oral recollection. In doing so, the mental image is transformed from an objective memory into a subjective thought. Cognition—*true cognition* as a processes that is separate and distinct from perception—is born of oral language, when words are "interiorized" into the inner voice of consciousness, the language of our own thoughts. At the mythic stage, the words of inner thought formalize the duality between the perception of objects and the cognition of subjects.

In the theoretic stage, visual memory is retrieved, not as a means of recalling mental images of objects, but as a means of objectifying oral words into written words. When we see the word as a written text, we turn it into a visual object. However, when we see this object, the written word "apple," we do not see the object apple, nor do we see a bunch of incoherent markings of black ink, we see a symbol representing "apple," a subject rather than an object, a thought rather than a thing. Thus, when we are in the literary mode of thought, perception is co-opted by cognition. When we are reading and writing words, we are perceiving symbolic subjects, not objects. If the right hemisphere of the brain is involved in understanding our environment as a whole—*cognitive-perceptual unity*—and the left hemisphere is involved in dissecting our environment into objective bits to be analyzed as subjective concepts—*cognitive-perceptual duality*—then the literary mode of thinking becomes a cognitive-perceptual hall of mirrors. In the literary mode, we think in subjective concepts (oral words), and perceive our environment in the form of subjective concepts (written words), which we then interiorize as our own thoughts (more words), that we then express as new concepts (even more words), and on and on in a circle. This process of abstraction completely detaches us both perceptually and cognitively from the real world of objects and events. It locks us up in a perceptual prison of the left hemisphere, where the right hemisphere is completely inhibited, and all that we perceive and conceive are the subjects of our own thoughts.[21] The abstraction of theoretic thought and the resulting duality of cognition and perception become the primary inhibitors of spiritual perception in the modern mind. This, at long last, is why I can see my dead father in a dream, but not while I am consciously awake. It is because my conscious mind is locked away in a cognitive-perceptual prison that only recognizes the products of its own thoughts.

Cognitive-Perceptual Duality: Two Heads Are Better Than One

> Control mechanisms that stabilize a system and help avoid oscillations are the rule rather than the exception in biology.—V.S. Ramachandran[22]

If the corpus-callosum is surgically severed (corpus callosotomy), the two hemispheres of the bran cannot communicate with each other. In the 1940's, Dr. William P. van Wagenen discovered that corpus callostomy was an effective treatment for severe epilepsy. The procedure was performed on thousands of epileptic patients. Beginning in the 1950's, Dr. Richard Sperry performed these operations and conducted extensive research on his "split-brain" patients. For his research, he was awarded the Nobel Prize in 1981. However, on the heels of this research came a slew of theories and ideas about hemispheric differences. Much of this literature was too simplistic, making it seem like the two hemispheres were completely different in every way, and that they were opposed to each other in function and in action. By the 1980's, the topic of hemispheric differences came in to disrepute. Any paper or book that dealt with hemispheric difference was labeled as "New Age" "pop-psychology" hogwash. Indeed, the notion that the left hemisphere is the "rational brain" and the right hemisphere is the "emotional brain," and that the two hemispheres oppose each other, is absurd. Equally absurd, however, would be the notion that the two hemispheres are exactly the same, and have the exact same function. Utter redundancy is maladaptive and organically wasteful. It would belie the fact that we all know, which is that the human brain is the most incredibly sophisticated organic mechanism the world has ever seen. Clearly, there is a middle ground. That the two hemispheres have differences in function is manifest. That the two hemispheres work in conjunction is equally manifest. That the two hemispheres have some redundant functionality—as in the case of language—is also clear. That the hemispheric redundancy in language function is central to the experience of consciousness is probably correct. Dr. Sperry himself believed that each hemisphere is conscious in its own way:

> [each hemisphere is] a conscious system in its own right, perceiving, thinking, remembering, reasoning, willing, and emoting, all at a characteristically human level... both the left and the right hemisphere may be conscious simultaneously in

different, even in mutually conflicting, mental experiences that run along in parallel....

In his book, Ian McGilchrist provides a plethora of research which demonstrates that the right side of the brain is much more involved in processing socio-emotional behaviors, thoughts, and feelings, while the left side is more involved in processing language and reason. Research done with "split-brain" patients displays quite incontrovertibly that both hemispheres simultaneously process concepts and engage in thinking and reasoning in parallel ways, though they can also function independently of each other, and often times do. The notion that one hemisphere can communicate an independently formed idea or concept to the other hemisphere is well established. The notion that this communication could be perceived as coming from an external source is also well established. The relatively common phenomena of dreams, visions, voices, and divine inspiration, perceived as emanating from an external spiritual source, all point to this fact.[23] Spiritual perception, the experience of a "sentient other" as a presence that is *external* to one's own mind, is an experience that has its origin in the right hemisphere of the brain. The increasing inhibition of this experience since the Paleolithic Age, and the more rapidly increasing inhibition since the Iron Age, is due to a shift in brain hemispheric dominance from right to left. The right-to-left shift was a neurological adaptation made to accommodate the human race's increasing need for tool use, language, literacy, and associated tasks. As the left hemisphere's dominance over all cognitive functions—especially language based consciousness—increased, the right hemisphere's input became increasingly inhibited. Spiritual perception, a right hemispheric function, has, in many people, become almost completely inhibited by the left hemispheric function: language based consciousness. When spiritual perception is experienced, when it slips past the bars of the perceptual prison governed by the left hemisphere, it is experienced as a foreign intruder on our perception, a strange, separate, sentient "other."

The left hemisphere, as McGilchrist summarized in his book through exhaustive clinical and experimental examples, invokes a perspective that is literal and analytical, focusing on exact details and parts of things that may be taken out of context. The point of view taken is self-reflective, self-conscious, abstract, and detached. The left hemisphere uses a mode of cognitive-perceptual duality to separate the objects it perceives from the subjects that it conceives, so that it can maintain a detached, analytic, aloof perspective. To recall a metaphor I used in the previous chapter, the viewpoint of the left is of the observer looking down at the maze, rather than the viewpoint of the person inside the maze. The right hemisphere invokes a holistic gestalt perspective, looking at things within their context, focusing on the relationships between things, rather than analyzing the specific things individually. The right viewpoint is one of cognitive-perceptual unity, the viewpoint from within the maze. The right tends towards the personal, the left towards the impersonal, as emotion, emotional memory, and thoughts about emotional relationships are processed in the right hemisphere.[24] When an infant sees, remembers, or recognizes his mother's voice and face, those thoughts and feelings are processed primarily in the right hemisphere.[25] Unconscious insight, intuition, imagination, and inspiration are predominantly right hemispheric functions.[26]

McGilchrist believes that the leftward shift in perspective is speeding up in the Digital Age, as a function of our increasing interactivity with computers and digital devices, and our decreasing interactivity with real people. A quick glance at the modern world of social networking seems to affirm McGilchrist's assertion. Only the left hemisphere, in conjunction with the digital interface of the internet, could associate the once cherished word—"friend"—the word that embodies the feelings of love and personal connection we have with others, with the process of gathering hundreds or even thousands of random acquaintances and complete strangers, connected by varying degrees of abstract separation, onto a social network spreadsheet. Only the left hemisphere could conceive of the verb, "unfriend."

A mind with two hemispheres working conjunctively but in different ways is a better problem solver than a mind that only has one system of problem solving in place. Hence, the bi-hemispheric structure and functionality of the brain is highly adaptive. The adaptability of "lateralization"—the localization of a function in one specific hemisphere of the brain—and "duplication"—the ability of the brain to process the same function in two separate locations—can be seen in many ways. For instance, the lateralization of manual operation functions, which results in right-handedness and left-handedness, is highly adaptive, because it is beneficial for humans to have a right hand that can function independently from the left, as mutual independence increases the level of sophistication of manual operation. Imagine trying to play the piano if you had a left hand that could not function independently of the right. Duplication of manual operations, *on the other hand*, also increases adaptivity, as one hand can substitute for the other in case of the loss or injury of a hand or limb. Similarly, thinking and reasoning are processes that are both lateralized and duplicated in the brain.[27] They are carried out in parallel form by both conscious and unconscious mechanisms, with both the left and right hemispheres specializing in its own way of thinking. You "think twice" about an important decision. You may be "of two minds" about some issue, or you say that you can't "make up your mind," as if your mind was debating with a different mind inside your brain. You "sleep on it" when the decision needs to be cogitated upon, whereupon you wake up in the morning with a "different view" of the problem, as if the answer "came to you in a dream."

When we are engaged in conscious thought, we are usually thinking in the mode of language, and we can even hear the sound of our language based thoughts in our heads as we think, the "internal monologue." However, we also engage in an "internal *dialogue*," in which the mind speaks to itself in a debate or discussion, with two separate viewpoints being espoused. The ability to deliberate with oneself is an extremely valuable intellectual asset, as it allows us to explore different possible solutions to a problem on an entirely hypothetical basis, so that we arrive at the best possible solution before making a decision and acting upon it. As McLuhan asserted, the greatest feat of consciousness is that human beings have learned to "act" rather than to "react." Instead of just responding instinctively to our environments, we think about our actions before we act upon them, and we can even withhold action or act counter-intuitively, if our thoughts instruct us to do so.

Although we are *for the moment* envisioning the left and right hemispheres as different systems, we must always remember that the brain is one system, creating one sense of consciousness. It is equally important to remember that nearly all of the brain is nearly always occupied with functions that are almost completely unconscious: "...very little brain activity is in fact conscious (current estimates are certainly less than 5 percent, and probably less than 1 percent)."[28] Sperry's work revealed that the different hemispheres function independently of each other, and specialize in different types of tasks: "...each surgically disconnected hemisphere appears to have a mind of its own, but each cut off from, and oblivious to, conscious events in the partner hemisphere."[29] But the fact that we are for the most part unaware of our own cognitive duality points to the incredibly sophisticated interactivity of the two hemispheres; they create the near perfect illusion of singularity. This is because consciousness, rather than being a single process of "higher thought," is actually a blend of processes that begin at much more basic levels of brain functioning.[30] Consciousness can be compared to a tree that begins quite humbly in a base of roots, before extending upwards into a trunk, and then limbs, and then thin branches, and then leaves. The canopy of leaves is likened to the "cerebral canopy" of consciousness that seems to exist independently; but in actuality, is at no point ever disconnected from its lower origins, the roots.[31] But while consciousness as a process has deep roots in a unified brain, the very apex of consciousness, the process of language based consciousness that controls most of our waking thoughts, is stationed in the left hemisphere of the brain.[32] The left hemisphere dominates functioning in language, especially literacy, as well as calculation, our sense of time, and all thinking that is literal, analytical, sequential, deductive, and reductive.[33] Furthermore, the left hemisphere is usually inhibiting the right hemisphere to a certain degree, in order to maintain a literal, focused, and analytic perspective.[34]

It creates and maintains this order with the "three Ls" of cognition under its disposal: "language, logic, and linearity"[35]—which can be summarized with one big L—*Logos*—the rational, logical, and literal system of thought that arose as a consequence of the advent of Literacy.

The cognitive mode of the left hemisphere— Logos, language based reason—is by definition incapable of processing spiritual perception, as this perception is both ineffable—inexplicable by *language*—and illogical—based on belief *without reason*. Furthermore, spiritual perception is always experienced as a feeling of "unity," a feeling of being integrated with something bigger and outside of oneself. The left hemisphere, however, functions by detaching itself, by creating a duality of object and subject, in order to maintain an abstract analytical perspective. Thus, the left hemisphere of the brain is both incapable of and *inhibitory* of spiritual perception.[36]

The left hemisphere is dominant when viewing familiar images that are complete and distinct, while the right hemisphere is dominant when images are incomplete, indistinct, only partially visible, or seen fleetingly. The left hemisphere is more comfortable focusing on the clearly understandable, while the right hemisphere displays an "affinity for all that is 'other,' new, unknown, uncertain and unbounded." The left hemisphere displays a distinct "affinity for what it itself has made," that is, language—which is based on signs such as the phonetic alphabet—which are concrete, fixed, sequential, and generally represent only one thing.[37] Perceptions that are indistinct and open to interpretation are likely to be "rationalized" by the left hemisphere to the point of non-existence. "Denial is a left hemisphere specialty."[38] Ramachandran observed this phenomenon in patients who had severe strokes that disabled sections of their brain's right hemisphere. When the left hemisphere is not tempered in its perception of the world by right-hemispheric input, the patients were often over-optimistic about their conditions, to the extent that they even denied having anything wrong with them at all, even when they were seriously disabled.[39] Because the left hemisphere tends to deny the existence of anything that it cannot recognize, objectify, or conceptualize—anything that is not completely under its cognitive control—the left hemisphere is likely to deny the existence of spiritual perceptions, whereas the right hemisphere is more open to these modalities.[40]

If a nonconforming perception is admitted entrance to conscious awareness by the dominant left hemisphere, it becomes "denatured" in the process, because it is analyzed as an object or a concept, a specific thing with a specific meaning, rather than as a phenomenon that exists primarily within its own context.[41] The literal consciousness that de-contextualizes and dissects in order to analyze, destroys the true nature of that which it sees by the process of its own analysis, because nothing that is alive and meaningful exists in a vacuum. A deconstructed poem loses its emotional core as a consequence of being deconstructed. A flower plucked from a garden dies because it was plucked. The innards of a dissected frog can tell you nothing of its prodigious hop or of its stentorian croak, because the dissection disemboweled him of his innate nature. Thus, the essence of a spiritual entity—God—is denatured when it is abstracted from its context of spiritual perception. When God is dealt with as an intellectual concept rather than as a perceptible being, he is de-animated—he loses his spirit—and becomes an imperceptible thought, rather than a personal other.

While the left hemisphere focuses on the "three Ls ... language, logic, and linearity," one could say that the right hemisphere focuses on the three Is: intuition, inspiration, and imagination.[42] Working together, conjunctively, the two modes inform each other quite well. However, as McGilchrist argued, when cognition and perception are dominated by the left hemisphere, we have a situation in which consciousness is for the most part a left hemisphere affair, while right hemisphere input is repressed or inhibited, left in the untended dustbin of unconscious awareness.[43] McGilchrist's believes that "the essential difference" between the hemispheres is that the right hemisphere is focused on "the Other, whatever it is that exists apart from ourselves." The right hemisphere is engaged in the field of "relationship, the betweenness, that exists with this Other." The left hemisphere, on the other hand, is "self-contained" within its own solipsistic world of logic and reason. It is "ultimately disconnected from the Other," because the rules of its own logic disallow the recognition of that which is not objectively known.[44] Language creates a "magic circle" around itself, a circle that can only be entered through word-shaped holes, a circle that circumscribes and imprisons conscious thought.[45] The right hemisphere provides an outlet through which we can unensnare ourselves, but the outlet is often shut off by the circle's tendency to close in on itself. "Modern man has been so trained to trust only thoughts driven along by chains of words that this inner knowledge is treated nervously."[46]

The sentient "Other," the sense of something outside of the closed circle of the conscious self—the "Other-I"—is what spiritual perception is reaching outwardly towards.

While the corpus callosum is the primary connective tissue between the two hemispheres, the main task of the corpus callosum is in most cases to *inhibit* or delay direct communication between the hemispheres. The tube created for communication has become blocked. The blockage began when we started speaking and thinking in words; it sped up dramatically when we began visualizing words, reading and writing them down; and as the process of literacy accelerates, the tendency for the left hemisphere to cut itself off from the right hemisphere accelerates as well. The tube, like a clogged pipe, becomes increasingly blocked as a result of the blockage itself. Meanwhile, the information being blocked—the intuition, inspiration, and imagination of the right hemisphere—is increasingly dumped into the untended dustbin of unconsciousness. If the "normal" state of consciousness is a state of neural *inhibition* of certain influences of the right hemisphere on cognition and perception, then spiritual perception could be considered an "abnormal" or "altered" state of consciousness, in which there is a temporary *disinhibition* of certain influences of the right hemisphere. When bi-hemispheric communication is temporarily disinhibited due to a seizure, a drug, a moment of ecstasy, an epiphany, a magnetic wave, etc., the feeling of connection with that which we do not perceive as ourselves comes over us like a wave of emotion. The perception of the "sentient other," because it is rarely experienced, therefore takes on a much more pronounced and dramatic effect. Because it is hardly ever seen, when it is seen, it is more than a normal experience—it is a revelation!

Intuition, Imagination, and Inspiration

> Consciousness is a witch beneath whose charms pure inspiration gasps and dies into invention.—Julian Jaynes

An intuitive thought is spontaneous. It comes to us out of the blue, rather than us coming to it via a process of concentration, focusing, reasoning, or deduction. Intuition, defined this way, is a right hemispheric function.[47] Everybody *intuitively* knows what intuition is, because we have all experienced it. Intuition is "knowing without thinking," or having a sudden insight that gives us a new or original perspective on a subject. Oftentimes, people attribute intuitive insights to dreams, as the image or idea came to them in their sleep. Since dreaming, like intuition, is also largely a right hemispheric function, it would not be a stretch to argue that dreaming and intuition are intimately linked. In 1865, Friedrich Kekulé envisioned a hexagonal ring of carbon atoms in a dream, that solved the puzzle he was trying to figure out, regarding the molecular structure of benzene.[48] Kekulé's discovery of the structure of the "benzene ring" would become the foundation of the chemical structure theory, and was the basis of the research that earned Kekulé three of the first five Nobel prizes ever awarded for chemistry. Similarly, Einstein experienced a sudden insight that led to his theory of relativity while dozing off on a train. The structure of the periodic table of elements came to Mendeleyev while he was in a dream.[49] There is an old saying, sometimes attributed to Wittgenstein, that our best thoughts always come to us within the context of "the three Bs: the bed, the bath, the bus." This is not to say that all great thoughts are completely intuitive. That's absurd. The point is, the mind, when grappling with a subject that it is extremely familiar with, will often reach a point of blockage, a point at which further progress is impeded, because rational analysis excels at deducing knowledge from that which is *already known*. In order to launch a foray into *new* knowledge, one must go beyond rational analysis, and take a leap outside of logic. That's what intuition does. Because intuition is illogical, it is often wrong.[50] In those cases, our right hemispheric intuitions are quickly disqualified and dismissed by our analytical left hemisphere. But in those instances when our intuition is right ... those are the "breakthroughs" that found new theories and build new edifices of knowledge. What is being "broken through" is the blockage, the inhibition that generally exists between the analytical and intuitive hemispheres of the brain.[51]

However, as every intuitive thinker knows, the farther away we get from the original intuitive insight, the more we think about our intuition rationally, the more we lose of its original inspirational power. For an intuition is a spontaneous thought arising from the right hemisphere. If that thought is reflected upon, it is being analyzed by the left side of the brain. The thought may bounce back and forth for a moment between the two sides of the brain like a ping pong ball; but with each bounce, the thought will become less intuitive, as the left hemisphere will do what it does best ... it will "grasp" the thought and hold on to it, focusing on it and deconstructing it. Hence, the more reflective we become about our own thoughts, the more abstract our thinking becomes, and the more detached we become from our more basic, spontaneous, intuitive cognitions. In this sense, abstract thought becomes like a positive feedback loop. Submitting our intuitive thought to analytical reflection makes the thought more abstract, and the more we think about it, the more abstract it becomes, until it has become complete abstraction.

Though intuition may be directly linked to instinct, making its origins millions if not billions of years older than logic, intuition is by no means retrograde or obsolete. It has continued to evolve, even if it has somewhat recently been eclipsed to a large extent by logic. Preliterate peoples perform great feats of thought using only intuition. Our prehistoric ancestors navigated the glacial landscapes without the aid of maps or compasses. The Truk Islanders in the South Pacific, a contemporary preliterate society, commonly sail hundreds of miles within a zigzagging maze of tiny coral islands, finding their way by "feel" alone.[52] Autistic mathematical savants are capable of astounding feats of calculation without even thinking about it—the numbers just come to them without any thought at all.

Batson (1982) developed a theory of religious experience based on intuition. As a template, he used Graham Wallas' (1926) four stage model of the creative process:

1. Preparation—thinking about a problem and reaching an impasse.
2. Incubation—giving up and relaxing, possibly going to sleep or having a drink.
3. Illumination—gaining sudden insight, inspiration, or "seeing the light."

4. Verification—going back to the problem and verifying the solution with logical reasoning.

Batson suggested that a momentary shift in cognitive dominance from left hemisphere to right hemisphere is taking place in stages 2 and 3. If, in the Preparation stage, the problem that has reached an impasse is a moral or existential crisis, perhaps a sense of meaningless in life, then an objective intellectual solution may be impossible to derive. And, because an existential life crisis is inherently emotional, the problem may require a socio-emotional rather than a rational deductive solution. Hence, the shift from left to right hemispheric dominance in the Incubation stage represents a change in thinking from the logical left hemisphere to the socio-emotional right hemisphere. This shift is perhaps induced by simply going to sleep and having a dream, or maybe a more purposeful method such as praying, meditating, chanting, or taking a psychoactive substance. In any case, a spiritual "Illumination" is experienced when the right hemisphere expresses an intuition that is clear and uninhibited by the left. The person will come out of this stage with a new outlook on his problem. In the Verification stage, he will try to make sense of this "cognitive restructuring" of the problem, and find a way to integrate this spiritual insight into his everyday life.[53]

To return to the case of Mohammad and his father, when Mohammad had a problem to resolve, he would think about it until he either resolved the problem or realized that he was stuck: the Preparation Stage. Mohammad would then go to the tree and sing a song or burn some incense or do whatever ritual deed he needed to perform in order to summon the mzimu of his father: Incubation Stage. Usually, his father's mzimu would appear, and they would talk: Illumination. Afterwards, Mohammad would go back to his own hut and think about what his father had told him, and try to integrate that into a meaningful resolution for his problem: Verification. Once again, we see that Mohammad's spiritual perception provides much more direct and practical access to his mind's wellsprings of intuition, imagination, and inspiration. Nevertheless, a modern secularist would criticize the process on the grounds that too much weight is given to "spiritual" insight, as the message of the "mzimu" is typically accepted uncritically as pure wisdom, rather than analyzed and verified with logic and reason.

A study by Barrett (1996) indicated that people process thoughts about God in both intuitive and rational ways. Barrett asked people to describe God. In response, most subjects described God as being omniscient, omnipotent, and omnipresent. Then Barrett told the subjects a story in which God does two things simultaneously. For instance, God saves a man's life while, at the same moment, he helps a woman find her lost purse. After a little while, the subject is asked to recall the story. In the subject's recall, God always saves the man's life first, and *then* he helps the woman find her purse. The key point is that when the subject must reconstruct his memory of a story—a task that requires not only memory, but also some imagination, to fill in the gaps of memory—God acts more like a human than like a god. In the reconstructed memory, God can only do one thing at a time, and he can only pay attention to one thing at a time. Like us, God is acting and thinking sequentially, rather than simultaneously. Hence, these people's "mental representations" of God's thoughts and behaviors were not the same as their conscious verbal descriptions of God's abilities. The latter attributes, the way people consciously described God, were referred to as "theological correctness," meaning that they were based on their conscious theoretic knowledge of theological doctrines that define the concept of God (the left hemisphere's logic-based approach). But the mental representations that people had about God, their "intuitive expectations," represent a more primary and basic cognitive process, an "implicit," intuitive, unconscious concept of God.[54] This divergence in subject responses shows that God is conceptualized in two different ways, and that the intuitive conceptualization is the more basic and primary process, as it is accessed much faster and does not require deliberate thought.[55]

Paradoxicality

> Try and penetrate with our limited means the secrets of nature and you will find that, behind all the discernible concatenations, there remains something subtle, intangible, and inexplicable. Veneration for this force beyond anything that we can comprehend is my religion.—Albert Einstein

"Paradoxicality" is a form of understanding and perception in which someone sees something in two different ways simultaneously, yet still comprehends the subject as one complete experience. Paradoxicality can be construed intuitively, but it is inaccessible to the logical frame of mind. Myths speak in a language of paradoxicality. Gods in myth are all-loving and beneficent, yet they are often angry, vengeful, violent, and withholding. Spiritual beings morph into different animals and personas, yet they retain their singular identities. Gods display temporal duality—they can be in two places at once. Miracles occur, defying the laws of nature. To appreciate myth, one must accept the paradoxes they portray, without questioning the logic behind it. "Mythos," "myth," "mystical," "mystery"—these words with the same Greek root speak in a language of paradoxical symbols, in which one thing can mean many things, and many things can represent a single thing. Paradoxicality is sensed when the right hemisphere accepts the experience as a whole, perceiving the outer event and the inner thought about the event—the object and the subject—as one integrated experience of cognitive-perceptual unity. Paradoxicality is accepted by the right hemisphere, but rejected by the left, which detects the illogicality of the experience, and denies it.[56]

In some situations, such as the dream state, paradoxicality is readily accepted, because the left hemisphere, during the dream state, is the side that is inhibited. In other situations, paradoxicality is readily accepted, because it is a mode of cognition that is set as a precondition for the situation itself. Paradoxicality, for example, is always associated with spiritual rituals. In some preliterate rituals, a shaman dancing in the skin of a leopard believes that he actually *becomes* the totem animal. His fellow participants in the ritual see a man in leopard skin; but they *perceive* a leopard spirit in their midst. In prayer, within the sacred confines of the temple or church, I speak to a presence who cannot be seen or heard. I am aware that dozens of people around me, and millions of people around the world, may be simultaneously praying to the same God, yet I believe that he is listening specifically to me. In Catholic Communion, a wafer is understood to be both a wafer and the body of Jesus. Catholic theologians call this state of mind the "*coincidentia oppositorium*," in which, during a heightened encounter with the sacred, things that normally seem opposed coincide to reveal an underlying unity.[57]

Paradoxical thinking transcends the logical, allowing the believer to transcend the Paradox of Faith, which is only seen as a paradox when comprehension is filtered through the sieve of language based consciousness. A logical thinker says: "Faith is a paradox, because it requires the belief in something that cannot be proven to be real." An intuitive thinker says: "God may not be objectively real, but he is spiritually real, and I have faith in his spirit, as long as I can feel it." Voila! There is no paradox!

Logical thinking functions according to the "laws of non-contradiction." It does not recognize anything that contradicts itself—that which is paradoxical—as being valid or even existent.[58] This rule of preclusion doesn't exist in the right hemisphere, which isn't bound by logic, and is therefore open to things that are paradoxical and ambiguous. So the phenomenon of God, which is inherently paradoxical, because he is both real and unreal, can only exist in the right hemisphere. The left hemisphere can only comprehend God when his existence is rationalized according to logical principles. Hence, the myriad of volumes of abstract theology published by literate theoretic believers over the past 3,500 years. Nevertheless, these logical principles, in the final analysis, always fall short of the standards of pure reason. Rationalization of the inherently paradoxical must always fall back on the believer's last stand.... Faith. But Faith itself, from a purely logical perspective, is ultimately paradoxical! Hence, the person whose thinking is governed by logicality becomes incapable of making the "leap of faith" that is necessary for a logical person to believe in the existence of God, because he is incapable of accepting an inherently paradoxical phenomenon as true or real. This is why the left hemisphere, in the case of God, so often trumps the right hemisphere, as the left controls the "means of argument"—logical language—while the right is largely silent.

This is not to say that the thinking of the true believer is always inherently illogical. Most people maintain multiple levels of representation for single concepts in their minds.[59] For example, when observing a sunset, you might say: "Ooh, how pretty, the sun is going down!" This is exactly what you're thinking; yet at the same time, on a different level of representation, you know very well that the sun isn't going anywhere; but rather, it's the rotating Earth that is turning away from the stationary sun. Similarly, the believer's mental representations of God are both logical and paradoxical, because God is a complex concept that exists on multiple levels of representation. There is the abstract God that modern monotheistic religions tend to purvey, the distant, hidden God—Barrett's "theological God." And then, for many, there is the personal God, the God whose voice can almost be heard, whose face cannot almost be seen, and whose presence is sometimes felt—Barrett's "intuitive God." The simultaneous conception of these dichotomous representations of God has been labeled by some cognitive psychologists as "the tragedy of the theologians."[60] While theologians such as Paul Tillich insist that one can never truly "know" God, and that he must be conceived of in completely abstract terms, such as the "existential ground of being"—most believers cannot even comprehend these extremely abstract concepts,[61] and instead feel a very intuitive and personal sense of God—much like the feelings one would have for another person. In the brain's dual-processing system, the theological God is processed by the "rational system ... a deliberative, analytical system that operates primarily in a medium of language." This system has a "relatively brief evolutionary history." The "intuitive God," on the other hand, is processed by the "experiential system," which "encodes information in a concrete, holistic, primarily nonverbal form." The experiential system has a "very long evolutionary history." The experiential system is the "controlling system," because "basic representations govern social thought unless care is taken to override them." Hence, when it comes to spirituality, "experiencing is believing."[62]

The "tragedy of the theologian" points out that theologians and atheists are very much alike in their thinking. If you read Kierkegaard and Hume in tandem, it is clear that these literate minds both dwell in the most abstract regions of logicality, yet they come to opposing conclusions. "One says 'I do not know,' the other 'I know—that there is nothing to know.' One believes that one cannot know: the other 'knows' that one cannot believe."[63] The logic of the left hemisphere can bring you to only one of two destinations: the absolute belief in the unknowability of God, or the absolute disbelief in God. The two stances are, in essence, quite similar. But the believer who actually gains substance and nourishment and meaning from his belief is not attaining those benefits from the left side of his brain. It is the emotional *experience* of God, the sensory *perception* of God's presence, the intuitive *awareness* of God's existence that make God real. These experiences are processed in the right hemisphere of the brain.[64]

Perception Is Virtual Reality

> If the doors of perception were cleansed, every thing would appear to man as it is, infinite. For man has closed himself up, till he sees all things through narrow chinks of his cavern.—William Blake[65]

Oliver Sacks summed it up quite neatly when he wrote: "One does not see with the eyes; one sees with the brain." Perception is an interpretive process that is almost entirely unconscious. Herman von Helmholtz, the "founding father of visual science," referred to perception as an "unconscious inference."[66] What we perceive is by no means a presentation of reality. Perception is a cognitive re-representation of a made-up virtual reality. The reason why perception must be unconsciously inferred rather than directly represented in the brain is that the amount of sensory stimulation that we are bombarded with in each second of the day is simply too much to handle. In order to "make sense" of it all, the stimuli have to be narrowed down through an extremely restrictive straining process. First, the total amount of stimulation that is received by the senses is tapered down into a very narrow range of sensory input that is actually transmitted into the brain.[67] Everything outside of that narrow range is filtered out of our perceptual awareness. Then that narrow range is filtered through a primary process of interpretation, in which only a few possible interpretations of the stimuli are enabled. Only those interpretations that arise in accordance with memory, reason, or imagination are recognized. Finally, those few elite possible interpretations are narrowed down to one accepted interpretation. That one remaining finalist is what we call "perception." It is by no means a recording or representation of the objective world. It is, in actuality, a subjective best guess at what is in our environment.

Perception is an active constructive process, a cognitive function of the brain, not the sense organs. What we perceive is immediately interpreted by the brain into a meaningful pattern, even if that interpretation is not entirely faithful to the sensory information being received. The mind not only organizes sensory experience, it actively constructs the experience itself, rearranging what is perceived and filling in gaps where it feels necessary, in order to create an illusory experience of the real world as a whole, even though we are not seeing the "real world" at all, and even though the constructed re-representation that we perceive as one whole and believe to be the "real world," is actually an assemblage of infinite bits of data, some of them taken in by the senses, but many of them constructed and inserted by our brains themselves.[68] Social psychology experiments have demonstrated what we already intuitively know—the mind presents us with images of what we truly desire. This happens in the form of dreams every night, and in more subtle and infrequent ways, in the form of hallucinations, mirages, and visual misperceptions. For example, one classic study demonstrated that when presented with a distorted image, hungry people will see food, while non-hungry people will see non-food related images.[69] In a Navy experiment, sailors who were deprived of food for up to 16 hours would actually see visions of food when no stimulus was present. The longer the sailors were deprived of food, the more likely they were to hallucinate images of food.[70] Other researchers found that religious individuals recognized religious words such as "priest" and "minister" significantly faster than non-religious words such as "price" or "bond," demonstrating that not only do we see what we want to see, even when it is not really there; but we are quicker and more ready to see the things that are important to us, as compared to the things that are not as important to us.[71] Clearly, believing is seeing, not the other way around.

What we perceive as reality is, as a rule, singular. Our perceptual faculties must choose just one interpretation when making its initial perception. Otherwise, life would be too confusing, for instead of making quick decisions when we have to, we'd get stuck like a deer in the headlights, trying to decide what our senses are perceiving. Imagine what it would be like if, while you were driving to work, every object in the distance came to your mind as several different interpretations co-existing in the same moment. "That thing up ahead is either a fallen road sign, a disabled car, a state trooper, a fallen tree, or a dead horse." You absolutely could not function if all of your perceptions evoked multiple interpretations ... you'd crash, or take the wrong exit, or never get to work. Instead, the mind immediately makes one interpretation, usually the one that makes the most sense at the moment, and you proceed accordingly. So, what we actually perceive is: "That's a state trooper up ahead." If you could take a snapshot of your perception at that moment, you would see a clear image of the state trooper in your mind, even if, after a few miles, you see that the object is actually a disabled car. Regardless of the initial misperception, the mind must always function as if it actually knows what it's perceiving, because the consequences of not being able to function due to multiple perceptual interpretations is far worse than making the occasional initial misperception.

Language-based consciousness, as it becomes more abstract, subjects itself to the discipline of logical, rational, objective reasoning. Thinking that is dominated by abstract logical reasoning adds a "logic filter" to conscious perception.

Every perceptual interpretation that is illogical gets filtered out. "That thing up ahead can either be a dinosaur or a holly bush shaped liked a dinosaur." Immediately, even before the dinosaur interpretation is made fully conscious, it is weeded out by the logic filter, leaving only the logical, sensible interpretation. However, our cognitive decisions about what is or is not logical are based on our beliefs. If you truly believed in the existence of dinosaurs, then the dinosaur interpretation would not be immediately weeded out—you might actually see the dinosaur in your mind—before you get closer and see that it's only a bush. Similarly, if that thing up ahead could either be a white sheet blowing on a clothes line or an angel, your initial interpretation depends entirely on whether or not you believe in angels.

We would not be able to function if we perceived the world around us as multiple coexisting realities. Life with one reality is complicated enough! So the mind filters our perception, squeezing it through a tiny "door," so that we are presented with only one version of reality at each given moment. Nevertheless, there is always another version of reality, another mode of perception, another way of conceiving the world that we are not perceiving. We go about our lives perceiving one reality, while an infinite number of alternate realities exist just outside our doors of perception. But the existence of that subliminal other is known to us unconsciously, as he was seen but not perceived, experienced but not processed, sensed but not fully interpreted. The experience of God for many people is similar to this perceptual netherworld in which a sensed other, an alternate reality, is felt but not fully perceived. For the believer, God is always there, just behind the door of perception, but one is not always aware of His presence, because the door is not open. However, there are moments of spiritual awareness when the perceptual field is temporarily flipped, the doors of perception are flung open—the figure becomes ground and the ground is made figure—and God's existence is made quite clear. However, because we can only perceive one reality at a time, the moment in which the alternate spiritual reality is perceived is a moment in which the primary reality of logic and reason are not in focus. This is why the mystical experience is always ineffable and insusceptible to rational explanation.

Belief is primary, perception is secondary. Our beliefs are preexistent to our perceptions, and because the interpretations of our perceptions are "belief-dependent,"[72] beliefs mold our perception ... we see what we believe. Because uncertainty and confusion are anxiety provoking, the brain automatically narrows down our perceptual interpretations into one singular, believable, rational representation of the world. It is the task of the left hemisphere of the brain to create a meaningful conscious explanation for our perceptual experience, even if that experience lay outside of our own conscious understanding. This is called "confabulation." For example, let's say you are walking at night. Suddenly, there is movement in the bushes to your left. You look to your left and see something indistinct moving in the darkness. At the same time, you hear a hushed whistling sound, and you see a soft bluish light shine briefly and then disappear. A rational explanation for all of these perceptions is that there was an animal scurrying in the bushes, the wind blew through the trees creating a whistling sound, and the moonlight, obscured by overcast, shone briefly through a break in the clouds. However, a person with a spiritual mindset could very easily perceive the conjunction of all of these perceptions as an encounter with a spirit. The perceptions themselves happened in an instant and then it was over. The understanding and interpretation of the perceptions, however, are now in the hands of the mind. The memory of the event can be twisted and contorted—confabulated—to reflect the individual's beliefs. The imagination takes hold, changing the memories to reflect hidden fears or anxieties. The mind confabulates, assigning meaning and significance to details that may not have even existed, and changing details to fit its needs. Perception is a conglomeration of fragmentary and incomplete sensory information, molded into a conscious model of an illusory whole with the creative assistance of memory, expectation, reason, intuition, imagination, desire, and most importantly, belief. So what is perceived in the end is entirely confabulation, an act of creative unconscious interpretation.

Perception imparts a complete picture, even when only an incomplete picture is present. In doing so, perception reveals the preference of the mind for totalities, complete pictures, even when a true totality is lacking. For instance, a rabbit seen behind a picket fence is perceived as a whole rabbit, not as a series of rabbit slices.[73] The mind intuitively "fills in" the missing rabbit pieces to construct or "re-present" the whole. Similarly, a "blind spot" exists in every human's visual field. Rather than perceiving this blind spot as a small black hole in our environment, our mind is constantly filling in this blind spot with the visual information it expects should be there.[74]

The mind also uses our memories and expectations to prime our perceptions, even before the sensory information is received by our senses. "Conceptual completion,"[75] the process of the mind perceiving stimuli before the senses, suggests that our perceptual machinery works in reverse.[76] We perceive what we expect to perceive, rather than perceiving what we actually see. For instance, let's say you hear what sounds like a "meow." Memory immediately makes an association and provides your "mind's eye" with a complete image of a cat, before a cat even enters your visual field. You glance to the right and see a tail sticking out from behind a couch. The image re-presented to our brain is an interplay between what you see (a fragmentary image of a cat), what you remember a cat is supposed to look like (a familiar image in your mind's eye of a cat), and your mind's configuration of what this particular cat *should* look like based on the color and length of its tail (a black cat for a black tail, etc.). If you were to look behind the couch and find a small child pretending to be a cat, with a cat's tail attached to her bottom, you would be very surprised indeed! Hence, the mind creates the perception of the cat, rather than the cat creating a perception in the mind. Visual perceptions "flow from top to bottom—from higher regions to the primary visual cortex—and the combined activities of all these areas lead to the perception of an imaginary cat by the mind's eye."[77]

The perceptual opposite of the blind spot phenomena and conceptual completion is "blindsight"—a rare condition resulting from neurological damage to a certain area of the visual cortex. The patient is blind, because the neural connection between her optical nerve and her cortex is severed. However, when prompted, the patient can point to a spot of light projected onto a wall, even though she can't see it. This is because another perceptual pathway linking the retina and the parietal lobe is still intact. Blindsight demonstrates that we do not perceive much of what we sense in our environment, and that what is perceived is completely determined by the brain, and for the most part interpreted and re-presented by the cortex.[78] In a very true sense, we are hallucinating all the time. The images that we see are truly re-presentations constructed by our mind. They are inspired by the "real world," but in no way are they objective copies of the real world. In fact, human beings never truly have any direct contact with what we may call the "real world," because everything we experience is filtered through the interpretative process of perception. There may not even be a "real world!" All of our perception, all of our experience, could simply just be a "dream within a dream."

Qualia

> Good Lord Boyet, my beauty, though but mean,
> Needs not the painted flourish of your praise:
> *Beauty is bought by judgement of the eye,*
> Not utter'd by base sale of chapmen's tongues.
> —Shakespeare, *Love's Labour's Lost*

Qualia are subjective perceptions, perceptions of things that cannot be explained by referring to other objective things. In discussing the phenomena of perceptual qualia, Ramachandran (1998) raises the example of a type of electrical fish that can sense electrical fields via special organs on its skin. An ichthyologist can dissect the fish and examine it, construing exactly how it uses its sense organs to feel electrical fields; but the ichthyologist, despite his analytical knowledge, will never know how it truly *feels* to sense electrical fields. Nor can you, nor can I. Similarly, as I read my son a book about bats that use echolocation to perceive their environment, he asked me: "What do sounds look like?" I was forced to answer: "Only bats know." Colors are qualia too. The experience of the quale blue is only accessible to those who share that particular form of subjective perception. I cannot explain the color blue to you if you are colorblind. Furthermore, the moment I first associated the thought "blue" with the color "blue," some time back in my tender toddlerhood, for the rest of my life, I could never un-see blue. I will never be able to look up at the sky on a clear day and consider a color other than blue.[79] "Indeed," Ramachandran adds, "we have recently shown that neurons in the brain have permanently altered their connections..." once a certain stimuli has been perceived and processed in a certain way.[80]

Perhaps spiritual perception is a quale, like seeing blue or feeling electrical fields? Can there be such a thing as a "God quale?"—a subjective perception that, once experienced—permanently alters the neural pathways in such a way that one is bound to perceive the God experience again and again and again? Perhaps, just as there are some people who are colorblind, some people may be spirit-blind. And just as I cannot explain in words the subjective perception of blue to someone who is colorblind, the most faithful believer can never explain the subjective perception of God to the spirit-blind. Like beauty, perhaps God is simply in the eye of the beholder.

Synesthesia

> Oh, could you view the melody of every grace
> And music of her face,
> You'd drop a tear;
> Seeing more harmony in her bright eye
> Than now you hear.
> —Richard Lovelace

Ramachandran (2011) believes that synesthesia is caused by the disinhibition of neural connections between disparate processing areas of the brain. For instance, a typical synesthete may report that he sees numbers in color—i.e., the number seven always appears blue, the number nine always appears red, etc. How does this occur so consistently, and in so many people? Also, why is synesthesia a phenomenon that can be induced chemically? Give an average person an average dose of LSD, and he will quite likely see numbers in color, or see music in the air, or tangibly feel the smell of a flower. According to Ramachandran, these neural connections must, for some reason, exist. Considering that human beings are analogical by nature—we think in terms of symbols and analogies—it should be no surprise that our minds are wired to make connections between many stimuli that may not be obviously related to each other. However, because it is important for our conscious minds to see the world in a rational, coherent way, most of these non-linear associations are inhibited most of the time. So most of us do not see numbers in color, because that would be distracting; and most of us do not feel the smell of a rose, because unless you're a poet or an aroma therapist, that association is not useful most of the time. Perhaps, like synesthesia, spiritual perception is a mode of sensation that potentially exists in everyone, but is turned off in most people most of the time ... a perpetual potential that is incessantly inhibited. Thus, spiritual perception is only experienced when these neural connections are disinhibited—when the conscious processes shutting off spiritual perception are themselves shut down.

Doubled Consciousness

> Who is this third who always walks beside you?
> When I count, there are only you and I together.
> But when I look ahead up the white road
> There is always another one walking beside you
> Gliding wrapt in a brown mantle, hooded.
> —T.S. Eliot, *The Waste Land*

The feeling of "doubled consciousness"[81] has been reported by numerous epileptics. It is the feeling of being outside of one's self. The feeling that you are observing yourself as if you were outside of your own body, like an outsider looking in on yourself. Consciousness is "doubled" because you are aware of the existence of both selves simultaneously—the observer and the observed. It is as if the two halves of the brain temporarily cease to function as a single mechanism; but rather, each half identifies itself separately as its own self.[82] The doubling effect that occurs as a result of some temporal lobe epileptic seizures may lead to drastic personality changes. In particular, epileptics following seizures often become much more spiritual, artistic, poetic, and musical.[83] Art and music, of course, are processed primarily in the right hemisphere, as is poetry and the more lyrical, metaphorical aspects of language. In any artistic endeavor, one must engage in "doubled consciousness," creating the art with one "I," while simultaneously observing the art and the artist with a critically objective "other-I." In *The Great Gatsby,* Fitzgerald expressed the feeling of "doubled consciousness" in a scene in which Nick Caraway, in the throes of profound drunkenness, looks out of a city window and ponders:

> Yet high over the city our line of yellow windows must have contributed their share of human secrecy to the casual watcher in the darkening streets, and *I was him too*, looking up and wondering. *I was within and without*, simultaneously enchanted and repelled by the inexhaustible variety of life.

Doubled-consciousness, the sense of being both "within and without" of one's self, is a moment of disconnection and disassociation between the two hemispheres of the brain, a moment when left looks independently at right and right looks independently at left, each recognizing each other as an uncanny mirror reflection of himself, but at the same time not recognizing the other as "I."

The sense of doubled consciousness also arises quite frequently in situations of extreme physical and psychological duress.[84] In his book, *The Third Man Factor*, John Geiger delineates the conditions associated with the perception of the "sensed presence": darkness, monotony, barrenness, isolation, cold, hunger, thirst, injury, fatigue, and fear.[85] Shermer added sleep deprivation to this list, noting that Charles Lindbergh, on his famous cross–Atlantic flight, recorded the perception of "ghostly presences" in the cockpit, that "spoke with authority and clearness ... giving me messages of importance unattainable in ordinary life."[86] Sacks noted that doubled consciousness is not necessarily an alien or abnormal sensation, we all feel it, especially when we are alone, in the dark, in a scary place.[87] We all can recall a memory from childhood when we could palpably feel the presence of the monster hiding in the closet, or that indefinable thing in the dark space beneath our bed. The experience of the "sensed other" is common in schizophrenia, can be induced by certain drugs, is a central aspect of the "near death experience," and is also associated with certain neurological disorders.[88]

To speak of oneself in the third person; to express the wish to "find myself," is to presuppose a plurality within one's own mind.[89] There is consciousness, and then there is something else ... an Other ... who is nonetheless a part of our own mind, though separate from our moment-to-moment consciousness. When I make a statement such as: "I'm disappointed with myself because I let myself gain weight," it is quite clear that there are at least two wills at work within one mind—one will that dictates weight loss and is disappointed—and another will that defies the former and allows the body to binge or laze. One cannot point at one will and say: "This is the real me and the other is not me." They're both me. Within each "I" there exists a distinct Other that is also "I." In the mind of the believer—this double-I, this other-I, this sentient other, this sensed presence who is me but also, somehow, not me—how could this be anyone other than an angel, a spirit, my own soul, or God?

Sacks recalls an incident in which he broke his leg while mountain climbing alone and had to descend the mountain despite his injury and the immense pain it was causing him. Sacks heard "an inner voice" that was "wholly unlike" his normal "inner speech"—a "strong, clear, commanding voice" that told him exactly what he had to do to survive the predicament, and how to do it. "This good voice, this Life voice, braced and resolved me." Sacks relates the story of Joe Simpson, author of *Touching the Void*, who had a similar experience during a climbing mishap in the Andes. For days, Simpson trudged along with a distinctly dual sense of self. There was a distracted self that jumped from one random thought to the next, and then a clearly separate focused self that spoke to him in a commanding voice, giving specific instructions and making logical deductions.[90] Sacks also reports the experience of a distraught friend who, at the moment she was about to commit suicide, heard a "voice" tell her: "No, you don't want to do that..." The male voice, which seemed to come from outside of her, convinced her not to throw her life away. She speaks of it as her "guardian angel." Sacks suggested that this other voice may always be there, but it is usually inhibited. When it is heard, it's usually as an inner voice, rather than an external one.[91] Sacks also reports that the "persistent feeling" of a "presence" or a "companion" that is not actually there is a common hallucination, especially among people suffering from Parkinson's disease. Sacks is unsure if this is a side-effect of L-DOPA, the drug used to treat the disease, or if the hallucinations are symptoms of the neurological disease itself. He also noted that some patients were able to control the hallucinations to varying degrees. One elderly patient hallucinated a handsome and debonair gentleman caller who provided "love, attention, and invisible presents ... faithfully each evening."[92]

Phantoms and Zombies

> There is in fact another being inside you that goes about his or her business without your knowledge or awareness. And, as it turns out, there is not just one such zombie but a multitude of them inhabiting your brain.—V.S. Ramachandran[93]

The "phantom limb" phenomenon is relatively common among amputees. The experience is that of still feeling and seeing one's limb and even having the perception of controlling it, well after the limb has been amputated. Ramachandran explains that these hallucinations exist and are so vivid because the neural pathways that have always been associated with the real limb have not adjusted to the absence of the limb. The perceptual brain, the captive audience of the nervous system, has no recourse but to confabulate the vision of a limb, in order to *make sense* of the sensations coming from the nervous system. The only way the perceptual brain can make sense of a deeply felt sensation—the feeling of having an arm—is to make up a sensory stimuli out of thin air that corroborates this sensation—the sight of an arm—thus the brain hallucinates the presence of the missing limb. If the unconscious mind can perceive phantoms limbs as a mechanism for dealing with a crisis of the body, then it is just as plausible that the unconscious mind can also create phantom beings as a means of dealing with a crisis of the mind. This notion, that God arises as an unconscious projection in response to an emotional need, was posited by Freud a century ago, though he did not equate his theory with the phenomenon of phantom limbs.

Nevertheless, Freudian theory is applicable to both the phenomenon of perceiving phantom limbs and the phenomenon of perceiving phantom beings, both of which are quite common.

Just as the unconscious creates phantoms attached to our bodies, it also harbors "zombies" within our bodies. The "how" pathway for behavior, which Ramachandran locates in the right parietal lobe, is in charge of automatic behaviors—complicated behaviors that we accomplish without thinking—and usually without even being fully aware of what we're doing. Driving long distances is an example. This is something we do on autopilot, while our conscious mind is occupied with deeper thoughts or fancier reveries. The driver is the unthinking actor within the brain, taking care of business while consciousness is either busy with something else, or is actually completely off-duty, as in the case of sleepwalking. The sleepwalking zombie is unthinking, unconscious. It is not "I," yet it is also not "*not*-I." It is the "other-I." Perhaps this is why zombie movies are so scary. They present us with an uncanny image of ourselves, not the consciously thinking selves of our normal state, but the lumbering unthinking selves of the unconscious beings that are constantly present within our own minds, lingering just below our threshold of awareness.

Cognitive-Perceptual Unities: Hallucinations

> *My father!—methinks I see my father.*
> *Where, my lord?*
> *In my mind's eye, Horatio.*
> —William Shakespeare, *Hamlet*

In my college glory days I indulged in a few psychedelic experimentations that seemed expected, if not obligatory, at the time. The drugs I tried—LSD, psilocybin (mushrooms), mescaline—all had somewhat similar effects, though to varying degrees. While I didn't have any spiritual or mystical experiences, the experimentations were genuinely eye-opening in the true sense of the words. I experienced many of the somatic and psychological sensations that are associated with spiritual perception. I felt in awe of the world around me, a deep sense of fascination with my surroundings, occasional feelings of trepidation, a realization of how small a part I was within the vastness of time and space—yet at the same time—a feeling of deep connection with its vastness, a sense of time itself being malleable, in that time could speed up or slow down depending on my thoughts and feelings, an insight into the paradoxicality of the world—how one thing could actually be two or three things, depending on how it was perceived—an ineffable sense of wonderment; and most importantly, the realization that my perception of everything around me was happening in my mind, and not as a product of my senses. I suppose I had covered that basic principle in my Intro to Psych class, but I didn't truly comprehend its significance until I experienced it for myself. During the "peak" phases of some of my psychedelic experiences, I could look at an object and simply by thinking about it in a different way, I could actually change its physical appearance. To be clear, I knew very well that my thoughts were not causing any physical change to the object. I merely understood that when my mind was in that particular mode of perception, the connection between my imagination and my perceptions were clearer and more direct. As if in a waking dream, I was able to conjure and manipulate my hallucinations. And in my most intense moments, hallucinations appeared that were not under my own conscious control. These moments were scary, and I can fully understand how, for some people, this uncontrollable hallucinatory experience could result in a terrifying "bad trip," a waking nightmare. I also gained, possibly, a bit of insight into the experience of psychosis.

My most vivid psychedelic memory was that of lying on my back on an East Village rooftop with a dear friend. It was a very windy night, and we were staring at the low flying clouds zooming past us overhead. Suddenly, I began seeing faces in the clouds. For some reason, they were the faces of U.S. presidents, like on the front of U.S. currency, all flying above me, seeming so close, extremely vivid and in detailed perfection. Some of them were smiling at me. I distinctly remember these visions to this day, over twenty years later. I had no conscious control over the visions, and I don't know where they came from or why I saw them. If my mind was so inclined at the time, those perceptions, combined with the other feelings I was experiencing, could easily have been visions of angels or demons, spirits or sprites, or even God himself. I believe that the difference between my hallucinatory psychedelic experiences and the mystical experiences associated with spiritual perception was simply a matter of interpretation. I think that if I had truly believed in and wanted to see or hear or feel God at the time, even on an unconscious level, and even without the aid of my conscious will, I would have.

Oliver Sacks recalls a similar experience of the ability to manipulate perceptual hallucinations, along with a likewise sense of the quasi-divine. After ingesting some amphetamine, LSD, and cannabis, Sacks stared at the wall and demanded of his mind to see "true indigo." Then, as if by magic, the color appeared: "Luminous, numinous, it filled me with rapture: It was the color of heaven..."[94] Sacks saw "true indigo" because he believed it existed and that he *could* see it. I saw presidential faces in the sky, not God, probably because I didn't believe He existed or that I *could* see Him. The fact that the form of hallucination is determined largely by belief is confirmed by a classic experiment by Hood and Morris (1981). They put college students in isolation tanks that have been proven to elicit dreamlike and hypnogogic imagery. Some students were primed to think about cartoon characters, others were primed to think about religious images. All of the student participants experienced imagery in the tanks. The ones primed for cartoon images saw cartoon images, the ones primed for religious images saw religious images. However, religious students experienced significantly more religious imagery than non-religious students. Furthermore, religious students reported seeing religious images, even when they were primed for cartoon characters. Most significantly, religious students who were primed for cartoon characters were more likely to see religious images than non-religious students who were primed for religious imagery![195] Clearly, the content of the intra-psychic imagery was determined by the individual's intrinsic beliefs, not just by the external stimuli. Hallucinations project our own inner beliefs, reflecting them back to us like a haunted mirror, showing us not the outer image, but our inner selves.

Hallucinations are experienced in varying degrees and intensity in about half of the general population.[96] They can also be induced by drugs, dehydration, illness, or any number of physical maladies, such as delirium or migraines, a host of physical activities, and most simply ... by nodding off or falling asleep. Even while we're awake, we're constantly hallucinating, in the sense that what we perceive is in no way a true depiction of the objective world around us.[97] Hallucinations are *perceptions*, not figments of the imagination. Brain-mapping studies over the past few decades confirm that hallucinations are unlike imagination and much more like perception, and since perception is formed in the mind and not the eyes, neither the mind nor the brain can tell apart hallucinogenic vision from reality.[98] Unlike visual imagery taken in from the senses, hallucination is the result of "bottom-up activation of regions in the ventral visual pathway."[99] The perceptions come from the unconscious part of the mind, and thus appear to our conscious mind to be as real as any real object in the real world. Hallucinations are the most vivid examples of the experience of cognitive-perceptual unity, a moment when an imagined subject is truly perceived as an external object.

So while hallucinations are certainly "all in your head," they're not experienced in that way, and they're completely different from other processes controlled by the conscious mind. Hallucinations originate from the *base* of the ventral visual pathway, an area that is removed from the actual sensors that receive visual input from the outside world (the eyes). But as far as the brain is concerned, not only are hallucinations perceived as "real," they are typically perceived as being "more real" than actual objects seen by the eyes, and certainly much more real than images conjured by the active imagination. This phenomenon is referred to as "super-lucidity"—the tendency for hallucinations to look "more real than real"—in that they are shinier, clearer, more distinct, and more vibrant.[100] The super-lucidity of hallucinations may be a result of the fact that, since they are intra-psychic perceptions, they are not filtered through the senses, and thus retain all the unfiltered luster of their unconscious origin. Hallucinogenic images may be akin to eidetic memories, which are more vivid and more detailed than typical mental representations, because they are drawn from a system of visual memory that is larger and richer than the system of visual memory used by modern consciousness, which has become primarily dependent on external storage memory systems for visual images. For instance, try to picture in your mind what Ulysses S. Grant looks like, without resorting to googling his image on your phone or computer, or trying to find a $50 bill. I can't consciously recall a clear image of Ulysses S. Grant. But when I hallucinated his face on that rooftop, his face was more vivid and clear than anything I'd ever seen before.

Some blind people see the most remarkably super-lucid visions in their mind's eye. They are "victims" of Charles Bonnet Syndrome, a neurological condition in which the mind, deprived of external visual stimulation, provides itself with its own internally originated visual stimuli. In essence, it is as if these people live their lives in the sort of "isolation tanks" used in the experiment mentioned above, forcing their perceptual brain to conjure its own visions. James Thurber, the famous novelist, gradually lost his vision and eventually became completely blind. In a letter to his ophthalmologist, he described the visions he saw in his mind's eye:

> Years ago you told me about a nun of the middle centuries who confused her retinal disturbances with holy visitation, although she saw only about one tenth of the holy symbols I see. Mine have included a blue Hoover, golden sparks, melting purple blobs, a skein of spit, a dancing brown spot, snowflakes, saffron and light blue waves, and two eight balls, to say nothing of the corona, which used to halo street lamps and is now brilliantly discernible when a shaft of light breaks against a crystal bowl or a bright metal edge. This corona, usually triple, is like a chrysanthemum composed of thousands of radiating petals, each ten times as slender and each containing in order the colors of the prism. Man has devised no spectacle of light in any way similar to this sublime arrangement of colors or holy visitation.[101]

The super-lucidity of religious visions may contribute to the quality of awe and wonderment that they purvey.

Bereavement hallucinations, hallucinatory experiences subsequent to the loss of a loved one, are also quite common.[102] Many doctors and psychologists consider these hallucinations, that often take the form of brief but incredibly meaningful conversations with the recently departed, to be a normative part of the grieving process. The mind has become so inextricably attached to the external love object—the mother, father, spouse, or child—it cannot adjust to life without him. Like the blind man whose mind invents its own visual input in the absence of external visual stimulation, the bereaved person's mind invents the presence of the lost one, in order to adjust itself to life without him. Consider the following recollection of a woman whose husband had recently died:

> I lay in bed trying to piece my life together. I lay there for hours. Suddenly, I felt Fred's presence beside me in the bed. I looked over and saw him standing beside me. He was dressed in his old work clothes and had a big smile on his face. He said, "Don't worry, Maud, I'm in heaven now. God has let me come to you. All our friends are here too. It's all true, what we believed about God ... this is only a temporary separation." I went to sleep and didn't wake for hours. The next day I felt good, the sun was shining again; there was meaning to my life. I know that God exists because I have experience of his presence.[103]

If we create deep emotional attachments with others, feeling them so closely that they are just like a part of our own selves, than the experience of losing that person to death might evoke an emotional "phantom" of that person, just as the mind creates a phantom limb when it loses a physical part of its self. The emotional phantom is a product of our mind's need to adjust to an emotional amputation, the loss of a being who was an emotional part of our own identity. The bereavement hallucinations of our Paleolithic ancestors were, perhaps, the primordial images that molded the archetypes of myth and religion: the martyred hero, the wise old man, the merciful goddess, the guardian angel, the personal gods....

The cognitive counterpart to the bereavement hallucination would be the deathbed hallucination, which Sacks observed on several occasions.[104] As the mind prepares itself for its final transition, the normative functions must rebuff the existential anxiety evoked by the imminent potential of non-existence. Even the most secularized mind reveals a spiritual bent when faced with the ultimate issue. Consciousness cannot conceive of its own end. "There are no atheists in foxholes."

Digital Zen

> We feel like angels trapped inside the bodies of beasts, forever craving transcendence.—V.S. Ramachandran[105]

The process of "Digital Zen" has the goal of creating a sense of cognitive-perceptual unity in the user. This experience of unity is similar to what a practitioner of Buddhist meditation may feel at the peak phase of his meditation, or to what a devout religious person may feel in the deepest moment of prayer, or to what a tribal shaman may feel while in the throes of a spiritual ritual. The reason that such a process is necessary is because the mind in its current "theoretic" state is imbalanced. The dominant left hemisphere controls cognition and perception, inhibiting the right hemisphere during every waking moment, disallowing the experience of pure intuition, imagination, inspiration, and spiritual perception. The goal of Digital Zen is to rebalance the mind by allowing the right hemisphere of the brain free expression through disinhibition.

While the ancient spiritual practices have the same function of providing a sense of psychological balance, they have become inaccessible and ineffectual for many modern literate people. The religion-based spiritual practices of the Western cultures require belief in God as a prerequisite. However, many modern people simply cannot believe, because their consciousness is governed by logic-based reasoning, which disallows belief in the paradoxical concept of God. The meditative practices of the Eastern cultures require intense and extensive practice and discipline in a mode of quiet unimodal introspection that is foreign to a generation of people who have grown up immersed in an environment of constant multisensory media stimulation. How can we expect someone to meditate for five hours, if he can't go without checking his Iphone for five minutes? The inner paths seem to have been shut off for the digital generation, but digital technology itself may open a new door to the transcendent state of spiritual unity.

When the perceptual and cognitive faculties are always "online" in the conscious mode, it is very difficult to turn them "offline" into a semi-conscious mode. Consciousness is the pinnacle of cognition, the chief executive officer of the mind. Just as there is no single person who can control the CEO of a company, there is no single cognitive function that can control consciousness. There is no dimmer switch for consciousness. We can shut it down completely by going to sleep, and oftentimes even that's difficult, prompting us to resort to drugs that literally knock us out. But while shutting down consciousness altogether allows us to dream, it doesn't allow us to be consciously reflective of our dreams while they are happening. Sleeping dreams are just as imbalanced as waking consciousness, only the balance has now shifted to the right hemisphere. The dream of my father may have been spiritually significant, but I can't really be sure, because I have almost no conscious recollection of that dream. What is needed is a semi-conscious state of awareness, in which both hemispheres of the brain are aware of each other, and brain activity is truly balanced. Because consciousness is the boss, it will have to find a way of dimming itself in a deliberate and "conscious" way.

The semi-conscious state I am referring to is a state of perceived unity—the state of spiritual perception—the unitive state aspired to by religious rituals and meditative practices. It is a state that is reached easily by Mohammad Farah, because his cognitive mindset and his cultural environment do not inhibit spiritual perception. It is also a state that can be achieved quite effectively via the proper application of digital technology. If you recall the Digital Dream process from the previous chapter, you will remember the digital helmet and virtual reality suit that are hooked up to both a digital media system and a host of neurological devices. The digital media system creates a virtual environment of real perceptions for the user, while the neurological devices monitor brain activity and also stimulate specific locations in the brain using electromagnetic waves. The technology is one interactive system, so that the media being projected is in sync with the neurological status of the user's perceptions and cognitions. The initiation phase of the Digital Zen process would be identical to the initiation phase of the Digital Dream. Using a combination of guided imagery and sounds that are synched to the user's brain waves, the user is drawn inwards into a state of semi-conscious awareness. Once in this state, variations of cognitive-perceptual unity can be experienced, which would give the user a sense of spiritual and psychological balance.

The Digital Phantom

> Abandon the search for God...
> Look for him by taking yourself as the starting point...
> You will find him in yourself.
> —Hippolytus, *Heresies*, 3rd century AD

"The true spiritual experience cannot be approximated by the virtual experience provided by digital media." That's what you may be thinking, but wait, let me explain.... First, let me remind you that *every* perceptual experience is a virtual experience that is constructed completely in the mind. The spiritual experience, in particular, is a virtual experience, because it aspires to encounter a metaphysical Other that exists in a dimension that is different from our own physical dimension. Spiritual perception is a reaching out into a virtual world of virtual others. The spirit who is perceived as a real object is similar in perceptual quality to the phantom limb that an amputee perceives and feels as a real arm or leg. The same phantom perception happens during the typical digital experience of playing a videogame. When we play, we project ourselves into the avatar that we are controlling on the screen. Indeed, this sense of identification, this vicarious sense of actually experiencing what the figure on the screen is experiencing, is the reason why videogames are so much fun. We feel a bit of physical anguish when our guy is destroyed by an alien's laser blast, and we feel a physical thrill when our guy destroys the aliens with his own blaster. The ease in which we project our own sensori-emotional feelings into external virtual figures is just another example of how humans are neurologically predisposed towards projecting our sense of selves outwardly. We are hardwired not just to experience the "Other," but to experience the "Other" as if he was an extension of ourselves, the "Other-I." With this ability hardwired into our neurochemistry, it's no wonder that we often perceive another presence even when none is there. From a perceptual standpoint, an actual "Other" existing in real physical space outside of us is not at all necessary in order for a complete perception of the "Other" to take place. Reality is, more or less, irrelevant.

In the future, the "realness" of virtual reality simulators will increase exponentially, giving us the sense that we're not looking at a screen, but that we're entirely inside the game. Virtual reality can truly create the sensation of cognitive-perceptual unity, the state of being "inside the maze" rather than "observing the maze." The ability to project the user's sense of self into the virtual reality dimension of a digitally created environment is already existent. The only part of the labyrinth left to add is the minotaur....

Persinger believes that the left temporal lobe coordinates our "sense of self" by managing our sense of place and time within our environment. The left temporal lobe must be in exact sync with the right temporal lobe, which coordinates the structure of memories that we have of ourselves in place and in time. If the left and the right get out of sync, even slightly, the integrated sense of self becomes dis-integrated or decoupled, resulting in the sense of a separate other, a "sensed presence," a sentient other. Persinger found that this sensation of "doubled consciousness" can be predictably induced by electrically stimulating the left temporoparietal junction within the brain.[106] Using this technology, Digital Zen can create a virtual setting in which consciousness is split in two, creating separate identities who can be represented by separate avatars. The left hemisphere's sense of self will be projected into the avatar that represents the conscious "I"— what Jung called the "persona" archetype—one's own image of oneself. The right hemisphere will then be projected into the avatar that represents the unconscious sense of self—what Jung called the "shadow" archetype—the "Other-I." This anomalous figure could be represented by a specific person (my father or Mohammad's father), by a mysterious or mythical figure that must be interpreted by the mind as it encounters and "plays" with the Other (a "digital phantom" or "virtual minotaur"), or, of course, by a spiritual figure (Jesus, Mary, Buddha, or God himself). The user could pre-program the specific figure he wants to be projected into his episode of spiritual unity, or he could leave it up to his own unconscious mind. He could even allow his digital media system to project randomly selected figures from a storehouse of spiritual figures online, or he could allow for other users experiencing similar episodes to merge their figures with his. The possibilities, literally, are endless—as is the labyrinth of the unconscious mind.

A more meditative version of Digital Zen could also be experienced. Spiritual prayer and meditation typically uses the device of an extended unimodal focus on a single object of devotion to facilitate the quieting of the conscious voice. The symbol points to a spiritual place of transcendence. Jesus on the Cross, the image of Buddha, the various mandalas and icons of diverse spiritual practices ... all foster inward reflection that eventually leads to a moment of cognitive-perceptual unity, in which the mind transcends the symbol and gets a glimpse or a sense of the meaning behind the symbol. Perhaps this is why Christianity spread so much faster and wider than its mother religion, Judaism. In forbidding "graven images," Jewish spiritual practice inhibited the visualization aspect of spiritual practice that is so helpful in reaching a sense of transcendence. Two thousand years ago, the Christians created a reformed version of Judaism that added the iconography of Jesus on the Cross, an incredibly potent visual symbol to meditate upon, and now Christianity accounts for a third of the world's believers (2.1 billion Christians), while Judaism accounts for less than a quarter of one percent (14 million Jews).[107] To return to meditation, the media used in Digital Zen enhances the visual, auditory, and tactile sensations that would draw the user into the intense and prolonged meditation upon the symbol that precedes the sense of transcendence. Through monitoring the user's brain waves and neural processes, the media system synchronizes the imagery and sounds with the user's mental state, in order to perfectly time the user's "launch" into the transcendent "peak" phase of the experience. At that point, at the moment of complete cognitive-perceptual unity, the figure of the symbol melds into the ground of the underlying meaning behind the symbol. To use the Christian example, the symbol of Jesus on the cross is meditated upon until the moment of "apotheosis"—the moment when the figure of Jesus the son dissolves into the ground of God the father—and the reality of existence is transcended. Digital Zen, because it is open to any iconography, any symbol, would facilitate a sense of transcendence and spiritual unity, regardless of one's beliefs or disbeliefs. The technology does not discriminate. All novices are welcome, no conversion necessary (but you must pay in credit or cash).

From a neurological perspective, the function of Digital Zen is not just to stimulate the areas in the brain that evoke spiritual perception, but to create an episode of hemispheric balance in the brain. Newberg and d'Aquili (1999) point to a function in the left parietal lobe of the brain that they refer to as the "Reductionist Operator." This function analyzes and deconstructs our environment from a detached perspective, in order to break things down to their basic units and see how they work. The Reductionist Operator is balanced by a parallel function in the right parietal lobe, the "Holistic Operator," that sees the world as a whole from an integrated perspective, in order to discern the gestalt or "big picture" of our environment. Clearly, a balance between these two operators is necessary. My principal argument is that the theoretic mindset pushes the balance further to the left, giving more weight to the Reductionist Operator, resulting in a sense of detachment that is inhibitory towards spiritual perception. But if the Holistic Operator in the right parietal lobe is activated via electro-stimulation, while the Reductionist Operator in the left parietal lobe is inhibited via electro-stimulation of inhibitory connections, then the balance can be shifted towards the right. The re-balancing of the hemispheres during Digital Zen will allow for the experience of cognitive-perceptual unity, an experience that is naturally evocative of a state of transcendent spiritual unity.

In particular, the transcendent state is achieved in meditation and prayer by a prolonged and intense unimodal focus on one stimulus, "a steady assault on one sense, like a tribal drumbeat."[108] Chanting or prayer are examples of the auditory method. "The simplest and most widely practiced form of spiritual exercise is repetition of the divine name, or of some phrase affirming God's existence and the soul's dependence upon Him."[109] Jews, Moslems, and Buddhists focus primarily on the auditory method in their rituals. The visual method is achieved by staring at an icon or a symbol or even by focusing intently on a well-known verse of a written text, such as the words of the Bible, the Koran, a prayer book, etc. Tactile methods include spinning in circles, rhythmic swaying, dance circles—any recurring movement that is repeated over and over again. All of these rituals have the same neurological effect, referred to as "deafferentation" by neurologists. An "afferent" is sensory input to a spot in the brain that processes this input. When the "afferentiation" of a specific sensation is extremely repetitive over a long period of time, the neurons become desensitized to the input, and begin to ignore it. For example, the sound of crickets chirping is at first extremely annoying to a city person staying in the country overnight. However, after a couple of hours, the mind becomes desensitized to the repetitive sound, because the auditory processing area of the brain has become "deafferentiated" to that particular stimulus. Soon, the city person no longer notices the crickets, falls asleep, and may even sleep deeper than he usually sleeps.

In Digital Zen, the digital media system can temper and synchronize the rhythm and intensity of a repetitive stimulus in harmony with the user's brain waves and his neurological processing of the stimulus. The process of deafferentiation, the blinding of the senses to a stimulus, would be hastened. At the same time, neuro-electro-stimulation of the regions that foster deafferentiation would also hasten the process. In this way, the state of spiritual perception achieved through deafferentation of all the senses will be reached much sooner. To use George Harrison's words—we could "see" and "be with" our "sweet lord"— but it wouldn't have to "take so long."

Waiting for God? Oh!

> *Dulcis Jesu memoria; Dans vera cordi gaudia:*
> *sed super, el et omnia; Ejus dulcis praesentia.*
> (Sweet is the memory of Jesus giving me true joys to the heart:
> but sweeter beyond honey and all else is his presence.)
> —12th century hymn[110]

The ultimate goal of any spiritual practice is transcendence from a state of cognitive-perceptual duality to a state of cognitive-perceptual unity ... "spiritual unity." For instance, when a modern Christian in his normal waking state gazes at the icon of the Cross, the dominant left hemisphere is processing the stimulus in a dual manner. There is the physical object that is perceived, the intersecting beams; and there is also the symbolic subject that is conceived, the spiritual meaning of the icon. The two experiences—the perception and the cognition, the object and the subject, the thing and the thought, the symbol and the meaning—are separate, a duality. But if gazed at long enough, with enough patience, devotion, and belief, the duality merges into a unity. Neurologically, the left hemisphere's cognitive-perceptual mode of dual thinking is deafferentiated, and the right hemisphere's mode of holistic unified thinking is disinhibited. The Cross and the meaning of the Cross are experienced as one. The figure of Jesus on the Cross melds into the ground of God. The worshipper understands that Jesus and God are one, and furthermore, that Jesus and God and *himself* are one, and even beyond that, that Jesus and God and himself and *everyone else* are one. The longer and deeper the experience of spiritual unity goes on, the more unified all experience becomes, until a point is reached in which everything that exists is experienced as one single entity ... the "Unio Mystica."

However, there is a problem for the modern Christian, or for the modern *anybody* for that matter. In order to achieve this state of unity, one must truly believe in the meaning of the symbol that is gazed upon. If belief is not there, the door to this mode of perception is shut. One could try to pry it open. One could gaze at the Cross and say to himself: "I will gaze at this Cross until I see God." But the mind, in its state of duality, sees the Cross as an object. If the meaning of the Cross is a subject, and if there is no true belief in that meaning, then there is no cognitive bridge between the object and the subject. The door to transcendence is shut, and the paradoxicality of the situation is the lock on the door. How can one thing, the Cross, be two things ... a physical cross but also a spiritual truth? There are methods of overcoming this inhibition, but these methods require belief, devotion, discipline, and practice. Digital Zen provides a means of overcoming this inhibition, and requires none of the prerequisites listed above. In the Digital Age, there's no reason for someone to think that he must "wait" for God to come to him, as the wait is likely to be endless and pointless, like the characters "Waiting for Godot" in Samuel Becket's play. If the mountain will not come to Mohammed, then Mohammed should come to the mountain.

When Mohammad Farah saw the mzimu of his father, the sight of his father's presence and the sound of his father's voice were crystal clear, pristine. When I saw my father in my dream, the vision was similarly clear. When Oliver Sacks saw "true indigo" in his psycho-pharmacologically inspired vision, the color was more colorful than any color he'd even seen before. The "super-lucidity" of these sense perceptions points to the fact that intra-psychically perceived images and sounds are akin to eidetic memories, in that they are extremely vivid and detailed. This kind of perception is inaccessible to the conscious minds of modern people functioning in the theoretic mindset, because the literal mind enhances a recall system for extremely abstract and complex concepts, at the cost of obsolescing a recall system for highly detailed and vivid memories of sense perceptions. It's as if your mind has to make a choice: "I could either read a book about George Washington crossing the Delaware, or I could stare at the painting of George Washington crossing the Delaware, but I can't do both at the same time." Reading the book gives you a ton of information about the episode that you can think about, but the sensory input is minimal—just a lot of black marks on a white page. Staring at the picture gives you a ton of sensory input about the episode, so that you can really get a sense of the cold air, the icy water, the foreboding overcast sky with a ray of light in the distance ... however, the amount of conceptual information is minimal—just an image of one moment. Both modes of perception are available, but the theoretic mind tends towards the conceptual mode.

The Digital Zen experience opens the door to the other mode of perception, the mode of direct sensory experience and the direct elicitation of episodic eidetic images that exist in the unconscious memory banks of the mind, but are irretrievable by the conscious mindset. The limitation of much of modern religion is that it is focused on the mythic/theoretic mode of studying doctrine, dogma, scripture, and verse. This mode provides the concepts of spirituality, but not the *objects* of spirituality—it is all thought but no experience—all cognition and no perception. Digital Zen opens the door to the episodic mode of perception, retrieving the super-lucid eidetic images stored in unconscious memory, and providing new spiritual images in three dimensional, interactive, immersive, high-definition format. The theoretic religious experience is reading about God in the Bible. The episodic religious experience, the digital experience, is meeting God in person.

CHAPTER THREE

The Stages of Spiritual Perception and Digital Nirvana

> When I was a child, I spake as a child, I understood as a child,
>   I thought as a child:
> but when I became a man, I put away childish things.
> For now we see through a glass, darkly; but then face to face...
> —1 Corinthians 13: 11-12

The roundabout journey of the development of spiritual perception begins before birth, in a state of "unitive consciousness,"[1] a state in which all things, in the mind of the fetus, are part of one whole.[2] Moving forward from this state of cognitive unity with everything, we develop—step-by-step—through a number of cognitive "dualisms."[3] At birth, the physical unity of self/mother is severed into a physical duality of self and other: I and Mother. But while the physical duality is obvious, the cognitive distinction between self and other in the mind of the infant is not necessarily a given. Other dualisms, such as the distinction between internal representations and external objects—the distinction between thoughts and things—the distinction between thoughts and the words that represent them, the distinction between words and the objects they represent, and the distinction between reality and fantasy, will all arise as the mind develops. Though the path will get complicated and torturous, please remember that the route plan itself is quite simple: In the initial stages, we begin with unity and we proceed towards duality; and in the final stages, the path becomes circular, moving from duality back towards unity. Our guide on this path, for the most part, is Jean Piaget, a towering figure in 20th century psychology, and the father of the cognitive-developmental paradigm of psychological inquiry. The vehicle driving the mind down the path of dualistic thinking is, for the most part, Language.

We begin life in a state of complete unity with an entity that encompasses us wholly, nurtures us, and instantaneously satisfies every physical and psychological need. In the womb, we are at one with Mother, at one with our environment, at one with Nature. There is no distinction between the inner and outer worlds. This state of psychological unity is the holy grail of spiritual perception, the mystical experience of oneness that is the ultimate goal of every spiritual practice or ritual. As we proceed from the moment of birth and beyond, the development of spiritual perception in the mind of the child retraces some of the steps of our preliterate ancestors. Spiritual beliefs in childhood are intuitive. God is experienced on a personal level. He is envisioned anthropomorphically, as a person, much like you or me. As the child's mental processes become more logical, his manner of thinking changes. Beginning with speech, and continuing with the mastery of reading and then writing, conscious thought becomes inextricably linked with language, as words become the fabric of thought. God becomes literalized, objectified, and concretized into a distinct figure, with specific features and commandments that are understood in literal, concrete terms. As the net of words broadens and spreads out across the burgeoning bubble of thought, that which cannot be expressed or conceived of in words—the ineffable, the indefinable, the irrational—becomes increasingly inaccessible to the conscious mind. God, who was previously understood and perceived intuitively, gradually becomes a puzzlement ... a problem of logic that must be solved. As the puzzle becomes more complex, the solutions become more abstract, until God is nothing more than a metaphysical concept, a metaphor, a symbol.

Nevertheless, for many people, God never becomes a conscious problem of logic, because his presence is felt unconsciously, and the experience of God is sensory and emotional, not logical or rational. Others still work through a conscious stage of analytical, critical doubt, and rediscover the experience of spirituality in a way that makes sense for them. Finally, there are those who experience a deep and enduring sense of spirituality that is not a mere continuation of the spirituality realized in childhood, but a breakthrough into a new perception of the spiritual dimension of life. Spiritual perception in this final stage is a return to the state of union with the eternal infinite that we all knew before birth, a state of egoless unity referred to by the Hindus as "Nirvana."

Since the days before recorded history, Nirvana has only been known by the spiritual specialists—saints, mystics, spiritualists, shamans—those people who just happen to be born with a highly acute sense of spiritual perception. The media of the Digital Age, however, may provide the technology and the alteration of sense perception that could make the internal experience of spiritual unity—the state of Nirvana—accessible to anyone who can master the digital technology. The ultimate frontier of digital media will be the space within the mind, the virtual journey inwards towards one's own spiritual center. We set off onto this journey into the frontier of the mind with a peerless guide, Jean Piaget:

> Let us imagine a being, knowing nothing of the distinction between mind and body. Such a being would be aware of his desires and feelings but his notions of self would undoubtedly be much less clear than ours. Compared with us he would experience much less the sensation of the thinking self within him, the feeling of a being independent of the external world. The knowledge that we are thinking of things severs us in fact from the actual things. But, above all, the psychological perceptions of such a being would be entirely different from our own. Dreams, for example, would appear to him as a disturbance breaking in from without. Words would be bound up with things and to speak would mean to act directly on these things. Inversely, external things would be less material and would be endowed with intentions and will.
> We shall try to prove that such is the case with the child.[4]

Stage 1: The Mother God—The Prenatal Period & Infancy

> Single is the race, single
> Of men and gods;
> From a single Mother we draw breath.
> —Pindar, 6th century, BC

The primary state of cognitive unity between the internal self and the external world is the psychological essence of spiritual perception. Every mystical tradition and every spiritual practice has as its primary goal the loss of the sense of ego, so that the self merges with a sense of something bigger than itself. The internal voice of the ego, created by conscious self-awareness, must first be silenced. Only then can it be reunited and merged with the entire self. This feeling of oneness, of spiritual unity, of boundlessness, of connectedness, of transcendence ... these are all reminiscent of the state within the womb. The timeless and boundless state of perpetual bliss experienced within the womb is the sensation we are seeking for when we look to Heaven or God for redemption or grace. Perhaps the moment of death offers this final return to unity, a timeless eternal moment of reunion and reunification, a reconnection of the psychological umbilical cord, as we merge into our earliest memory, which would seem indistinguishable from our earliest dream.[5]

Otto Rank believed that the "Birth Trauma" of initial separation is the primary anxiety—the mother of all anxieties—which we re-experience, to various degrees, whenever life makes us feel disconnected from others or ourselves. Despite the birth trauma, infants still experience a state of virtual symbiosis with Mother, a state of cognitive unity that is reinforced with physically intimate acts such as breastfeeding, holding, rocking, and co-sleeping. In the mind of the baby, because his every need appears to lead directly to a satisfaction of that need from Mother, there seems to be a continuation between his internal mental state and the external figure of Mother.[6] "Mother and I are one." If the infant is a "narcissist," as Freud suggested, it is not because the infant is egocentric, because the infant has no ego, no sense of self that is differentiated from the external world. The infant places his own needs above everything else because he is not only unable to understand that there *are* others, but because he cannot even understand that there is a *self*—in the sense that his "self" is different or disconnected from the world around him. The infant lives in a state of total unity, in which the internal and external worlds are undifferentiated parts of the same whole.[7]

In the state of spiritual oneness experienced in infancy, not only is there unity with the Goddess of Life—"Mother and I are One"—but also with the almighty God of the Universe, the god who controls the movements and actions of the Goddess with the pure power of his own thought ... the baby himself. In the mind of the infant, he himself is a sort of god; but not a god that rules above the world, a god that is at one with the world.[8] The sense of intrinsic connection and unity between the internal world of mind and the external world of objects is the basis of the notion of "magical participation"—the belief that our own thoughts can cause a change in some external body.[9] In the infant, this is the belief that a desire for mother causes her to appear; or that the cry for mother actually brings her to him (rather than mother hearing the cry and using her own will and volition to come). Magical thinking persists in the mind of the child until it is gradually disqualified by rational logical thinking, during the school years. Magical thinking, nevertheless, is still primary not only in the minds of children, but in the thinking of preliterate societies, and also in the thinking involved in spiritual or religious belief. So, while the 6-year-old child believes that wishing for snow on a Sunday will cause it to snow before morning; in a preliterate society, it is believed that a ritual such as the "moon dance" actually causes the new moon to be born, or that a "rain dance" actually causes the clouds to appear and throw down water.[10] In post-literate rituals, magical thinking is found in the belief that God can hear our silent prayers, and that his answer to these prayers will be made manifest. In all of these cases, the belief is predicated on a sense of continuum between the internal state of the believer, and the external forces with which it is connected. Spirituality, in essence, is the feeling of connection between within and without. This feeling was once the only feeling that we experienced.

Not only cognition, but perception itself is unified in infancy.[11] The infant perceives mother and bottle not as a separate subject and a separate object, but as extensions of his self that he can control with the power of his own thought.[12] To add to this sense of internal/external unity in the mind of the infant, is the probability that infantile perception is primarily "intermodal" or "sysnesthetic"—

the infant does not perceive the different modalities of sense perception—but experiences all perception as a whole. So, in the case of the nursing experience, the infant doesn't think: "Mother's face looks this way, and Mother's voice sounds this way, and Mother's milk tastes this way, and Mother's body smells this way, and Mother's skin feels this way." Rather, the infant experiences mother as an intermodal, undifferentiated whole—one sense, unlabelled, and un-separated from the infant's sense of self—with all sensations and all feelings melded into one. The experience cannot even be referred to as "Mother," because the whole experience of mother is completely undifferentiated from the self. If a mind with language could experience the infantile state, perhaps it could label it only with the word: "'Mother-I-World"; or more succinctly: "All."

Alison Gopnik's (2009) model of "lantern consciousness" may also shed "light" on the nature of infantile perception. "Lantern consciousness" is an unfocussed awareness in which one is "open to the whole undifferentiated world." It is common in infants, according to Gopnik, but attainable to adults only in altered states of consciousness, such as meditation, when there is a similar feeling of "losing oneself." Lantern consciousness is not achieved by disconnecting with the world, but by "becoming part of the world," entering a state in which "everything is illuminated." The functional opposite of lantern consciousness is "spotlight consciousness," a state in which we are extremely focused, even to the point where we may "lose ourselves" in an activity, becoming unaware or "un-conscious" of anything else. While spotlight consciousness is achieved through activity, lantern consciousness is achieved through passive receptivity.[13] As we grow older, we experience less moments of lantern consciousness, as we are forced by our environment to engage our minds primarily in the focused mode of spotlight consciousness. In a sense, our mind is molded to gradually lose sight of the forest in order to focus on trees; and as we focus only on the trees, we filter out our ability to see that there may be fairies in the forest as well.

In a provocative article, Prince and Savage (1966) suggested that the "mystical experience" is actually a state of regression to a primary infantile experience of nursing. They point out that standard aspects of the mystical experience—ineffability, noeticism, unity, and ecstasy—are also core aspects of the nursing experience as well. The nursing experience is *ineffable* because the stage in which it was experienced was preverbal. It is *noetic*, an experience of knowing something deep and personal, because there is a feeling of passively "drinking in" something of deep nurturing value from an external entity that is infinitely bigger than us.[14] The sense of *unity* is evident, as the act of breastfeeding recapitulates the recently severed symbiotic relationship between fetus and mother, in which the baby is physically attached (latched) to its mother: "Mother and I are one." And above all, both experiences are inherently emotional. It is a reciprocally *ecstatic* experience of love-giving and love-taking, in which both participants are not individual selves, but united in a primary "fusion" of two bodies into one.

In his study of priests, Rossetti found that a "personal devotion to Mary" was one of the strongest overall predictors of a priest's happiness and of priestly spirituality as a whole, causing Rossetti to note: "There is probably more of a devotion to her in the priesthood than currently known."[15] Because Mary symbolically represents the relationship with Mother that at one point is always entirely unitive, the figure of Mary in Christianity represents a "concrete" and "palpable" sense of unitive consciousness that is both physical and spiritual at the same time. "The veneration of Mary is the surest and shortest way to get close to Christ in a concrete way."[16] Because Mary was a real woman, not a god like God or a demigod like Jesus, and because she was a mother, like the physical mother we all experienced, she is less conceptual, less metaphysical, less imperceptible than God or Jesus. She is the physical presence we can perceive viscerally and emotionally with our own senses and feelings. When Christians report a vision of the divine, it is almost always a vision of Mary. Rossetti provides a priest's experience as an example:

> Praying with a young woman who had lost a child, like Mary did, he invoked Our Lady's intercession. Then, the priest wrote, "As I was encouraging her to confide in this special, loving woman, I felt a presence enter my office, a presence of ineffable sweetness.... The experience was real and perceptible, palpable for both of us.... Mary was real."[17]

Though on the surface the Abrahamic religions seem androcentrically focused on a male God, the veneration of a sacred mother or feminine aspect of divinity is ubiquitous. In Islam, she is recognized, among many other names and figures, as Fatimah. In Judaism, she is recognized as the Shechinah—the feminine aspect of God, the "bride of God"—who is also the spiritual presence of God. On the Sabbath, the most sacred of all Jewish holy days, the Shechinah is welcomed into the midst of the community, and felt as a palpable presence throughout the holy day. It is important to note that when the presence of God is truly felt on Earth, it is always ascribed to the sensation of the Shechinah, as this is the only aspect of God that descends from the highest of high places in order to comfort and commune with her children.

The mystical experience of spiritual perception expresses an inner drive towards the sense of unity that began when our natural state was, indeed, a state of symbiosis with another entity larger and inclusive of ourselves. Separation from that united state is unconsciously perceived as the ultimate tragedy of life—the "birth trauma," separation anxiety, the "Fall of Man"—which pulled us unwillingly out from the womb of Eden to suffer in the cold detached world of separateness. Reunification with that united state is the ultimate goal of all spiritual practice and of all mystical experience.

Stage 2: The Magical God—Toddlerhood and Early Childhood

> And out of the ground the Lord God formed every beast of the field and every fowl of the air and brought them unto the man to see what he would call them; and whatsoever the man would call every living creature, that was the name to be thereof.—Genesis 2:19

The child sketches his image of God in his mind's eye, just as the artist sketches his image of the portrait he will paint onto the bare canvass. Though the pencil sketch is eventually overlaid with several layers of oil paint, the sketch doesn't disappear, nor does its formational effect on the finished portrait diminish over time. Though invisible and inaccessible, it exists underneath. What does the sketch of God created in very early childhood look like? Inevitably, invariably, it must be a reflection of how the toddler perceives and understands his world, and himself.

Deborah Kelemen, a developmental psychologist, refers to children as "intuitive theists."[18] The mind of the small child, not yet governed by language—much less logic, reason, or abstract reflective consciousness—is inherently intuitive. Thoughts of God are not based on holy books or dogma, they come from the small child's impression of the world around him, a world that he intuitively knows and feels to be intimately connected with, a world that he is a part of, a world that is a part of him. Emerging from the infantile state of cognitive unity, the child has the innate sense that all matters and beings are woven into each other in one great fabric of interrelation. Perhaps the only word that can adequately define this deep sense of unity within and without of the self is: "Spirit."

The term "animism" is derived from the Latin word "anima," which means "spirit" or "soul." To animate something is to project a spirit into that thing, transforming it from a thing into a being. Piaget defined "animism" in children as the inability to "distinguish the psychical from the physical world." The small child retains the infantile inability to "recognize any definite limits between his self and the external world."[19] The sun is alive to the little boy because it shines on him and follows him as he walks. The stone is alive because it likes to roll down the hill, the river is alive because it likes to flow downstream. The child hits the door because the door slammed on him on purpose. He hugs his teddy bear as he would his mother, because he loves Teddy, and Teddy loves him.[20] Animism represents a sense of "adualism" between the thought that we have about an object and the object itself. The inner thought and the outer object, to the small child, are connected.[21] The subject, the child's cognition about the object, and the child's perception of the object are joined in a state of cognitive-perceptual unity. The outer world, therefore, becomes animated—alive and conscious—because the child is alive and conscious, and the inner world and outer world are one in the same.

The ability to create a cognitive separation between a detached "I" and other objects and beings that are disconnected from "I" comes from language-based consciousness. Words generate the first cognitive duality, the initial severing of the inner thought from the outer thing.[22] Language begins with the process of naming things. A word, in its most basic sense, is a name for something within our environment. Once we can point to something and name it—"Mommy"—we can differentiate it by name and therefore by thought from that which is "not Mommy." Similarly, once we can regard ourselves by name—"Jimmy!"—we can differentiate our self from everything that is not the self, everything that is "not Jimmy." Just as Adam was tasked by God to name all the beasts and birds in the Garden of Eden, so too is the small child tasked by Mommy with naming all the people and things in his house. While Mommy thinks that Jimmy is learning his words, the cognitive leap that is being formed is (like the serpent in the Garden), far more subtle. In naming himself and everything around him, Jimmy is nailing down the concept that there is an "I," surrounded on all sides by things that are "not-I." This disconnection between thought and thing at the earliest stage of language development gives rise to a budding sense of cognitive duality. However, what initially arises is a transitional phase in which thoughts are cognitively attached to the words that denote them.

"Nominal realism" refers to the "real" connection between the thought and the word attached to it.[23] Names of things, for the very small child, are conceived as being a part of the things themselves. Piaget discovered proof of nominal realism when he observed the common belief in small children that a thought about an object resides in the mouth,[24] not in the mind, because the thought is expressed primarily through the word.[25] Piaget noted many examples of nominal realism. I will cite just one, in which the psychologist is interviewing a 7-year-old child:

PSYCHOLOGIST: You know what it means to think?
CHILD: Yes.
PSYCHOLOGIST: Then think of your house. What do you think with?
CHILD: The mouth.
PSYCHOLOGIST: Can you think with the mouth shut?
CHILD: No.

PSYCHOLOGIST: With the eyes shut?
CHILD: Yes.
PSYCHOLOGIST: With the ears stopped up?
CHILD: Yes.
PSYCHOLOGIST: Now shut your mouth and think of your house. Are you thinking?
CHILD: Yes.
PSYCHOLOGIST: What did you think with?
CHILD: The mouth.[26]

With the integration of words, there arises the duality between an inner sense of self and external objects—each have words to distinguish them—but then the words themselves get wrapped up in the thing. Hence, a doll named "Teddy" could not possibly be renamed something else, because "Teddy" is a part of the doll, as much as the fur or the legs are a part of the doll. Names are perceived as physically real, in that they are an indivisible aspect of the thing itself. This reification of the word is, I believe, at the heart of most magic and religious ritual. In magic, we recite the magic spell, and the magical power of the incantation—the magic of the en-*chant*-ment, the magic words themselves—cause a physical change in the world to occur. When we wish upon a star, it is the wish itself, the words, that cause the physical change. Similarly, when God created the universe, he did so through the power of words. "God *said* 'Let there be light'; and there was light" (Genesis 1:3). When we pray to God, it is with words spoken either aloud or silently. There is spiritual power in those words, if they can truly reach the ears of God and sway him to alter the universe. The 3rd Commandment warns us to never take the Lord's name in vain; for there is power in the name itself. Similarly, when one says: "Speak of the Devil and he will appear," we must remember that in olden days, this saying was not referring to mere coincidence or even superstitious synchronicity. The belief was: If you speak the Devil's name, the power of the name itself, once uttered, will cause the Devil to appear. A similar theme is found in "Rumpelstilskin" and dozens of other fairytales and folktales. Among Jews, it's traditionally forbidden to name a child after a living relative, because the name of the person betakes part of the soul, and so two souls will become confused and adulterated when the bodies that are housing them are given the same name. Kabbalah, the mystical tradition in Judaism, is primarily obsessed with the spiritual power found in holy words, especially in the "tetragrammatron," the ineffable four-letter name of God.[27]

The language that adults use, which is the language that children hear, is inherently animistic and anthropomorphic.[28] This is because on a neurological level, our imagistic thoughts precede by a microsecond our linguistic interpretation of these images into words. On a cognitive level, just as imagistic thinking preceded linguistic thinking in the evolution of our species, images precede words in the thinking of preverbal toddlers. Thus, our words often take on the more holistic, animated, personal nature of the primary images that gave birth to them. We say animistically that "the sun is setting," though we know perfectly well that the sun does not move. We say that "the sun is breaking through the mist," as if it were really trying to accomplish this task. We even instill "quasi-magical" intonations in our speech, when we say: "Red sun in the morning is a sailor's warning," as if the sun were trying to warn the sailor of foul weather to come. Piaget, however, is quick to remind us that animistic language does not *cause* animism in children. Rather, animistic language in children and adults reflects the retention in thought at the pre-linguistic level of the animistic mindset. Thus, animistic language, which is cognitively "regressive," shows a "convergence" between a natural way of speaking in adults and a natural way of thinking in preliterate children and preliterate peoples.[29] While the adults may *say* that the sun is setting, he *knows* it is not true. The child, on the other hand, not only says that the sun is setting, he actually *thinks* that the sun is descending in position—and what's more—the sun is setting because *he knows* it's time for him to say goodnight, and so he must reluctantly depart for the evening. The perception of the sun as an active participant in the world, one that thinks and feels and is also aware of us, recalls the perception of God in its most pristine state—the presence that is always there, even when it's not seen—the presence that has will and reason, sees all things, and presides over all.

The Anthropomorphic God

> So God created Man in his own image, in the image of God created He him...—Genesis 1:27
>
> Men create the gods in their own images.—Aristotle, 3rd century BC
>
> There is an universal tendency among mankind to conceive all beings like themselves.... We find human faces in the moon, armies in the clouds...—David Hume, 1757

In his book, *Faces in the Clouds* (1993), Stewart Guthrie argues that "religion may best be understood as systematic anthropomorphism: the attribution of human characteristics to nonhuman things and events."[30] We tend to project life and consciousness into things, because it is a perceptual gamble that is adaptive ... "it is better for a hiker to mistake a boulder for a bear than to mistake a bear for a boulder."[31] The animistic mode of perception, while dominant in preliterate societies and preliterate children, is also present in the perception of literate adults, and is always active on a latent level. When we read about a hero in a story, we perceive the letters or "characters" on the page not just as mere objective marks, but as a real live person—a "character" who speaks and breaths and is as animated as any person in real life. "No sum of 'characters' creates a 'character.'"[32] That God is nearly always perceived and imagined as a character who is conceived in anthropomorphic dimensions by both children and adults, regardless of age or literacy, points to an anthropomorphic tendency in spiritual perception that has been noted throughout history. Xenophanes[33] wrote that if horses had gods, those gods would look like horses. Voltaire wrote that a cockroach's notion of God would probably be an immense and omnipotent cockroach.[34] Tremlin noted that "only theologians and religious specialists present them [gods] as radically "Other".... Mel Gibson's portrait of the "Passion of Christ" will always be more compelling than Paul Tillich's obtuse depiction of god as the "Ground of Being" (1973)."[35]

Robert Coles (1990) observed that when children draw a picture of God, they always draw God as a person, not as a thing; and the drawing is nearly always that of a face—the face of God—surely the most personal part of a person's person. Despite the prohibition of the 2nd Commandment against the making of "graven images," anthropomorphic religious iconography is omnipresent in Christianity. The emergence of the Christian faith itself may represent a reaction to a deficit in its mother religion, Judaism, which always took the 2nd Commandment a bit more literally, absolutely forbidding the creation of any images of God. Without the image of a human face or human form, without the human-like deity to connect with on a perceptual level, the internal mental image of God seems vacant and empty, leaving a "God-shaped hole" in the mind where an anthropomorphic image should be.[36] For the ancient Jews in biblical times, the anthropomorphic trend in spiritual perception was satisfied in the presence of divine kings, potent sacrificial rites, prophets who heard God, a holy temple—God's actual home on Earth—which housed the Ark of the Covenant, from which God's voice was actually heard, and to top it all off, the ancient Jews were apparently all worshipping idols anyway.[37] But when the divine kings were defeated and replaced with imperial governors, when the holy temple was destroyed, the Ark and sacred relics lost, the sacrificial rites abandoned, and the prophets deafened to the voice of God, the anthropomorphic need was met by the emergence of a messiah, the presence of God in human form. In keeping with the Greco-Roman setting of the Judean colony, the messiah was soon elevated from a man who was selected by God, to a man who was God.

To return to the small child, his perception of the realness of magic and of dreams is, for Piaget, another indication of animism and nominal realism, the fusion of inner thoughts and external things.[38] Just as the child makes little distinction between the object and his thought of the object, he makes no distinction between the dream experience and the experience of dreaming, because he does not recognize that the process of dreaming, like the process of thought, is separate from that which is being dreamed of. Therefore to a small child dreams are real. They are not inner experiences of pure imagination, but external experiences that actually happen in the outside world. If the child dreams of Disneyworld, he believes that the dream occurred at Disneyworld, not within his own mind.[39]

Dreams occur in the real world, not in a "dream world," and what happens in dreams is as real as what happens in reality. This is why nightmares are so much more terrifying for small children than they are for adults, as adults in literate societies have learned to dissociate themselves from the dream experience, realizing that the dream, like our thoughts, is merely a product of the mind, a virtual reality that is not objectively real. Dreams, to literate adults, are subjects, not objects. Dreams, to little children and preliterate adults, are objective—they really happen in the real world—they're not "just a dream," not just in the mind. Magic is also real to the child because he isn't aware that the thoughts in his head become symbols when they are put into words. He regards the word as *part* of the thing, not as a *representation* of the thing, because he is unaware that the words he is using are in fact symbols.[40] This pre-symbolic unity will divide itself into symbolic duality when the next major cognitive shift occurs, in school-aged childhood.

Language based consciousness liberates our thoughts from the shackles of time and space. Our inner monologue is unbound by the present moment and the present place, allowing us to reflect in a "decoupled mode of interaction"—to engage in conversations silently with ourselves or with imaginary people on a completely hypothetical basis.[41] This ability allows us to prepare for future interactions, running through a variety of potential scenarios, and it even allows us to engage in conceptual conversations that could never actually exist. We can interact in the decoupled mode with our dead fathers, with ancestors or historical figures that we've never even met, and yes ... we can even converse with God. It's this propensity to engage in conceptual conversation that psychologist Marjorie Taylor[42] believes is at the root of the childhood tendency to create and maintain relationships with imaginary friends. The animistic tendency in children drives them to seek out relationships with things. They project consciousness into objects such as teddy bears and animals such as their dogs. Then, because they can, they engage in conversations with these imaginary conscious objects. These conversations, for the child, seem as real as the conversation they have with other people—or even more real—because while the small child often feels frustrated that he cannot express his ideas fluently in words, the imaginary friend always understands everything the child says, and he never speaks in words that the child cannot understand. Richard Dawkins, in *The God Delusion*, suggests that the imaginary friends of early childhood provide the cognitive template for all future "delusions" of God. He recounts the personal experience of a real girl and her imaginary friend.

> Another child, a girl, had a "little purple man," who seemed to her a real and visible presence, and who would manifest himself, sparkling out of the air, with a gentle tinkling sound. He visited her regularly, especially when she felt lonely, but with decreasing frequency as she grew older. On a particular day just before she went to kindergarten, the little purple man came to her, heralded by his usual tinkling fanfare, and announced that he would not be visiting her any more. This saddened her, but the little purple man told her that she was getting bigger now and wouldn't need him in the future. He must leave her now so that he could look after other children. He promised her that he would come back to her if she really needed him. He did return to her, many years later in a dream, when she had a personal crisis and was trying to decide what to do with her life. The door of her bedroom opened and a cartload of books appeared, pushed into the room by ... the little purple man. She interpreted this as advice that she should go to university—advice that she took and later judged to be good. The story makes me almost tearful and it brings me as close as I shall probably come to understanding the consoling and counseling role of imaginary gods in people's lives. A being may exist only in the imagination, yet still seem completely real to the child, and still give real comfort and good advice. Perhaps even better: imaginary friends—and imaginary gods—have the time and patience to devote all their attention to the sufferer. And they are much cheaper than psychiatrists or professional counselors.[43]

While I agree with Dawkins on the basic idea that imaginary friends provide a good example of how children in particular and people in general create non-physical subjects with which they relate, and this relationship with a non-physical entity is certainly relevant to the construct of spiritual perception, I must emphasize my central point: Spiritual perception does not begin, nor does it end, in early-childhood. Spiritual perception develops in every person, in a path that roughly parallels the evolution of spiritual perception in the human race. My purpose in quoting the story that Dawkins relates above, is that the girl in the story intuitively knew that at a certain point in childhood—significantly, the point when she enters a system of fulltime formal schooling—she was expected to leave behind the magical, animistic thinking of early childhood, in favor of the logical, rational, concrete, and literal thinking of school-aged childhood.

In preliterate societies, where formal schooling does not exist, the imaginary friend is never expected to depart; but perhaps, is molded into a new form. In some traditional Native American societies, a boy upon reaching adolescence goes on a "vision quest" to find his "guardian" or "animal" spirit. What the boy may be doing on the quest is not so much finding something new, but re-acquainting himself with something old—the boy's imaginary friend—who must now die, transform, and become reborn into a "guardian spirit." Thus the spiritual death of the boy and his rebirth into a man is paralleled by the death and rebirth of his accompanying spirit. Take the case of someone like Mohammad Farah, who as a boy had a host of mzimus of deceased ancestors to relate to: dead grandfathers, dead grandmothers, dead uncles, dead aunts, etc. However, when the moment came that makes the young man reflect on himself as a man and as a father—when Mohammad's own father died—it was only his father's mzimu that he related to from that point onwards. Hence, as some preliterate societies believe, it is not necessarily we who choose our guardian spirits, but it is our guardian spirits who choose us.

Stage 3: The Symbolic God—School-Aged Childhood

> At present our system of education seems almost a guarantee that while we teach them how to use words and concepts, we wipe out this other world of beauty and higher reality which so many children live in.—Aldous Huxley

Piaget believed that self-conscious awareness comes about as a result of interiorized language. The moment when we begin to think in words is the moment when we begin to understand ourselves as a separate "I"—"if by 'I' we follow William James and mean that element of the self which watches the life of the rest."[44] This knowledge of the self as a subject separate from other subjects creates a split in the sense of self, an inner duality between the self that is living and the self that is observing itself as it lives.[45] The awareness of oneself as a distinct, private, and separate identity changes not only our perception of ourselves, but our perception of the world. Rather than having a unified perception of the world and our thoughts about the world, our perception is split into a duality of the perceived objects in the world and the conceived subjects in our mind that may or may not be directly related to a perceived object. When thoughts become abstracted into words, our experience of the world becomes "disassociated" from the world. As Piaget pointed out, the process of "dualization" or "dissociation" actually occurs gradually through a series of steps. First there is the detachment of the inner world from the outer world: Mommy and I are not one. Then there is the detachment of the thought from the object: Thinking of Mommy does not cause Mommy to appear. Then there is the detachment of the word from the object: The name "Mommy" is not a part of Mommy ... Mommy by any other name would still be Mommy. And then, finally, the distinction between objects and subjects: Mommy is alive like me, but Teddy is not alive like me.

At this final point, we begin to refrain from projecting consciousness—a soul—into other nonhuman things, because we realize the inherent difference between that which is conscious like ourselves, and that which is not conscious. We stop seeing the world animistically. The sun is no longer seen as a watchful majestic presence residing on his throne in the Heavens. It becomes merely a massive orb of heat and light floating in space. The subject has become an object; or as Martin Buber would put it: the "Thou" has become an "It." At the same time that animistic thinking wanes, the "Age of Magic" of childhood also dusks.[46] What cognitive adaptation causes the mind to abandon animism and magic as viable ways of understanding the world? In a word: Literacy.[47]

The shift from preliteracy to literacy concretizes words in the mind, turning them into concise and concrete literal symbols, as opposed to vague, fleeting, imagistic notions. The shift in the perception of language—from auditory to visual—also facilitates the concretization of language. The age old oral tradition of reciting nursery rhymes and fairy tales to children, for example, has been replaced in the modern world by the storybook and picture book.[48] In this we are giving children "an eye for an ear,"[49] by placing the focus on the written word and the drawn picture. An oral story allows the storyteller to choose his own words. In this way, the meaning, emphasis, and content of the story are left in the control of the storyteller's imagination. The story could be custom fit for the child who is listening. An oral story also allows the listener to imagine—*image-ine*—his own mental image of the characters. The story is experienced primarily as an internal imaginary scenario in which the child's own imagination creates the imagery. Thus, the listener is an equal partner in the storytelling/story-creating process.[50]

A written word and drawn picture, on the other hand, literalizes and materializes the stories and sounds into exact, specific, unvarying forms. With a picture book or storybook, the story is told and imaged by the writer and illustrator. They control and dominate the creative process. The storyteller is merely a narrator of the written words. The images present themselves fully formed in the illustrations. The child is merely a consumer of these images and words. A passive listener, he takes no part in the creative process. The implicit knowledge that the creation of an external objective picture for the eye to see actually *inhibits* the creation of an internal subjective image for the inner-eye to imagine, may be at the root of the biblical prohibition against the "graven images" of God.

In the 21st century, the movement in education towards digitalizing the classroom experience—students in the classroom looking at computer screens rather than listening to the teacher, and online classes replacing traditional classes—presents another method of giving students "an eye for an ear." The traditional classroom experience, in which learning is achieved through a dialectic interchange between the student and the teacher, as well as the interchange between the students themselves, is exorcised from the education process when it is replaced by a purely digital mode of interchange that offers no true dialectic between anyone, no personal interchange, no in-the-moment interpersonal interactions, and no real human exchanges whatsoever. The process of education in this system is reduced to an information delivery system. When the digital replaces the personal, education (teaching children how to think), is replaced by information (showing children how to process data).

A Critical Period for Spiritual Development

> There was a time when meadow, grove, and stream,
> The earth, and every common sight, To me did seem
> Apparell'd in celestial light,
> The glory and the freshness of a dream.
> It is not now as it hath been of yore;—
> Turn wheresoe'er I may,
> By night or day,
> The things which I have seen I now can see no more.
>
> Whither is fled the visionary gleam?
> Where is it now, the glory and the dream?
>
> Our birth is but a sleep and a forgetting:
> The Soul that rises with us, our life's Star,
> Hath had elsewhere its setting,
> And cometh from afar:
> Not in entire forgetfulness,
> And not in utter nakedness,
> But trailing clouds of glory do we come
> From God, who is our home:
> Heaven lies about us in our infancy!
> Shades of the prison-house begin to close
> Upon the growing Boy,
> But he beholds the light, and whence it flows,
> He sees it in his joy;
> The Youth, who daily farther from the east
> Must travel, still is Nature's priest,
> And by the vision splendid
> Is on his way attended;
> At length the Man perceives it die away,
> And fade into the light of common day.
> —William Wordsworth, from "Intimations of
> Immortality from Recollections of Early Childhood"

In 1967, Eric Lenneberg, following the linguistic theories of Noam Chomsky, proposed a "critical period" for language development. According to his theory, if a person does not acquire a first language during childhood, it is unlikely that the individual will be able to acquire and master a language after childhood. I propose a similar critical period of development for spiritual perception.

During my first year of graduate school, I had a part time job as a teacher in an after-school program at a Reform Jewish Temple in Greenwich Village, Manhattan. My students were 1st and 2nd graders. One day after reading a story about a Biblical event (I can't remember which), I told the children to draw pictures about the story. One little girl raised her hand and asked: "Can I draw a picture of God?" I hesitated. "He was in the story," she argued correctly. So I said "Sure." Two things of interest then happened. First, my assistant who, like me, was educated at an Orthodox yeshiva, told me that the child, in fact, *may not* draw a picture of God, as it would be breaking the 2nd of the Ten Commandments (no graven images). I told my assistant that this was a Reform temple, and that people here didn't follow the letter of the law so literally. Moments later, the little girl showed me her picture of God. He was, indeed, a kindly looking old gent with a long white beard and glasses. (God is nearsighted, who knew?) "Very nice," I said. A moment later, my assistant approached with an open copy of Deuteronomy. He read me the passage that forbade the making of graven images, in Hebrew, no less. "Very nice," I said.

As children, we anthropomorphize God, envisioning him as a person just like you and me. This conception of God is helpful for children as it allows for their more basic animistic tendency to guide their thoughts and perceptions about a concept that is a bit too abstract for them to conceive of in a meaningful way. Though their thinking has become less magical, it is still "concrete"—it is tied down to the real world—and must conceive of things in terms of concrete concepts. As adolescents, our thinking becomes "formalized," more abstract. We begin to understand abstract concepts; but initially, the concepts themselves are understood quite literally, with little room for varied interpretations. The young child, in drawing a picture of God, was understanding God in the best way she could. My young assistant, an adolescent, by pointing to the letter of the law as it was written in the holy book, was expressing his understanding of God in the best way he could. As for me, the best I could do was to try and understand each different viewpoint, while also realizing that my own personal viewpoint seemed somehow vacant or deficient. A part of me wanted to actually care deeply about either the "real" image of God, or the "real" prohibition against the image. Unfortunately, it just didn't matter to me either way.

Yet, I could distinctly remember being a child like the one who drew a picture of God. I remember going to Yeshiva, praying three times a day to a God who I believed existed, and engaging in all of the other rituals and traditions. But at a certain point, I began to doubt the existence of God. After a long period of doubt, in which no experience of God's presence came about to reaffirm my belief, I simply stopped believing. At first I felt guilty about my faithlessness; but in time, that too faded into nonexistence. What happened? I believe that my spiritual perception ceased to develop in childhood because my spiritual practice was not reinforced at home. Though I learned about God and prayed at school, I never once prayed or studied with my mother and father. I said no blessings at home, I ate un-kosher food, I did not keep the Sabbath, etc. Because my spiritual training was inconsistent, because I had one foot in the religious world and the other in the secular world, my spiritual perception failed to proceed forward. For some people, spiritual perception, like other abilities, needs to be practiced on a daily basis. "If you don't use it, you lose it"—or you never develop it in the first place. On top of that, spiritual perception, for some people, must be upheld consistently, like the consistent weeding of a garden. Otherwise, the seeds of doubt will take root, grow, and eventually take over the garden. Finally, spiritual perception, like language, needs to be formalized in childhood, before the mental force that wields the power to dissolve spiritual perception (language based consciousness), assumes total dominance in the mind. Spiritual perception, an abiding sense of the presence of God, must be strong and present at the developmental moment that language based consciousness takes control. If it is not there, it runs the risk of being lost forever....

> Whither is fled the visionary gleam?
> Where is it now, the glory and the dream?

My personal story and my personal theory related to my story are not universal. What is universal is the tendency for children to have a wide range of perceptions that go way beyond objective observations of the real world. Whether these perceptions are called spiritual, mystical, magical, or fantastical, is merely a matter of interpretation. Also universal is the tendency for children in literate societies to lose most of these non-objective perceptions, as Huxley noted:

> Strange openings and theophanies are granted to quite small children, who are often profoundly and permanently affected by these experiences. We have no reason to suppose that what happens now to persons with small vocabularies did not happen in remote antiquity, in the modern world ... the child tends to grow out of his direct awareness of the one Ground of things; for the habit of analytical thought is fatal to the intuitions of integral thinking, whether on the "psychic" or the spiritual level.[51]

It is not the establishment of schooling itself, but the mode of thought that children are compelled to acquire in school that changes their perception—narrowing it—in order to frame their understanding of the world in accordance with the rules of logic and reason. The frames of logic and reason, manifested in the forms of written words and numbers, become solid, concrete, in the age of schooling. For some children, the frames close in to become the barrier to the perception of anything that is illogical or unreasonable.

> We live in a secular world. To adapt to this world the child abdicates its ecstasy. (*L'enfant abdique son extase*: Malarmé.) Having lost our experience of the spirit, we

are expected to have faith. But this faith comes to be a belief in a reality which is not evident. There is a prophecy in Amos that a time will come when there will be a famine in the land, "not a famine for bread, nor a thirst for water, but of *hearing* the words of the Lord." That time has now come to pass. It is the present age.[52]

"Ecstasy," the "stepping out" of oneself, becomes impossible when the frames of logic and reason close in on each other, like the mythical stones Scylla and Charybdis, barring the exit of consciousness into unreason.

After literacy leads to the cognitive domination of language based consciousness over thought, magic and fantasy are only indulged at the cognitive level of "make-believe." At the same time, thoughts about God must grow up as well. In the concrete stage of cognitive development, school aged children must conceive of abstract ideas in ways that relate to the real world of objects and beings that surround them. As gods and spirits are less likely to be perceived directly, the child needs to concretize his internal image of God in a way that makes sense to him. At this stage, children equate their parents with the notion of God, not on a literal level, but as a mental template for what an all-powerful, all-knowing, ever-present, occasionally wrathful but for the most part loving and nurturing god would be like.[53] Parents and religion reinforce this metaphor by referring to God(s) as the "heavenly father" and "holy mother," and by generally representing God as a divine father to his mortal children. Parents often use a psychological "coalition with God"[54] as a means of reinforcing their authority in the home. They threaten their children with punishment from God for misbehaving, and warn their children that God will punish them if they neglect the 5th commandment, "Honor thy Parents." Eventually, the child's parental conceptualization of God must move beyond the concrete template of God as Father/Mother, when reason and logic push it further into abstraction. A "crisis" occurs in childhood when the child's mind, now governed by reason, understands that his parents are not and could not be gods, or anything remotely like gods.[55] The reconfiguration of God as an abstract entity who cannot be visualized or heard, who is not present in the world, and who is not felt as an emotional extension of mother and father, is a critical juncture in the path of spiritual perception ... for many it's a straight turn onto a dead end.

Stage 4: The Broken God—Adolescence

> We lose the power of a dream and other unconscious experience when we reduce them to rationalized words, for they then become "signs" rather than "symbols."—Rollo May[56]

According to Piaget, in adolescence, cognitive functions reach the "formal" stage of operations. Adolescents can think at a higher level of abstraction. They can engage in hypothetical-deductive reasoning, seeing multiple viewpoints simultaneously while understanding concepts from a detached perspective. Algebraic notions such as the unknown quantity or the possibility of an unsolvable problem are beguiling to the child, who must relate his understanding to a real-world concrete example. These notions are now accessible to adolescent thinkers. A small child can add 5 apples to 10 apples, or subtract 5 apples from 10 apples, or even multiply 5 apples by 10, or divide 10 apples by 5, but it will be difficult for him to calculate the unknown quantity of apples: $5 + n = 10$, because "n" is a completely abstract concept, un-relatable to any concrete image or idea. The concept of God in childhood, a concrete construct grounded in both the parental conceptual template and the animistic/anthropomorphic mental image, has the potential to become completely abstract in adolescence. If it does, questions may arise. The adolescent, now gifted with the ability to reason at an advanced level of abstraction, engages in hypothetical deductive arguments about God.

"If God can do anything, could he create a stone so big that he himself could not lift it?"

I asked this question to my rabbi in 6th grade. He was quite frustrated by it, explaining that questions like that are pointless, and are only made by troublemakers who want to belittle those things which are uplifting. I could see his point, but at the same time, the question came from a place of curiosity, not of malice. I was honestly trying to figure out what this thing "God" was on a rational level, because the old way of thinking about God, the "big old man in the sky" way, was no longer working for me.[57]

In adolescence, symbols are seen as abstract representations of a concept or feeling, not as concrete things in-and-of-themselves. For example, if you read Edgar Allan Poe's "The Raven" to an adolescent and ask him what the raven is, he is likely to tell you that the raven is a symbol for the man's loneliness or grief. If you read the same poem to a child and ask him the same question, he is likely to tell you that the raven is a bird that can somehow magically speak. The point is, though the child obviously perceives the symbol of the raven and gets a sense of its meaning on an intuitive level, the symbol is not perceived as a representation of something else, it is perceived as what it actually seems to be, a bird. If the "big old man in the sky" is a symbol for the concept of God, then it is a living and working symbol for most children who believe in God in the concrete fashion typical of childhood. But if at one point—adolescence, typically—the symbol is seen not as a representation of God himself, but as a representation for a concept so abstract that it cannot be conceived of in any true physical way, then the symbol of God is then recognized as a symbol—and *a symbol that is recognized as a symbol is a broken symbol.*[58]

For instance, a child thinks of Santa Claus as a real man (or elf) with magical powers who comes to your house on Christmas Eve bearing gifts. This is a living, working symbol of the Christmas spirit, because the child is not aware that the symbol only exists in the mind, he thinks that the symbol is physically real. When the child realizes that Santa Claus is not a real man, that he doesn't come to your house on Christmas—but rather, he is a cherished but abstract symbol of the Christmas spirit, with no real physical form—then the symbol, while still potent, is broken. When God ceases to be conceived as a physical presence, but only as a metaphysical concept, he ceases to be "real" on the physical plane. He remains a symbol, but a broken symbol. No longer *God*, he becomes just *a god*.

Rollo May, following Paul Tillich, made a distinction between a symbol and a sign. A sign points to one thing. A white flag on a battlefield is a sign, it means one thing: "surrender." An American flag to someone living in a far-off place where America is just a vague idea is also a sign, it means: "that far off land called America." But to me, the American flag is a *symbol*. It means much more than a land or a country. It somehow encapsulates and represents all the things I associate with America, all the ideals, all the paradoxes, all the things I am proud of as an American, and all of the things I am ashamed of as well. These associations cannot be encapsulated in one term, or even in a thousand terms, which is why the power of the symbol is so potent. The symbol represents what we feel and sense and intuitively know, but which cannot be completely grasped or precisely defined with one term. Symbols, in this sense, while not irrational, are somewhat elusive to rationality and reason. How could one thing mean so many things? How could one thing be so significant, yet also so un-definable? The power of the symbol is in the emotions and sensations it evokes, not in the rational thought it indicates. This is why, as May and many others noted, symbols are the language of myth, dreams, and the unconscious. They go beyond reason, they transcend conscious reality. Symbols present paradoxes that are anathema to the rationalistic mindset that prefers specific signs with concrete single meanings over ambiguous symbols that have many meanings and are oftentimes paradoxical.

Adolescence, the stage of formal operational reasoning—the stage of abstract symbolic thinking—becomes the stage of utmost duality: the duality of consciousness and unconsciousness, of sense and nonsense, and of the real and unreal. Adolescence is the stage in which paradoxicality, one of the essential qualities of spiritual perception, is most likely to be rejected. There is much irony and little coincidence in the fact that the same stage of life in which paradoxicality and the sense of the unreal is first rejected by the conscious mind, is also the same stage in life when many adolescents begin to explore and experiment with drugs and experiences that might give them an artificially inspired sense of the paradoxical, the fantastical, the psychedelically unreal.

A new tool in the hands of an eager user is prone to be overused. To the man with a hammer in hand, the world is perceived as a series of nails.[59] To the man with a new Iphone, the world is perceived as a series of instagrams, texts, and tweets. To the adolescent with the new tool of hypothetical-deductive reasoning, the world is perceived as a series of conceptual problems that could all be solved through the application of reason and logic. There may then arise a nascent narcissism grounded in the belief that all old answers are wrong and must be righted, that the truth is neither relative nor unattainable, and that reason and logic, when properly applied by the conscious self, will discover and reveal the universal truth that underlies all things. This is an eager tool-user seeking signs, not symbols. The eager seeker is likely to reject symbols as "meaningless" emblems used to control the minds of children and of the thoughtless unseeing masses. Mythology, whose primary function is to provide meaning to life, becomes meaningless to a person whose spectacles for perceiving symbols have been broken. The symbolic stories and figures are now seen as fables and allegories. *Myth*—the connection between humanity and divinity—becomes just *a myth*—an old story that is untrue.[60]

Whereas the stage of late childhood could be seen as an age of "disenchantment," an age when the magical qualities of the world are dissipated in the base solution of conscious realism; adolescence could be seen as an age of "disillusionment," an age when the illusions of childhood are revealed by abstract conscious reasoning to be nothing but shadows and reflections. The idol worshipper of old smashed his idol, but only after the symbol had already been broken—only after the idol was no longer perceived as God—but only as a symbol for a god. Just so, the adolescent becomes an iconoclast, smashing the idols around him as he searches for an unambiguous sense of truth, something that is a sign rather than a symbol ... something that is not just an "illusion." What spirituo-religious options are available to the rebellious adolescent mind?

Adolescence, the stage of utmost duality, tends to be a time of absolutes and extremes. You either love me or you hate me! A musician is either totally awesome or he totally sucks! In terms of religion, you are either a "theist"[61]—completely invested in the traditional conception of God as a real entity, and accepting all of His precepts—or you are an "atheist"—completely rejecting God as an illusion, and as a consequence, rejecting all the precepts and dogma of the associated religion. I certainly became a self professed "devout atheist" for my entire adolescence. The atheist who has no faith and no sense of spiritual perception is likely to judge all theists as conformists, mindless followers, blind sheep. I made this mistake myself. It is, of course, a classic case of the pot calling the kettle black. In this case, it is the blind (spiritually blind), mistaking his darkness for light, and calling those not similarly benighted, "blind." For the "spiritual theist," the person who is both spiritual and religious, spiritual perception could just be a continuance of the sense of God that existed in childhood. If the perception of spirit is strong enough, a sense of faith grounded in spiritual experience and spiritual practice will trump any sense of doubt raised by abstract formal reasoning. William James called this type of person the "once-born." He is born into a faith that he feels to his core, and he retains both his faith and his spiritual feeling throughout childhood, adolescence, and adulthood. Here, indeed, is the person who doesn't believe in God ... he *knows*.[62]

There is, of course, the non-spiritual theist—the conformist, the hypocritical bible thumper who praises God while robbing old ladies blind—but this phony is of little interest to us right now. More relevant to us is the spiritual nontheist. The one who feels spiritually, has a sense of spiritual perception, but has rejected the traditional religious creed that he was raised in. Abstract reasoning will point out clearly the paradoxes and contradictions within any system of dogma; yet the individual may still feel distinctly a sense of spiritual perception. In this case, it is certainly not uncommon for an "enlightened" individual to reject religion, but not the spirit—to identify oneself as a "spiritual" person—but not as a "religious" person.

There are also those who undergo a sudden and abrupt conversion experience. Adolescence is a time when sudden religious conversions to a church or cult are quite common. Sometimes the experience is enabled by a hallucinogenic drug, sometimes a psychotic break, sometimes a traumatic experience, sometimes it is found in the search for identity, a search for a community, or a search for a notion of universal truth. Regardless of the path, I believe that the sudden conversion is usually a series of back-steps to an earlier stage of spiritual perception, in which symbols were real, God was perceptible, tangible, accessible, concrete, and the answers to everything were clearly defined by an all-powerful, all-knowing, authoritative father figure, who guides his children into the ever-loving and all-encompassing embrace of the unitive mother. The sudden conversion experience, in which God is suddenly felt to be real and present, is "sudden" only in the sense that the same spiritual perceptions, experienced earlier in life, had been forgotten. A moment of spiritual perception, for the person experiencing spiritual blindness, is startling and revelatory. "To the blind, all things are sudden."[63]

Stage 5: The Paradoxical God—Adulthood

> As children must have the whooping cough, the college youth must pass through the stage of conceit, in which he holds in slight esteem the wisdom of the best.—John Lancaster Spalding, 1901

I can't be sure if most people continue to develop after childhood, much less adolescence, in this made-up area I'm calling "spiritual perception." The idea of a stage-wise model of perceptual development, in which perception is apparently the strongest in the initial stage, and then diminishes for the following three stages, seems rather suspect and paradoxical in-and-of-itself. But wait ... it gets even more absurd! In the latter stages, perception ceases to diminish, and even begins to develop in potency again. The miracle of this spiritual rebirth is drawn from the gift of life itself, or more specifically, from experience. As we grow older, we realize that not everything makes sense, and it is rather presumptuous to assume that most things should make sense. As we grow older, we experience wonders that astound even the most rational of minds: the miracle of birth, the marvel of love, the mystery of death, and the majesty of the world renewed. As we grow older, hopefully, we become more tolerant of people whose beliefs are different from our own, whose experience of life varies from our experience, and whose philosophy is altogether different, yet altogether as valid, as our own. Perhaps, if lucky, we grow wiser. We realize that the disillusioning conceit of youth is in-itself an illusion. The narcissism of conscious omniscience becomes tempered by the reality that one does not know everything, one cannot know everything, and that most things will never be known by anyone.

Paul Ricoeur wrote of a "second naiveté" which can occur later in life, long after the first naiveté of childhood has dimmed. It is a "willing naiveté," we go into it with our eyes open, and we are aware of the paradox it entails.[64] The second naiveté is a reconsideration and an acceptance of that which is so often rejected in the previous stage. There is a revaluation of the importance of myth and symbol in life. The myth is accepted, but it is a paradoxical acceptance. The myth is accepted as an old story that is factually untrue, which nevertheless speaks to an otherwise inexpressible truth that goes beyond facts. Symbols, spiritual symbols in particular, are approached again in the light of this *untruth which is true*. God is accepted as a paradox. He is a symbol for that which cannot be completely understood; but the symbol in-and-of-itself has spiritual value. Furthermore, it is accepted that the notion of spirituality cannot be summarily dismissed, just because it cannot be understood. Once the paradox is accepted, we can accept both God, and the concept of god. While the pure imagination of childhood, the imagination of real magic and concrete gods, is not accessible; the adult can acquire an "ironic imagination,"[65] in which the paradox of belief is accepted, and the mystery of existence is embraced. While the acceptance of the paradox doesn't open the door to spiritual perception, it at least releases the lock.

For me, the stage of adulthood marked a step forward from a cynical and rigid stance of devout atheism, to a more open and accepting stance of curious agnosticism. This shift in perception, perhaps, marks a potential return towards unity. If God can be perceived as an entity that transcends and connects both the real and unreal levels of existence, then he can exist as both an internal subject and an external object. As for now, all I can say for myself is that I neither believe, nor do I know. I have no faith, but I do not doubt the possibility of anything; while I simultaneously doubt the existence of absolutely nothing. I'm neither religious nor spiritual. If I had to label myself something other than "agnostic," I'd say that I'm "hopeful."

Stage 6: Nirvana

> The sharp edge of a razor is difficult to pass over: thus the wise say the path to Salvation is hard.—Katha-Upanishad

There are those who experience a deep and enduring sense of spirituality that is not a mere continuation of the spirituality realized in childhood, but a breakthrough into a new perception of the spiritual dimension of life. William James called this person the "twice-born." Evangelicals call this person "born again." The experience is the perception of being reborn into the unitive state that was previously experienced in the womb.[66] It is the closing of the circle of development, a moment of unity, in which the two ends of the circle meet and join each other, and the unity of the self is, once again, reintegrated and whole. The ancient symbol of Uroboros, the serpent swallowing its own tail, purveys the mystical element of unity and circularity that best illustrates this idea. Spiritual perception in this final stage is a return to the state of union with the eternal infinite that we all knew before birth, and that we'll all hopefully return to in the moment of death. The mystics call it by many names, the most common being the Hindu term for a state of egoless unity: "Nirvana."

To summarize the stages of development using Donald's model as a structure, we can see spiritual perception in the mind of the fetus and infant as an experience of an episodic mindset. He is in a state of cognitive-perceptual unity, as he sees no distinction between the cognitive thoughts in his mind and his perceptual observations of the world. Everything is experienced as One. In toddlerhood, the mindset is mimetic. The toddler uses preverbal gestures to express himself, demonstrating that he understands that specific signs refer to specific things; but his expressions and thoughts are still preverbal, indicating that a detached sense of consciousness does not yet exist. The early childhood years reflect a mythic mindset. Children interiorize language, and thought quickly becomes enmeshed in the words that represent thoughts. The anthropomorphic and animistic trends in early childhood—the belief in mythical entities and stories as being literally and concretely true—demonstrates that children believe in words as "real things" in and of themselves, not just as signs and symbols for other things. The mythic mindset embraces magic, mystery, fantasy, and imaginary beings of all kinds. School aged childhood marks an entrance into the theoretic mindset. The old word for elementary school—"grammar school"—denotes the truth about the purpose of schooling. Children must conform their thinking to the grammar of literacy and mathematics, they must format their mind in the theoretic mode of thinking, so that the hardware of extra-somatic memory will be accessible to them. At this stage, magical and animistic thinking is first marginalized and later abandoned in favor of logical and literal thinking.

At the next stage, adolescence, the theoretic mindset is "formalized," pushed even further into abstraction. The adolescent mind at the point of ultimate duality can reflect upon its own thoughts as objects rather than subjects, and detachedly scrutinize his own beliefs. In the subsequent stage, there is a retrieval of the mythic mindset, when the adult realizes that something of value was lost when the symbols of myth, upon the scrutiny of logical analysis, were abandoned or forgotten. And in the final stage, the mimetic mindset is retrieved when the individual deliberately uses physical rituals such as meditation or prayer to subdue the theoretic mindset. The ultimate goal of the final stage is a complete reversal of cognition, a moment when the cognitive-perceptual duality of the literate individual is "flipped" into an episodic experience of unity, a moment of true and pure spiritual perception ... Nirvana

The ultimate frontier of digital media will be the space within the mind. The ultimate journey will be the inward journey toward one's own spiritual center. A Digital Uroboros may be imagined in the benign figure of the fiber optic cable. The snake swallowing its tail becomes the feedback loop connecting the inner dimension of spirituality with the outer world of digital media. In the future, instant nirvana will be just a mouse click away....

Digital Nirvana as a Virtual Death

> Whoever worships another divinity than his self, thinking, "He is one, I am another," knows not.—*Brihadaranyaka Upanishad*

Neonatologists and neuropsychologists have revealed that fetuses spend most of their time asleep, and that most of their sleep time is spent in REM. Fetuses are usually dreaming, but what about? While it may be impossible to consciously know or understand our earliest dreams, it is entirely possible that somewhere deep in the recesses of our unconscious mind, memories of our earliest dreams are stored. Perhaps a deliberate process of engaging and exploring our dreams, such as the Digital Dream process discussed previously, could bring us back to these primordial fetal dreams. If so, then the mystical state of unity we perceived before we were born—the state of Nirvana—could be re-accessed and re-experienced, with the help of digital technology.

Three. The Stages of Perception and Digital Nirvana

Andrew Newberg, a pioneer in the new field of neurotheology, refers to the mystical state of unity as a state of "Absolute Unitary Being" (AUB). This state of unity can be achieved through mystical spiritual practices—meditation, chanting, prayer, etc.—but it is also experienced in less deliberate ways. The near death experience (NDE), for example, shares many common perceptual experiences with the spiritual state of AUB. Newberg argues that NDE imagery and ideas can be found in preliterate spiritual rituals and in Paleolithic cave art, inferring that the NDE is an inherently spiritual experience of unity.

The feeling of "oneness with the universe," a ubiquitous feature of the NDE, is something that certainly may have been experienced as a primary sensation in the dreams of the fetus. As the final life perception, the NDE represents a closing of the circle of development, the moment in which our mind regresses to its earliest memory, its earliest dream, the fetal dream. Another universal perception of the NDE is the feeling of being in a dark tunnel and being irresistibly drawn towards an opening from which emanates a bright light. This does seem to eerily resemble what must be one of our earliest memories, the memory of birth. If the NDE is actually the cognitive re-experience of the fetal dream and/or the birth memory, then it may be that the beginning and end points of life, birth and death, are connected through a mutual experience, making these points not a true beginning or end, but a continuum ... the serpent swallowing its own tail.

Dr. Olaf Blanke, a Swiss neurologist, was conducting a brain mapping test on a 43-year-old woman in order to find the neural origin of her epileptic seizures. Blanke's patient had a sudden out-of-body experience (OBE)—a distinct sensation that her conscious sense of self was outside of her own body—when her angular gyrus, a part of the temporal parietal junction, was electrically stimulated. This effect was later replicated in other studies.[67] The OBE is another universal feature of the NDE. Certainly, the OBE could be seen as a primary experience of both birth and death. At birth, it is the feeling of the self being taken out of the body with which we have been completely unified both physically and psychologically for our entire existence. To be taken out of Mother is to be taken out of oneself. Similarly, at death, we feel the essence of what we recognize as our true selves—our sense of consciousness, our soul—being taken out of our physical bodies. Truly, birth and death are parallel experiences.

In his book, *Proof of Heaven: A Neurosurgeon's Journey into the Afterlife*, Eben Alexander describes in detail what he experienced while on the brink of death in an extended meningitis-induced coma. Dr. Alexander's account of the "underworld" is very evocative of womblike imagery. His description of being "a lone point of awareness in a timeless red-brown sea," accompanied only by the sound of a beating heart, and his experience of timelessness, of being atone with his surroundings, and even the distinct smell of blood, all point to a possible primal memory of the womb. Similarly, Alexander's exit from his womblike "underworld" is evocative of a birth experience. He describes a "light" approaching him, an "opening" that he passes through, and the entrance into a new world, upon which: "I felt like I was being born. Not reborn, or born again. Just ... born.... It was if I were being born into a larger world, and the universe itself was like a giant cosmic womb." Though Alexander refers to the "underworld" as a "vast muddy womb," he doesn't make the direct connection to the primal memory theory that I'm suggesting. Nevertheless, he does admit: "My situation was, strangely enough, something akin to that of a fetus in the womb.... In this case, the "mother" was God, the Creator.... I could sense the infinite vastness of the Creator, could see how completely minuscule I was by comparison." Alexander also reports that he experienced a lot of the other neuropsychological aspects of cognitive-perceptual unity that are experienced by the fetus and infant:

- Synesthesia: "Seeing and hearing were not separate in this place where I now was."
- Cognitive-Perceptual Unity: "Everything was distinct, yet everything was also a part of everything else, like the rich and intermingled designs on a Persian carpet ... or a butterfly's wings."
- Unity Between Internal Thoughts & External Objects: "Imagine that every time your mood changed here on earth, the weather changed instantly along with it. That your tears would bring on a torrential downpour and your joy would make the clouds instantly disappear."
- Nirvana: "The blurring of the boundary between my awareness and the realm around me went so far at times that I *became* the entire universe." "The very fabric of the alternate dimension was love and acceptance..."
- Preverbal Cognition: Thoughts coming from the angelic figures "bypassed language ... thoughts entered me directly ... the 'voice' of this Being was warm and—odd as I know this may sound—personal."

Was Alexander's experience an NDE, an OBE, a dream, a hallucination, or a spiritual revelation? Dr. Alexander insists that his experience was a spiritual journey into the afterlife, *not* one of the psychological phenomena mentioned above. For my purposes, the distinction between any of these psychological experiences and a spiritual journey is not a distinction that needs to be made. They are all experiences of spiritual perception. Dr. Alexander's book was a bestseller because people are interested in this sort of experience. They want to experience it for themselves, though not necessarily by nearly dying from meningitis.

Newberg and d'Aquili (1999) believe that the feelings and sensations associated with both the NDE and the OBE are the result of the deafferentiation of the orientation association area (OAA) in the posterior superior parietal lobe. The OAA regulates your sense of your physical self in space, keeping a mental tab on exactly where your body is in relation to the physical world, and maintaining awareness of what part of space is a part of your body, and what part of space is not part of your body—the "I"/"Not-I" distinction. When the OAA is deafferentiated for any reason, we lose that sense of space between "I" and "Not-I." Our sense of "I" may feel like it's floating out of ourselves—an OBE—or we may feel that our "I" is melding into its surroundings—the state of "AUB"—spiritual unity, Nirvana. Newberg and d'Aquili found that the OAA was deaffentiated during the peak phases of meditation in Buddhist meditators and at the peak phases of prayer in Franciscan nuns. At the moments when these test subjects experienced a sense of "transcendence," the OAA in their brains was in a state of hypo-functionality. Neuro-technology could reproduce this deafferentiation using electromagnetic waves transmitted directly into the OAA. This process would give the user a sense of being outside of his own body—the perfect launchpad for a trip into a virtual path leading to our earliest memories and dreams—the dreams and memories of events that occurred while we were still in the womb.

Newberg & d'Aquili believe that the NDE occurs due to the deafferentiation of certain areas in the temporal, parietal, and occipital lobes, combined with the hyper-activation of other areas such as the hippocampus, which would account for the vivid recollection of memories—seeing your life flash before your eyes—as the hippocampus regulates the flow of information between short-term and long-term memory. Given the number of feelings and sensations associated with the NDE, the experience is doubtlessly the result of multiple activities within the brain, most of which we have no data on, because you cannot ethically run a study in which subjects are nearly put to death in order to see what's going in their brains as they die. Newberg and d'Aquili suggest that the NDE may have an evolutionary function, in which case the experience should exist, at least in a rudimentary form, in other primates. So, theoretically, NDE research could be done on chimps and gorillas, though you would run into similar ethical problems, compounded by the fact that chimps and gorillas can't recall their experiences verbally. A better research option would be to utilize the psychedelic compound Dimethyltryptamine (DMT), a naturally occurring chemical in the brain that elicits many of the experiences associated with the NDE.

Dr. Rick Strassman, Clinical Associate Professor of Psychiatry at the University of New Mexico School of Medicine, did extensive clinical research with DMT, a chemical that is manufactured in small amounts in the brain, and is also found in many plants and animals. DMT is the active ingredient in *ayahuasca*, a brew used in the shamanistic rituals of Amazonian tribes in Peru. The drug causes brief but extremely powerful psychedelic effects, such as hallucinations, OBEs, a sense of the presence of mystical "others," and a sense of spiritual unity, awe, and inner peace. The feeling of "transcendence" experienced by most of Strassman's test subjects prompted him to refer to DMT as "the spirit molecule." He believes that DMT is produced by the pineal gland in minuscule amounts, but is released in large amounts during specific "transitory" moments in life, such as the moment of birth and the moment of death. This would explain why the psychedelic effects of DMT are so similar in nature to NDEs. Strassman also found that his patients, though conscious while under the effects of DMT, experienced REM, prompting him to suggest that DMT evokes dream imagery, and may even elicit a "waking dream" state in which super-lucid intra-psychic imagery is perceived. This particular finding supports my own hypothesis, that the NDE is actually a cognitive replay of the fetal dream experience at birth. Strassman relates his hypothesis that DMT elicits the NDE to the Tibetan Buddhist concept of *bardo*, found in the ancient mystical text, the *Bardo Thodol*, a.k.a the "Tibetan Book of the Dead." Bardo is the "intermediary state" between death and rebirth.[68]

The brain may have evolved the mechanism of releasing large amounts of DMT as a specific way of dealing with moments of extreme transition, such as birth and death, which would be extremely traumatic if they weren't processed in the right way. If the birth experience is associated with a large release of DMT from the pineal gland, as Dr. Strassman suggested, then Otto Rank's theory of the "birth trauma" would be incorrect, as the chemicals flooding the brain at that moment are causing the infant to feel comforted, united, and embraced by a loving "other." So, rather than coming into this world as a traumatized refugee, we arrive as tranquil passengers in a state of transcendent bliss. This primary experience would then be saved in our memory banks as an eidetic memory, our first memory, our earliest dream. The memory would only be recalled when a similar flood of DMT is released at the very specific moment that evokes the same exact mental association ... the moment of death. Imminent death causes DMT release, which then recalls and replays the memory of birth, in the form of the NDE. The imagery and feelings experienced at this moment allow the mind to process the passage of death in ways that make sense, and prevent the adverse feelings of horror, dread, and shock. This is adaptive, because not everyone who nearly dies actually dies, so these people avoid the extreme anxiety that could give them a heart attack, and it also prevents the development of post-traumatic stress symptoms afterwards. Furthermore, NDEs help to relieve the anxiety related to mortality salience of entire groups of people, because the NDE survivors report to their cohort that life continues after death, and there's a nice warm fuzzy place that we get to go to when we die, so there's nothing to be afraid of. The end result of this dying memory of birth is the universal spirituo-religious theme that death is merely a rebirth. This belief is not only comforting to the people who nearly die, it's comforting to everyone who is born and has to live a life that is condemned to an inevitable death!

People who study NDEs tell us that the experience usually has life-affirming and tremendously positive benefits for survivors. Afterwards, these people appreciate life more, have less anxiety about death and less anxiety in general, they no longer "sweat the small stuff" and typically re-prioritize their lives in order to spend more time with family and friends, and do things that are existentially important to them. They also typically believe that their experience was spiritual in nature, and many people who survive NDEs become more spiritually oriented.[69] If DMT is, in fact, the chemical agent that initiates the NDE, it could be used in studies to track the functioning of the brain during replicated NDEs, in a completely safe setting. Once we know exactly what is going on in the brain during an NDE, we could use electro-neuro-stimulation and digital media to create a virtual NDE, without having to use drugs. The virtual NDE—the experience of Digital Nirvana—would then allow users to reap all of the psychosocial benefits of a real NDE, without having to take drugs that have unpredictable and uncontrollable effects, and without actually having to nearly die. Digital Nirvana, the virtual "bardo," could provide instant "rebirth" for the world-weary user in need of spiritual renewal.

In the foreseeable future, digital media and neuropsychology can offer this sort of spiritual experience to anyone ... safely, securely, and discreetly. Since the days before recorded history, Nirvana has been known only to the spiritual specialists: saints, mystics, spiritualists, shamans, prophets, and those who just happen to be born with a highly acute sense of spiritual perception—to those "blessed" with a mind given to divine "openings and theophanies"—or to those who happened to knock on death's door, but did not pass through it forever. For as long as human memory can look back, the path to nirvana has always been obscured, hard to find, and nearly impossible to tread: "the sharp edge of a razor." The media of the Digital Age, however, will provide the technology and the alteration of sense perception that could make the internal experience of spiritual unity—the state of nirvana—accessible to anyone who can master the digital technology and assume the necessary psychological mindset. Though nirvana may not be consciously accessible to everyone, it is experienced by everyone at least twice: in the preconscious stage of life proximate to birth, and the post-conscious moment preceding death.

Ray Kurzweil argued that a key aspect of technological invention is "transcendence." When the materials of a new invention are assembled correctly, the invention "transcends" the materials themselves, by allowing the user to do something that could never be done before, even with the same materials. For example, when Alexander Graham Bell configured existing telegraph technology into a form that could transmit sound, his invention transcended his materials.... "For the first time, a human voice was transported, magically it seemed, to a remote location."[70] Carl Jung believed that dreams provide a "transcendent function," in that they allow the conscious mind to be guided and lifted by the ancient wisdom of the unconscious. Perhaps the digital neuro-technology of the near future will provide humans with transcendence on a variety of levels. The technology itself will transcend its materials, inventing a new form of intra-psychic spiritual experience that never existed before. By reproducing the NDE, Digital Nirvana will allow the user to transcend his own consciousness, bringing him in touch with unconscious images and perceptions that would otherwise be inaccessible to the conscious mind. And furthermore, Digital Nirvana will give us insight into the oldest questions: Is there something more to existence than the physical world? Is there a spiritual dimension ... a soul that transcends the physical realm? What, if anything, happens to us after death? Digital Nirvana would truly transcend the digital technology itself, bringing us into the realm of the spiritual—the magical—for as we have seen in our own generation: "Any sufficiently advanced technology is indistinguishable from magic."[71]

CHAPTER FOUR

The History of Spiritual Perception and the Digital Idol

> Language does for intelligence what the wheel does for the feet and body.—Marshall McLuhan[1]

Spiritual perception has its origin in a form of cognition that is far older than humanity itself, the episodic mindset. However, it is unlikely that nonhuman animals such as chimps actually perceive spirits, because it is unlikely that they believe in spirits, or have any concept of spirituality whatsoever. Because perception is grounded in belief, we must first have a concept of spirituality to believe in, before we could perceive spirits around us. Therefore, we must look towards the mythic mindset of Paleolithic humans to find the conceptual origin of spiritual perception. Once the concept of "spirit" is born, once the mythology of the spirit world exists, then preceding mindsets can be retrieved to complement the mythology and bring it to life: mimetic actions can be channeled into rituals that reenact the myths, and these rituals can evoke the episodic mindset, in which the spirits we believe in actually appear to us "in the flesh." Although the episodic and mimetic mindsets are older than mythic cognition, the entire virtual dimension of spirits cannot exist without the conceptual beliefs formed in the mythic stage.

Conceptual thinking is only possible once thoughts are objectified into individual blocks of cognition. Words, clearly, are the mind's best tool for objectifying thoughts. Without a word for an abstract concept, we cannot really grasp the concept, because there's nothing for the mind to hold onto. While a chimp can conceive of an apple by recalling an image in his mind of an apple, he cannot conceive of an invisible god of the apple groves, because such an image does not exist in the chimp's mind, which is circumscribed by an episodic mindset. Chimps are prisoners of their own perception, because they cannot conceptualize something that cannot be visualized as an image, and they can only conceptualize images that they've seen before. Chimps can see with their eyes and they can envision what they've seen before in their mind, but they cannot imagine—*image*-ine—an image that they've never seen before, because they don't have the cognitive tools to create a new concept out of abstract thought. They don't have the magic Word.

A story comes from the Kabbalah,[2] telling us that every human being is given a finite number of words by God before he is born. Once you speak all of the words that you have been predestined to speak, you die. This parable is typical of Judaic thinking in general, and of Kabbalistic thinking in particular, as it places a mystical significance in the elements of language. According to the Kabbalistic interpretation of Genesis, God's initial act of world creation was performed through speech: He said "Let there be light," and the power of the words themselves brought light into being. The same interpretation goes on to explain that the process of creation is ongoing. God continues to speak, and as he speaks, his words create the universe out of nothingness. When God ceases to speak, the world will cease to exist. Rav Nachman of Breslov, a titan in early Jewish thought, said that God created Man so he could hear him tell tales. These mystical beliefs about language point to a life circumscribed by words, a life in which existence is brought into being by words, and in which existence itself is given meaning through the holy words of the Torah. Not only do our first and last words have vast existential significance, but every word spoken between them must be valued at a price far higher than gold. For in words, we express everything we know and would like to know, everything we intend to do and everything we wish we could do, everything we experience and anything we can imagine, everything we are, everything we were, everything we will be, and everything we wish to be. Words define us as human beings.

Marx and Engels, the authors of the historical materialist theory of society, pointed out that human beings have always had an interactive dynamic relationship with their tools. When a man uses a tool, not only does he change his environment by using the tool, the use of the tool changes him. A farmer wielding his plow in the field develops a hunched back due to bending over all day. A cab driver in his car develops a hemorrhoid from sitting all day. A computer programmer develops carpal-tunnel syndrome from typing all day. Indeed, as Engels pointed out, the anatomy of the human hand evolved as a function of the use of the tools he created.[3] Though it is said that the opposable thumb made advanced tool use possible, it is more correct to say that advanced tool use *created* the opposable thumb in humans, as an evolutionary adaptation to hand-tool technology. Similarly, language is a technology. Words are tools. The human mind has evolved in dynamic interaction with the mind-tool of language, just as the human hand has evolved in dynamic interaction with the use of hand-tools. Language, the "extension of consciousness," gives form to our thoughts and filters our perceptions, so that all we know is that which comes to us through the word-sized holes in our heads.[4] Humanity is truly defined as *homo loquax*—the talking ape. Hence, to understand our relation to God, we must first understand our relation to ourselves, which involves an understanding of how language has shaped the way that we humans perceive and construe ourselves and the world around us.

The Birth of Language

> Confine the thought, to exercise the breath; And keep them in the pale of Words till death. Whate'er the talents, or howe'er design'd; We hang one jingling padlock on the mind.—Alexander Pope, *Dunciad*

What is a word? A word, quite simply, is an analog ... a thing that signifies something else. The spoken word "apple" signifies an object—apple—even though the word doesn't look, sound, feel, smell, or taste like an apple. So, the mind that spoke the first word must have been a mind that was able to conceive of an analog. He had to be clever enough to create an abstract sound that signified a specific thing, though the sound itself had no sensory connection to the thing. So when did humans become clever enough to begin using words? The evidence suggests that humans did not have either the physical[5] or psychological[6] ability to use language in the symbolic form that surpasses mere animalistic signals and gestures until about thirty to sixty thousand years ago, making it a quite recent evolutionary acquisition for the human race. It was at this time that we find clear indications that humans were using symbols in their thinking—signs such as cave paintings, engravings, small sculptures, jewelry, and ritual burials. The emergence of language coincided with and probably made possible an "explosion" in the creation and the use of new types of stone tools, which in turn allowed ancient humans to engage in more complex hunting strategies, and to master the technology of fire. These cultural tasks presuppose the existence of somewhat complex social organizations, indicating that the Upper Paleolithic[7] was a time in which great developments occurred in the social areas of the brain, especially the area of language—as language evolved as an adaptive mechanism for sophisticated interpersonal communication and interaction.[8]

The Birth of Time and Space

> Since Man from beast by Words is known, Words are Man's province, Words we teach alone.—Alexander Pope, *Dunciad*

Animal language—gestures and noises—exists only in the proximate and in the present.[9] Your dog has no way of telling you about something that happened in the past, nor can he refer to something that will occur in the future, nor can he point and gesture to something that isn't there. All of his communications must refer to the here and now. As John Locke said: "Beasts abstract not." But because human language is symbolic and abstract, we can use words to refer to things that are not *present* in terms of space (things that are not here), and we can also use words to refer to things that are not *in the present* (things that are not now). Hence, while animals do have a sense of time and space, it is extremely limited, as the time is always right now, and the space is always right here. Language gives humans the ability to free our expressions and our thoughts from the temporal and physical restraints of the present, exponentially expanding our imaginations into the abstract reaches of infinite time and space. With the advent of words, the past as recalled through our memory, and the future as created by our imagination, could now be conceived, cogitated upon, grasped like a hand-tool, and expressed to others.

The Birth of Consciousness

> My mind to me a kingdom is; such present joys therein I find;
> As far exceeds all earthly bliss, which God and Nature hath assigned.
> —Sir Edward Dyer, 16th century

Language evolved as a means of communication with others. Its first expression was through the voice. However, at a certain point in time, language was co-opted by the brain for use in private thought, ideas which were not necessarily communicated to others. This cognitive adaptation was quite clever, as symbolic language is an excellent tool for grasping and manipulating thoughts, which could then be used to master one's environment. The consequences of this cognitive shift, however, would be immeasurable. The "interiorization" of language created the "internal monologue"—the inner voice, the voice of the mind, the voice of thought, the voice of consciousness—which is aware of itself and of its own thoughts. It is only when we can hear our own thoughts about ourselves that we can say with any real certainty that the human being has an ego,[10] a sense of self, an "I." Or, as Descartes put it, "Cogito ergo sum," ("I think therefore I am.") But the nature of the ego is that it is a reflective self, a self that is abstracted and somewhat split off from the real world. Hence, the birth of the ego, as a corollary to the interiorization of language, results in a somewhat distanced, abstract, self-conscious sense of self.

When we think to ourselves, we often tend to think about what *other people* may be thinking about us. In order to do this, we must infer a mental state—consciousness—into other people's minds. Cognitive psychologists refer to the ability to infer mental states in people as "Theory of Mind." The first order Theory of Mind is the simple realization that I have a mind of my own, i.e., "cogito ergo sum." I can think about myself ... I am "sentient." Thus, humans are self-defined as *homo sapien*, the ape who is wise. The second order Theory of Mind is the assumption that other people have minds of their own—that we are surrounded by sentient others. And a third order Theory of Mind assumes that other people assume that we have minds as well. This order of Theory of Mind results in the tendency for our thoughts to focus on the "sentient other," the people around us whom we assume are thinking about us. This could be seen as the ego doing what it always does, reflecting upon itself, but through the imagined viewpoint of another person's consciousness. Hence, the teenage boy agonizes over what he thinks the cute girl in class may be thinking about him. Higher levels of Theory of Mind can go on infinitum, i.e., I think that you're thinking about what I'm thinking, and I know that you know that I know that you're thinking about what I'm thinking, etc. My point in explaining Theory of Mind is that we're always aware of our own thoughts, and we're also always aware of the thoughts of others, even though other people's private thoughts are actually only inferred by ourselves. That is, the private thoughts of others are just our own thoughts that we project outwardly onto other people.

Humans also have the perceptual tendency to detect "agents" or living beings within their immediate environments. This is an adaptive evolutionary mechanism. If you live in the forest, and if you hear a rustling behind some bushes, it's adaptive for you to instinctively assume that something—a lion or a tiger or an enemy warrior—is lurking behind the bush. Justin Barrett pointed out that a "hyperactive agency detection" system is extremely adaptive, even if it's wrong most of the time.[11] If you hear the bushes rustling and instinctively assume that the cause is a potentially dangerous agent, you'll immediately take precautions that may save your life. Even if 9 times out of 10, the rustling is caused by something other than a dangerous predator, it's still far more adaptive to detect an agent who's not there (a false positive), than to *not* detect an agent when it is there (a false negative). Nine false positive costs you very little, while one false negative might cost you your life! Hence, our instinctive sensory responses include a "hyperactive agency detector."[12]

Hyperactive agency detection exists in animals other than humans, and it's a feeling we've all felt at one time or another. Maybe you were walking home late one night, on a shadowy isolated street, and then you thought you saw something move in a dark alley, and your heart leapt to your throat.... Similarly, we can all remember the terrors we had in childhood of the monster who lived in our bedroom closet, or the thing that lived under our bed. When we combine our perceptual tendency to hyper-detect a sense of the "other" in our environment with the tendency of our conscious minds to project into that "other" presence a conscious mind, then the basic recipe for spiritual perception comes to fore.[13] We humans are hardwired to perceive within our immediate environments a sensed presence of a sentient other. The sensed other can mean anything from seeing faces in the clouds to seeing spirits in the sky or even angels in the heavens. A false positive of a sensed other, such as a hallucination, is only abandoned as being a misguided intuition if it cannot be explained. If the sensed other can be explained, as in the case of a preexisting belief in the omnipresence of spirits, then not only is the perception not dismissed, it's actually harbored and remembered as a salient and significant confirmation that spirits do actually exist, because you saw or heard one yourself.[14]

Animals may hyper-detect a predator in those rustling bushes 9 out of 10 times, but once the perceived danger is gone, they just go about their business as usual. Fortunate non-conscious beasts that they are, they have no conscious inner-voice to ponder the question of what the rustling could have been, or if the agent that caused it could be somewhere else, or if it will come back later. The ignorant animal is blissfully unconcerned with anything that is not in the here and now. The sapient human, however, cursed with consciousness, must ponder these nerve-wracking questions. The conscious human will not only detect an agent when none is there, it will infer a conscious mind into that unknown agent—a sentient other—and it will probably assume that the sentient other may continue to exist, even if it's unseen and unheard. Unlike animals, conscious thoughts are not limited by the cognitive constraints of the here and now, nor are they limited to images or concepts of things that actually exist in the "real" world.

Of course, it's also quite possible that perceptions of the sentient other cannot all be chalked up to Hyperactive Agency Detection and Theory of Mind. It's also possible that there actually *is* something out there, just below the threshold of our conscious perception. If we admit that we perceive a lot of things that we don't fully see or hear, isn't it just as likely that we *do not* fully perceive a lot of things that we don't see or hear; but rather, just get a slight sense of the presence of the imperceptible thing? To return to our friend the dog ... when Fido lifts his head and raises his ears in alertness, we do not assume that he hears nothing. To the contrary, we assume that he hears *something*; but that something is just below the perceptual threshold of our human auditory senses. Indeed, it's a common belief among preliterate peoples, both ancient and contemporary, that dogs can sense the presence of spirits. That's why they bark in the night in response to what their masters perceive as an unseen and unheard presence. So, what cognitive psychologists call Hyperactive Agency Detection and Theory of Mind, may actually be components of a system of spiritual perception that responds to the presence of metaphysical rather than physical beings. Obviously, this is pure conjecture, but anything's possible, as Freeman Dyson, a preeminent scientist in the field of quantum physics, suggested: "I find it plausible that a world of mental phenomena should exist, too fluid and evanescent to be grasped with the cumbersome tools of science."

Spiritual Perception

> In the perception of the senses, consciousness of the object is distinguishable from consciousness of self; but in religion, consciousness of the object and self-consciousness coincide.—Ludwig Feuerbach[15]

There is a *dual* character within the human mind—the conscious and the unconscious—that gives rise to the distinct feeling in the conscious side of our awareness that we are being accompanied by a mysteriously invisible sentient other. The French novelist, Alphonse Daudet, expressed his awareness of this duality of self, in his *Notes sur la Vie*[16]:

> Homo duplex, homo duplex! The first time that I perceived that I was two was at the death of my brother Henri, when my father cried out so dramatically, "He is dead, he is dead!" While my first self wept, my second self thought, "How truly given was that cry, how fine it would be at the theatre." I was then fourteen years old.
> This horrible duality has often given me matter for reflection. Oh, this terrible second me, always seated whilst the other is on foot, acting, living, suffering, bestirring itself. This second me that I have never been able to intoxicate, to make shed tears, or put to sleep. And how it sees into things, and how it mocks!

While Daudet was able to recognize the "second me" as an internal being, the Paleolithic mind would surely not have been so sagely introspective. When the rustling behind the bushes is heard, and the agent detected is found to be nothing—no-thing—then sentience and agency, which have already been assumed, are ascribed to a nonphysical being such as the spirit of the wind, or the spirit of the bushes, or the spirit of a lion. Because the sentient other itself is immaterial, composed of thought and feeling and perception rather than physical matter, because it is no-thing, it's easily conceived as a nonphysical being. In this sense, agency detection and theory of mind, when combined, become functionally autonomous. They function independently of their original purpose. We may continue to detect an agent or spirit, even when there's no rustling bush to evoke the senses; and we may continue to infer a conscious mind within that other being, even if there's no real being around us. Thus, the sentient other is not interpreted as a second I—but rather, as a separate You—a spiritual being.

Death and the Birth of the Soul

> To be, or not to be, that is the question...
> To die to sleep ... perchance to Dream; Aye, there's the rub
> For in that sleep of death, what dreams may come
> When we have shuffled off this mortal coil
> Must give us pause...
> But that the dread of something after death
> The Undiscovered Country, from whose bourn
> No Traveler returns, Puzzles the will
> And makes us rather bear those ills we have
> Than fly to others that we know not of
> Thus Conscience does make Cowards of us all...
> —Shakespeare (*Hamlet*, Act III, Scene 1)

The ego, the self aware voice of consciousness, believes that he is the "master of the house."[17] He believes that he and he alone controls cognition; and he, rather arrogantly and solipsistically, often disregards cognitions that he doesn't recognize as his own. However, there are many cognitions that are unconscious and exist below the radar of consciousness. Instinctive and intuitive cognitions, such as agency detection and theory of mind, are prime examples of unconscious cognitions. We don't think about them, we just have them, as they arise from cognitive processes that predate the existence of language-based conscious thought in the brain. So, when the conscious ego encounters a cognition or perception arising from some aspect of the unconscious mind, it may experience this mysterious sensation as an external other—a thing that is not within the ego's circumscribed circle of consciousness—a sensed, sentient other.

The most logical conclusion for the conscious mind is that the sentient other does not dwell inside the "house," as the conscious perceives this "kingdom of mind" as a walled off space. The sentient other is therefore perceived as an external entity—a physical, separate other—who is nonetheless sensed internally as well.

At the same time, abstract consciousness makes it possible for us to look into the foreseeable future and ponder the inevitability of our own death.[18] Knowledge of our own mortality is made salient,[19] not just because we are aware of death—we can assume that animals are also aware of death, and fear the threat of it—death is dreaded because our conscious ego exists, and cannot bear the thought of not existing. While animals are alive, they don't necessarily exist in the way that humans do, because they have no conscious ego, no sense of self, no idea of what it is "to be," and therefore no idea of what it is "not to be." To go back to Descartes, if there's no "cogito," there's no "sum." An animal exists in the moment, and is unconcerned about what may happen tomorrow, as it is more-or-less unaware that tomorrow exists. Humans, however, can foresee tomorrow, and they can foresee death, and they can reflect on their own existence, as Hamlet does in his famous soliloquy. It's the inability of consciousness to conceive of its own end that makes the "Undiscovered Country" such a dreaded destination. Hence, it's not really "Conscience" that makes "cowards of us all," it's Consciousness.

But what if consciousness didn't end? What if consciousness continued to exist, even after the body has died? If this belief is held, then Death itself is defeated, when the mind creates an immortal spiritual double of itself in the form of a "soul." This assumption is essentially the perseveration of Theory of Mind past the moment of death, and it's the central theory of Jesse Bering's (2011) book, *The Belief Instinct*. Saying that belief in the existence of a soul is merely an extension of Theory of Mind is, of course, too simplistic. Also, saying that the belief in a soul and an afterlife is merely a cognitive mechanism that humans have devised to cope with mortality salience is also, of course, too simplistic. However, it's a start....

The soul is not consciousness, nor is it conscious. The soul can best be described as a phantom of consciousness, the sense of dual-self that only comes into existence once the conscious "I" awakens and senses another presence, the unconscious "I," within the interior space of the mind. Once again, this comes about as a result not just of language, but of *interiorized* language, the inner voice of consciousness that creates a sense of inner duality. If there's a speaker, an internal "I" that's expressive, then there must be a listener, an "Other I" that's receptive. Interiorized language is the abstractor, the author of cerebral distance, the echo chamber of the mind, the mechanism that creates the mental distance between the "I" and the "Other I."

This sense of a sentient other that is not a part of one's own consciousness and not perceived as oneself, is the sense that lends credence to the universal human tendency to believe in the spiritual side of human nature ... the soul. The sense of the sentient "Other I" is spiritual perception in its most basic form. It is the "I" reaching out towards that which it knows is there, but cannot touch, taste, smell, see, nor hear. The "Other I" is sensed as both an internal *and* an external stimulus—for everything that is perceived by our senses is assumed to have an external origin—even though all perception is, ultimately, a product of the internal world of the mind. Hence, the spiritual experience is always inherently paradoxical.

God's presence seems to come from *without*, but it is perceived from *within*. God, the ultimate sentient Other, is somehow closer to "I" than one's own sense of "I."

The Birth of God

> Imagination ... is the drive to turn everything into a Thou, the drive to pan-relation—and where it does not find a living, active being that confronts it but only an image or symbol of that, it supplies the living activity from its own fullness.—Martin Buber

Spirituality begins with consciousness. Any being, even a dog, can comprehend the existence of his physical self—his body—as something other than the physical self of someone else. But consciousness is not a physical object, it is a metaphysical process. When the body dies, the physical self remains, as a corpse. Yet, the metaphysical self, consciousness, seems to disappear when the body dies. It's really the only glaring difference between a dead person and a sleeping person. In fact, many preliterate peoples look upon sleep as a temporary death,[20] in which the soul leaves the body to go on night-flights that are called "dreams."[21] For the ancients, this problem of metaphysics—"Who am I, if I am not just my physical body?"—is traditionally answered with the spiritual solution: "I am my soul." Thus consciousness, the metaphysical self, becomes associated with the soul, the spiritual self. While we all can agree that the dog has a physical self, and that the dog is aware of his physical self, it's doubtful that the dog has a *metaphysical* self, and even more doubtful that the dog is *aware* of his metaphysical self. Only we humans are conscious, somewhat, of the duality between our physical and metaphysical selves. At the same time, however, we are obviously not fully conscious of our unconscious selves.

So, to summarize quite briefly, the sense of inner duality that arises as a result of the interior dialogue of language-based consciousness is the mother of the soul. Mortality salience, the anxiety that arises when we can look into our future and conceive of our own inevitable death, necessitates the individual and cultural belief in souls. Theory of Mind, the awareness of other people's consciousnesses—the awareness of other people's souls—is the mother of spirituality; for if the world is filled with souls, than a spiritual dimension to life must exist in parallel with the physical dimension. And Hyperactive Agency Detection, the tendency to project and perceive sentient others in our presence, even metaphysical sentient others, i.e., spirits, is the mother of spiritual perception. God, in essence, is the grandchild of all of these mothers.

Spiritual perception in the Paleolithic reflected an "animistic mode of perception,"[22] in which spirit inhabited everything. Stone Age people didn't necessarily assume that consciousness was the singular possession of humans alone. If *they* could have private thoughts, why not animals, or trees, or rivers, or mountains? And if consciousness was equated with spirituality, then the animals and trees and rivers had souls just like us. The animistic mode of perception gave rise to the ubiquitous theme of talking animals, which exists in every mythology and every system of folklore, fantasy, and fairytale. Animism is also a primary mode of thought among small children, who seem to be quite open to the notion that animals can talk and have humanlike feelings and thoughts. However, animism also brought about a problem for Stone Age hunters ... guilt. If an animal has a soul, just like us, then killing an animal is tantamount to murder. The ethical problem of animal murder was resolved through the spiritual solution of ritual. It would be ok to kill an animal, as long as the animal's soul was taken into account somehow. So, rituals of atonement with the animal's soul—the earliest hunting rites and sacrificial rites—came about. For example, when the Bushmen of the Kalahari put down an animal with a poisoned arrow, the hunter must remain with his victim, "crying when it cries and participating symbolically in its death throes."[23]

A key feature of the animistic mode of perception is that, just as there's no clear distinction between the animal world and the human world, there's no clear distinction between the physical world and the spiritual world. The two worlds are one in the same. This mode of perception is much different than the conscious mode that distinguishes very clearly from the physical and the spiritual, the real and the unreal, and the conscious and not-conscious. The animistic perception of preliterate people is illustrative of a mind that has language-based conscious reasoning, but is not yet *dominated* by it. Similarly, small children who perceive the world animistically are also preliterate—their way of viewing things is much more intuitive and imaginative—as it's not yet dominated by language based conscious reasoning.

What is it like to perceive the world in a way that is not dominated by language-based consciousness? The only thing a modern adult could compare it to would be the way we perceive things while dreaming, because dreaming is really one of the few states that we regularly experience in which our thinking is not dominated by consciousness. In the dream state, things do not have to make sense. Our understanding of what we perceive actually determines the quality of what we perceive. So, if you see the sun, and the sun seems to be talking to you, then it actually *is* talking to you. There's no strict voice of consciousness telling you that you're just imagining the sun talking to you. There's no voice of reason telling you that what you hear and see cannot be true. The doors of perception in the dreamland of "dim Eden" are wide open. And what did we hear in "dim Eden," if not "the voice of God, walking about in the wind of the day."[24] In the world of animistic perception, each man was a prophet, each woman an oracle, each individual a beholder of his own spiritual realm ... and everyone heard and saw and felt his own personal perception of God.

The spiritual lives of prehistoric peoples are a mystery to us, but we can make some guesses about what was important to them by looking at the relics they left behind—cave paintings, stone sculptures, burial sites, etc.—and also by looking at people whose lives are very similar to the lives of our prehistoric ancestors: contemporary hunter-gatherer societies. Anthropologists who have studied these people by living among them have reported that animistic thinking is ubiquitous in these cultures. Contemporary hunter-gatherers live in a world full of spirits, whom they interact with on a daily basis. Nearly every act they engage in is in some way a spiritual act, because it involves a potential interaction with one of the spirits, who are everywhere. Spiritual perception for a pantheist[25] is always turned on. This is somewhat similar to a modern religious person, such as an Orthodox Jew, who is always mindful of God, and therefore commits every act in a way that is mindful of God's presence, such as always saying a blessing before eating or drinking, always abstaining from non-kosher food or drink, always wearing a yarmulke on his head to remind him of God's presence above, etc. However, this mindfulness of the spiritual is in-and-of-itself a sign of disconnection from the spiritual plane, as indicated by the fact that the individual must consciously *remind* himself that the spiritual is there. Contrastingly, the individual in the animistic mode of perception is not even conscious of a *difference* between the spiritual and physical planes. In tribal cultures, there's no word for the "supernatural," because the world of humans and the world of the spirits are one in the same. Only in literate societies do we see the idea of a plane of existence that's separated from the natural plane—the "super-natural"—which cannot be directly experienced or perceived.[26]

In the tribal ritual, when a shaman appears in the costume of a totem animal, such as a leopard, both the shaman and the observers take part in the ritual transfiguration. They don't see a shaman in leopard's skin. What they actually perceive is the shaman *becoming* the spirit he's embodying. Animistic perception—spiritual perception—is both within and without. The internal image is unified with the external field of perception. We see what we believe. This is in stark contrast to the observation of someone who is in the perceptually distanced mode of language based consciousness—the person who is aware of himself as he is observing someone else—the inner observer observing the outer observer observing the other person. This person sees a shaman in an animal costume symbolically representing an animal spirit. He is perceiving a concept, a *symbol*, not an actual animal spirit. The person in the animistic mode, on the other hand, perceives the *actual* spirit.[27]

It's fairly common among hunter-gatherers in North America, Africa, and Australia, for everyone to have a "guardian spirit"[28] who protects them. These individuals encounter their guardian spirits all the time. Oftentimes the guardian spirit takes an animal form, especially among groups who share communal guardian spirits, "totem animals," who represent the ancestral protective spirit of not just one person, but the entire society. Totems have the benefit of being personal—any individual can encounter and interact with the animal spirit at any time—while also being communal, allowing for communal rituals that provide connection and atonement with the totem. These communal rituals not only evoke spiritual perception, they also instill a sense of identity and community within the group. As language based consciousness gradually became the more dominant mode of awareness, the ever-present guardian spirit became less and less accessible, because the mind that perceives through a filtered process of logical deduction does not perceive the world, it perceives its own cognitive re-representation of the world. Perceptions that seem to defy the logic of normal sensed awareness would either be reinterpreted in order to "make sense" in accordance to the way that the world is logically perceived, or the perceptions would simply be filtered out of conscious awareness. The door of perception closed by language based consciousness has word shaped holes in it. Any perception that cannot fit through these word shaped holes—any thought that cannot be interpreted into words that "make sense"—becomes stranded on the unconscious side of this door of perception.

The heyday of the personal god dusked gradually. At first, the guardian spirit came naturally, the individual received frequent "calls" from his guardian spirit, either in dreams or in states of wakeful spiritual perception ... waking dreams. In time, the spirits began to refuse to take the initiative to "call," so the individual would have to take the initiative and find his guardian spirit by means of a ritual, such as a "vision quest." The initiate would scale a mountaintop or search the woods.[29] As the spirits got harder and harder to find, more elaborate rituals were developed to evoke the transcendent mode of spiritual perception. Harrowing ordeals, powerful hallucinogenic drugs, and frenzied sacraments were contrived. Eventually, direct spiritual perception became somewhat unattainable to most individuals outside of the dream state and the "ecstatic" or "trance" states evoked by elaborate rituals. At this point, shamans become essential figures in the tribe, as they were the individuals whose spiritual perception was still acute, and so they were the guides who led there tribesmen through the rituals that led them inwardly into the episodic mindset, in which the direct sensory perception of the spirits was experienced.

It's important to note that at this stage, spiritual perception is not about dimly sensing a vague spiritual feeling, it's a powerful visceral union of the body and mind with the spirit. The ritual participant enters the spirit world, has direct physical contact with the spirits, and oftentimes is transfigured into a spirit himself. It's a complete "possession" of the body and soul. Renowned anthropologist, Clifford Geertz, bore witness to these rituals in a preliterate society in Bali. He described the experiences of the participants who actually *became* the spirits in the throes of the ritualistic trance. They experienced the presence of the spirits and the transformation into the spirits themselves as "genuine realities," not as symbols or metaphors for a virtual or metaphysical reality.[30] Another anthropologist, Karl Luckert, suggests that ritual provides a psychological return to a primordial form of "unitive consciousness," a state similar to the animistic mode of perception which was dominant in the Paleolithic Age. Luckert calls it "prehuman flux." It was a time when "all things were interchangeable," because the same spiritual essence was instilled in every being and every object. The sense of primordial flux can be re-experienced in the trance state that accompanies ritual. It allows the individual's spirit to momentarily transcend his human body and transform into a totem animal or a god.[31]

In the Paleolithic Age, spiritual perception was experienced by *everyone*, and it was potentially accessible *all the time*. In the Mesolithic Age, spiritual perception was still experienced by everyone, but it was relegated mostly to the "Sacred Time" of rituals and dreams. Furthermore, the existence of spiritual specialists such as shamans and spiritual implements such as idols and sacred objects, presupposes the notion that the average person often needed help or guidance in engaging the spirits. In the Neolithic, among agricultural civilizations, the two worlds, the spiritual and the physical, the natural and the supernatural—Heaven and Earth—were finally rendered apart. Beginning in the Neolithic, direct communication with the gods was accomplished primarily through the Divine King. "He was simultaneously divine and human and the mediator between the divine and human realms."[32] For the average person, spiritual perception still existed, especially in ritual and in dreams, though much diminished. But even though spiritual perception continued to diminish as agricultural societies progressed through the Neolithic Age, religiosity—spiritual beliefs and practices—did not diminish at all. In fact, the picture painted by archaeological and anthropological records seems to indicate that religiosity *increased* during the Neolithic.

This inverse relationship, religiosity increasing as spiritual perception diminishes, could be analogized to a man who attempts to engage his girlfriend more vigorously, as he senses that she's becoming disinterested in him and begins to disengage. The more she disengages, the more he struggles to engage. I see this inverse relationship between spiritual perception and religiosity as a basic trend that began in the Mesolithic and continues through the modern day. It certainly explains why most people in the modern world are still very religious, even though most people in the modern world don't ever see or hear God. The less perceptible our God becomes, the less personal our God is to us, the more distant He seems—the more we try to connect with Him, the more we try to win Him back—the more we strive to gain favor in His disengaging eyes.

Living Idols

> Their idols are silver and gold, the work of men's hands.... They that make them shall be like unto them; yea, every one that trusteth in them.—Psalm 115

As we enter the Bronze Age,[33] God and Nature, once one and the same, are now separated by a "firmament," with the gods in the Heavens and humans down below. The Divine King, still a central figure in the spiritual and political lives of the people, was the primary medium between the two worlds; but the king, to the average peasant, seemed as distant, as inaccessible, as imperceptible as the gods themselves. The average person then, as today, needed a means of personal communication with a god who was personal and perceptible to him. Idols provided this day-to-day spiritual connection. The idols of the Bronze Age kingdoms of the ancient Near East were revered as living beings. They were fed, bathed, dressed, and in almost every way imaginable, treated as if they were alive.[34] Communities shared large communal idols, while individual households held their own personal idols.[35] Every day, either through the communal idol in the temple or through the personal idol in the home, each Bronze Age individual experienced spiritual perception with his own version of God. Personal and communal idols in the Bronze Age were more than just spiritual symbols, they were experienced as the embodiments of gods themselves. The idol worshippers, perceiving their personal gods through the lens of a sense of spiritual perception that was still largely unfiltered by abstract consciousness, actually heard the voice of their gods through the mouths of their living idols. One of Julian Jaynes' most provocative arguments in his "bicameral mind" theory was that ancient idols served a "hallucinogenic function."[36] When gazed at long enough—within the proper frame of mind, within the proper framework of belief, and within the proper mode of expectancy—the living idol always spoke directly into the mind of its worshipper. According to Jaynes, the ancient "bicameral" mind was hardwired for this form of spiritual hallucination.[37]

One good hint that this type of spiritual perception was actually going on can be found in the ways that the eyes of ancient idols were carved and painted. Eye contact is a primary form of communication in humans, expressive of deep emotion and conviction. Amongst primates, many mammals, and humans, direct eye contact is often interpreted as an aggressive gesture, or at least as an indication of an intention to interact with the individual you are staring at. Lovers gaze longingly into each other's eyes, as do mothers and their newborn babies. "There is a kind of stress, an unresolvedness about the experience, and withal something of a diminution of consciousness, so that, were such a relationship mimicked in a statue, it would enhance the hallucination of divine speech."[38] The eyes of ancient idols were much larger than human eyes, with eye sockets containing translucent gemstones, or with eyeballs that were painted in bright colors, outlined heavily in black, so that the eyes appeared livid, shining, wide-open, glaring outwardly, hypnotically.[39] The eyes of living idols were designed for communication, for eye-to-eye contact with their worshippers, for spiritual perception.[40]

A second focus of attention in ancient idols was the idol's mouth, which was often bigger in proportion to the idol's body. The idol's mouth in these cases was usually open, and the lips were usually painted more brightly than the rest of the face, with the exception of the eyes. This inordinate amount of focus on the idol's mouth would make sense given the assumption that the idol's worshippers expected to hear the voice of their god through the idol's mouth. Cuneiform tablets from ancient Sumerian sites describe elaborate rituals for cleansing the mouths and opening the mouths of idol-gods, in order to "renew the god's speech."[41] Numerous passages from ancient texts clearly indicate that the words of gods were spoken through statues and idols. Here's an example from the Bible:

> For the king of Babylon will stop at the fork in the road, at the junction of the two roads, to seek an omen: He will cast lots with arrows, *call to his teraphim for advice*, he will examine the liver.—Ezekiel 21:21[42]

The ancient Hebrew word "Teraphim," used multiple times in the Bible, is now somewhat of an enigma. It's generally translated as "personal idols" or as "household gods." Excavations in Iraq of Bronze Age Sumerian sites in what was ancient Mesopotamia have found that in nearly every household there was a "shrine-room" dedicated to the storage and/or worship of household idols.[43] From the context of the Biblical passages, it's clear that among the people living in ancient Canaan and other areas in the ancient Near East, Teraphim were worshipped like idols. They were small, shaped like human heads, were kept as personal items by their owners, and were highly valued. There was a designated place for them in each and every household, where they spoke to their owners.[44]

> For *the teraphim have spoken* vanity, and the diviners have seen a lie; and they have told false dreams, they comfort in vain.—Zechariah 10:2

What can be surmised from the biblical sources as well as a plethora of alternate sources is that idol worship in the Bronze Age was ubiquitous, that individual people or households generally owned their own personal idols, and that these living gods were believed to speak to their owners/worshippers.[45]

It seems somewhat inconceivable that the biblical Israelites were incessantly engaging in idolatry, despite the fact that it was directly forbidden by God, and despite the fact that the biblical Israelites had direct sensory proof of God's existence on Earth, in the physical Ark of the Covenant. Nevertheless, anyone

Four. The History of Perception and the Digital Idol

reading the Bible will see that the sin of idolatry was the number one problem for the Israelites, and archaeological artifacts from ancient Canaanite sites substantiate this record. The issue here is that the ancient Israelites were at a stage of spiritual-perceptual development that required a concrete and direct sensory perception of their gods in order to experience them. In other words, it's not that they didn't believe in the one true God, "Yehovah," they did; but in order to experience Yehovah, they needed a medium such as an idol to connect with him on a sensory level. Alternatively, the idea that there is one true God does not necessarily preclude the existence of minor deities, such as angels, spirits, demons, regional gods, and household gods. In fact, the Bible explicitly expresses a henotheistic model of the spiritual world, in which one principal God is recognized, while limitless other gods and spiritual entities exist. Hence, the sin of the Israelites was that they recognized other gods in addition to Yehovah, the one true God of the Israelites, and that they engaged in idolatry rather than strict monotheism.

The Talmudic sages offer a different perspective on "Avodah Zarah," the Hebrew term for idolatry (literally: "strange worship," i.e., worshipping of the gods of strangers'). Idolatry was empowered in the days of the ancients by the "Yetzer Ha'Ra," the "evil inclination" that exists in everyone. This concept is somewhat similar to the Christian concept of "original sin," or the Freudian concept of the "id," the primal drive that fuels our libidinous appetites.[46] According to the sages, in the ancient days, the Yetzer Ha'Ra was expressed through two primary acts: the sexual act, and Avodah Zarah. The desire to worship idols was as powerful as the desire for sex, because the drive to commune with the spirits was physically fulfilled, just like the act of sex, when the spirit would actually appear to you and speak with you. Idol worship was so tantalizing because it was always effective. This recalls Jaynes' concept of the "hallucinogenic function" of idols, the notion that the mind of ancient peoples were hardwired to experience direct sensory spiritual perception when worshipping their idols.

If idol worship was so fulfilling and so effective, and if the drive towards it was so strong, why is it no longer so? The Talmudic sages recall a story from the days before the destruction of the First Holy Temple. The devout among the people of Israel were agonizing because so many of their fellow Israelites had fallen victim to the Yetzer HaRa by worshipping idols and engaging in forbidden sexual acts. (The sexual and spiritual drives were oftentimes combined into single acts of sexual worship, making the practice doubly pleasurable, and doubly illicit.) The most pious of the generation congregated in the Temple and prayed to the one true God to extinguish the drive of the Yetzer HaRa. God heard their prayers and granted their request. Immediately, idol worship ended. The gods associated with the idols, no longer having an audience, disappeared. At the same time, the rooster lost interest in the hen, and there were no more chicks. The bull lost interest in the cow, and there were no more calves, and so on. The most pious quickly reconvened in the Temple and prayed again to the Almighty, requesting that the Yetzer HaRa be reinstated, but only in half part. Once again, the Lord listened and granted their request. So the sexual drive, though corrupting, was allowed to remain in the hearts of men, for the sake of reproduction; but the visceral spiritual drive that empowered idolatry was excised. From that point forth, there was no direct sensory perception of any spiritual form. So nobody saw or heard any gods, not even the one true God. Just as the Yetzer HaRa for sex has its good side and its bad side, so too did the Yetzer HaRa for spiritual communion. The bad side was expressed through physical communion with "strange gods," lesser spirits, and demons: idol worship. The good side was expressed through physical communion with the one true God: spiritual perception.

Obviously, we can still express our desire for communion with God through prayer and rituals of devotion, but God will not appear to us directly, because the ability to perceive God in a sensory form was lost to the minds of humans. So now, although God is still here, he's in a state of "Hester Panim." He has a "hidden face." He's no longer visible to the naked eye, but only sensed as an unseen presence.

Iconoclasm

> I will destroy your high places, cut down your incense altars and pile your dead bodies on the lifeless forms of your idols, and I will abhor you.—Leviticus 26:29–31

The archaeological ruins of ancient societies as well as the historical narratives that have survived through the ages suggest that it was standard practice for invading armies to make a point of burning the temples, decapitating the sacred statues, crushing the altars, and smashing the idols of their conquered foes. A vestige of this practice can be seen today, in flag burnings, the burning of leaders in effigy, the burning of sacred books such as the Bible and Koran, etc.[47] Though these acts of iconoclasm are now perceived as symbolic acts of psychological warfare and propaganda; the origin of the practice may very well be in the ancient belief that a god could actually be destroyed, if you destroy its physical embodiment on the earthly plane. One of the reasons why the voices of the gods retreated so hastily up to the Heavens during the era of the Bronze Age Collapse,[48] was because so many gods were literally killed, either at the hands of bellicose men, or by the fury of Nature, during the tumultuous periods of destruction in the second millennium BC, when perpetual warfare, diasporas, massive floods, tsunamis, earthquakes, volcanic eruptions, fires, and other calamities, not only dispossessed people of their homes, but dispossessed them of their souls as well, by killing their gods.

As a brutal method of dominating a subject people, the toppling, smashing, or beheading of the conquered peoples' idols would be quite effective. This was more than just a blow to the enemy's morale, more than just a symbolic stroke. Destroying the idol killed the god. Iconoclasm in the Bronze Age was deicide. In killing an enemy's god, it snuffed out their collective spirit, vanquishing the protective and commanding deity of the community, and silencing the voice of authority through which the peoples' will was directed.

Killing the god cut off the individual's intra-psychic connection with his own soul, and it also cut off the people's collective connection with the communal spirit. The invading people, after destroying the gods of their vanquished foes, would then erect their own idols, establishing their own god as the new god of the conquered people. The conquered ones may, at first, be forced to bow and worship the new gods at the point of a sword. But soon, the powerful function of spiritual perception would kick in, and the people, upon gazing at the living idol, would hear its voice as clearly as their old god. The vision and voice of the new god they beheld was all the more powerful, as it was this god who defeated their previous god, the soldiers being just pawns in the chess game of the gods. The conquering god, in all likelihood, was not loved but feared, much like the gods that came before him, and the ones to follow as well. Machiavelli's famous dictum about princes[49] is a restatement of our own archaic thoughts about gods.

Perhaps this is why the great Neolithic and Bronze Age cultures built such stalwart monuments for their spirit-gods and the souls of their divine kings. If the monuments themselves evoked the visions and voices of spiritual perception, as the living spirit of the deities were entombed in the monuments themselves, then the people would have realized the potential vulnerability of their gods, and thus the vulnerability of their own societies. If an invading horde could completely conquer and control a society—in body, mind, and spirit—simply by destroying the physical embodiment of its god, then it would make sense to make this physical embodiment as close to indestructible as possible. If you cannot destroy the monument that houses the god, then you cannot destroy the god, and you cannot conquer its people. Hence, 6 million ton pyramids in Egypt and massive stone monuments such as Stonehenge—that survive, un-toppled, to this day—though the voices of the spirits once entombed in these sacred mortuaries have long since been silenced.

In the Bible, we see clearly the need for perceptible gods during the Bronze

Age. While in Egypt, the Israelites worshipped the Egyptian gods, who were viscerally represented in both massive communal idols and plentiful personal idols, as well as embodied in the divine king himself—the Pharaoh—whose massive temple-tombs (the pyramids), ascended directly to the Heavens. Shortly after their exodus, while Moses was atop Mt. Sinai for forty days, the Israelites demanded an idol that they could see directly, and with whom they could have direct spiritual contact. Aaron fashioned a golden calf for the Israelites, which was a "living idol"—it came out of the fire fully formed—and moved and spoke like a living creature.[50]

After the debacle of the golden calf, the Israelites were provided with another living idol, the Ark of the Covenant, which housed the tablets written by God himself: "two tablets of testimony, tablets of stone, written with the finger of God" (Exodus 31:18). God spoke directly to Moses from the cover of the Ark:

> And there I shall be met by thee, *and I will speak with thee* from above the cover, from between the two cherubim which are upon the ark of the testimony, of all which I command thee concerning the children of Israel.—Exodus 35:22

The living idol of the Ark, enshrined in the portable Tabernacle, sustained the Israelites as a relatively small tribe of wanderers in the wilderness. But when the Israelites entered Canaan and spread across the land, becoming a nation, the Ark was no longer directly in their midst. That's where we see a return to idol worshipping. Teraphim, new golden calves, and communal idols were erected throughout the land. While the building of the Holy Temple by Solomon in Jerusalem created a culture of pilgrims to the holy city—where the Hebrews could gain some access to their perceptible god—the recurrent and ubiquitous sin of idolatry remained the primary concern in the Bible throughout the days of the prophets and the kings.

From the ashes of civilization following the Bronze Age Collapse in the ancient Near East, rose a spectrum of new world orders, and a flood of drastic changes in culture and society. The new empires of the Iron Age[51] saw a progression in agricultural technology, an increase in trade commerce between nations, and an increase in governmental and commercial bureaucracy. These developments required new tools. Not just physical tools, like new iron plows and new sailing ships and new working implements; but—much more importantly— new *cognitive* tools to manage the more sophisticated systems of agriculture, commerce, and government. In particular, these new cognitive tools were: financial currency, mathematics, and literacy. Each development would have a significant impact on the way we think, on the way we perceive the world around us, and on the way we experience the spiritual aspect of our existence.

The Birth of Money

> Money alone sets all the world in motion.—Publius Syrus, 42 BC
>
> Render therefore unto Caesar the things which are Caesar's; and unto God the things that are God's.—Jesus, Matthew 22:21

Richard Seaford, in his book, *Money and the Early Greek Mind* (2004), points out that the use of money as an abstract value system was, along with mathematics and literacy, a paradigm shift in the mind of the ancients.[52] Before money, an object or commodity could only be assessed by its face value. A chicken was worth a chicken, a loaf of bread was worth a loaf of bread. Though you could trade a chicken for a loaf of bread, this was by no means a standardized form of exchange. At a certain point of sophistication, civilization required the standardization of commercial exchanges, necessitating the substitution of the actual object with a sign or token. A chicken is now worth a silver coin, a loaf of bread is now worth a copper coin. This transfiguration of worth from the actual object to a symbolic object is a conceptual abstraction of the same order that took place with the birth of language, in which the object "apple" is transfigured in the mind and onto the tongue into the word "apple," the word being a conceptual analog or symbol of the object. Money, like language, is a cognitive leap forward into the abstract. "Money talks because money is a metaphor, a transfer, and a bridge."[53] However, because money is "extra-somatic"—because it exists outside of the mind and the body of the individuals who use it—money represents a progression into the "theoretic" stage of cognition. It drives us even further into abstraction, because money creates a world unto itself, a virtual hall of mirrors in which money is both the cause and solution to all of life's problems.

Money in the ancient world, of course, was only used by a few people—traveling merchants, businessmen, craftsmen, aristocrats, bureaucrats, etc.—but the use of money obviously spread amongst the peasantry slowly but surely over time. As an abstraction, money wrenches the mind away from a focus on life in the present—"What am I doing right now?—towards a focus on a hypothetical life in the future that's dependent on money—"*If I were a rich man...*" Money, and the single-minded obsessive meditation over money that most people in the modern world spend so much of their time engaged in, is an abstraction—as well as a *distraction*—from experiencing life in the present moment.[54] The mind that strains the perception of his world through the filter of money—"How much will this cost me?" "How does this action pay off?" "How can I turn this thing into a profit?"—is a mind that is turned off to the non-fiduciary, non-commercial, non-conscious mode of experience. The lens of money-mindedness is too constricted to let in the light of spiritual insight, which cannot be quantified or valued in dollars and cents. God is too big to fit through a dollar-shaped hole in the head. This is why Saint Paul said that "the love of money is the root of all evil"; and why Jesus told the Pharisees to focus not on the value of the coin, "things which are Caesar's," but on the value of that which is *invaluable*, "the things that are God's."

Services and goods are directly related to the people we service or provide, or the people who service or provide for us. Dollars exist alone in abstraction. The abstraction of goods and services into a symbolic currency promotes a sense of detachment from the real goods and services that the money symbolically represents, creating a different perception of the relationship between the people in the community. The person "grasping" the dollar may have no sense of the services or goods that the dollar signifies. In grasping the dollar, one can conceive that the dollar is "mine" in complete abstraction, without directly relating it to another person through services or goods. In creating the abstract detached sense of "mine" and "mine alone," money creates greed and avarice, and thus becomes the "root of all evil."[55] When money becomes digitalized into electronic numbers, it becomes even more abstract, and thus severs it more from the people and goods it represents. Only a man who perceives money in a completely abstract sense can, as CEO of a corporation, pay himself a 100 million dollar salary, in the same year that he lays off ten thousand workers. Only in complete abstraction could he rationalize that he somehow works 4,000 times harder than his average worker, so that he deserves to be compensated 4,000 times more than his average worker, despite the fact that his entire existence depends upon the goods and services provided to him 100 times daily by average workers who are somehow unlike himself.

The Birth of Math

> What is a number that Man may know it?
> And what is Man that he may know number?
> —Warren McCulloch

The mathematical requirements of a tribal culture living in a hunter-gatherer society are minimal. Basic counting skills using the digits and toes, knots on a string, tallies drawn with a stick in the dirt, and other rudimentary methods are quite satisfactory. These methods date back to the Paleolithic. In an agricultural society, formal mathematics becomes quite important. A shepherd must calculate the annual increase or decrease in his flocks. A farmer must calculate the seasonal yield of his harvest. Furthermore, the farmer must be able to predict the perfect time of year to sow and reap his crops, a task that requires an accurate calendar, the construction of which requires advanced mathematics.

And, when the seasonal sacrifices to the divine king or gods are transformed into imperial government bureaucracies levying taxes on farmers and herders and merchants; and when the merchants begin to engage in large scale commerce and trade, suddenly, counting on your fingers and toes just doesn't cut it anymore. More sophisticated math is required.

Money, the abstraction that transformed concrete objects into abstract concepts, was a key factor in the need for merchants and bureaucrats to devise a more sophisticated method of quantification. Mathematics as a field begins when we designate a specific symbol—the numeral "9"—to designate a specific quantity—the amount of 9 things. This small bit of symbolic abstraction may seem trivial, but the repercussions are anything but so. Once 9 exists as an abstract concept, not tied down to a specific number of fingers and not directly tied down to a concrete amount of objects—*once the number is known to Man*—not as a specific group of things in the outside world but as a mental representation in the inside world of cognitive operations, then an entire universe of mathematical thought is opened up. 9 can be added to, subtracted from, multiplied by, or divided by other conceptual numbers, using other conceptual symbols, such as +, -, x, and /. The number becomes an analog—a symbol for something that only potentially exists in the real world—as opposed to a direct representation of a real thing. Once the number 9 exists as an abstract concept, another purely abstract number—0—can be conceived, which then opens up the entire field of higher mathematics.

Math was a magical illusion, created in the human mind ex nihilo, a new concept that didn't exist there before. But now, once it exists, the mind cannot un-conceive of it. Now the mind is forever bent in the direction of thinking about quantities in terms of numbers, just as the mind is forever bent in the direction of thinking its thoughts in terms of words, once the word was known to Man. This analogizing or abstracting of a concept is almost exactly the same as what happened when language was born in the Paleolithic. A real perception (9 fingers) becomes an abstract concept (the number 9). Thus, math represents an extension of the language based mode of abstract reasoning that began with verbal language, and now extends into another form of symbolic language. However, math, like money, is also a progression into theoretic culture, because mathematics is primarily extra-somatic. While verbal language is, in the ancient world, an *oral* mode of thought and expression, mathematics—from its outset—was a primarily *written* mode of thought and expression. In order for tallies of numbers and calculations to be useful, they must be documented ... written down and saved. This initial step into the world of writing will have massive implications later on, when verbal language itself changes from a solely oral mode of thought and expression into a *written* mode of thought and expression.

The Birth of Literacy

> Whence did the wond'rous mystic art arise,
> of painting speech and speaking to the eyes?
> That we by tracing magic lines are taught
> how to embody, and to colour thought.
> —William Massey

As with the invention of money and mathematics, literacy marks a leap—our biggest leap—into the vast foggy frontier of theoretic cognitive abstraction. The Greek alphabet, derived from the earlier Phoenician alphabet,[56] arose around 1100 BC. Literacy spread throughout the ancient Near East in the 8th century BC, when the Assyrian empire tried to implement a uniform culture throughout its colonies by exporting the Aramean alphabet and script and demanding its use by all of its scribes throughout the empire. In ancient Greece, the first literary texts were the recordings of the poems, epics, and hymns of Homer and Hesiod, about 800 BC. These were transcriptions of oral traditions. The first prose—text composed originally and intentionally for the written format—arises in the sixth century BC.

True writing as we now know it, writing based on a phonetic alphabet—is "meta-language"—a graphic language used to denote an oral language. Hence, writing is also "meta-abstract," an analog used to denote another analog, a symbol pointing to another symbol, an abstraction abstracting another abstraction. Literacy is so abstract that it has the power to detach our thoughts so far away from the real world context of the original subject, that we quite literally become lost in our own thoughts, in a way that oral language cannot mislay us. The migration of language from the tongue to the page completely changes our relation to both the subject of the word and the creator of the word. A word that you speak to me is direct, in the moment, face-to-face, *personal*. A word that you write to me is inherently less direct, un-present, inherently *less personal*. One could even write a message to no one in particular—as I'm doing right now—which in the oral world would be impossible. The fact that, over time, words have become the fabric of our thoughts, the web with which we weave our every idea, becomes crucial here. If our conscious thoughts themselves become less personal, first through oral words, and then through written words, then what has happened to our soul, which is, in essence, our own perception of our unconscious selves? What has happened to our soul? We have lost it, in the abstractions of our own cognitions. What, may we ask, has happened to God? With our souls lost in the dark haze of abstraction, we have no inner lighthouse to point us to God. Poor lost souls, with our thoughts detached from the world, we seek God in the Heavens; but God has never left the Earth ... *we* did!

In Sanskrit, the world's oldest written language, the term "Devanagari" refers to the alphabet of the Sanskrit language. Devanagari literally means, "the language of the gods." Similarly, in ancient Egyptian, the phrase that means written language is literally translated as, "the speech of the gods."[57] Indeed, to the peasantry of the Iron Age, the possessors of this new mode of thought—the aristocratic and cultural elite—may have seemed liked gods, as literacy not only denoted nobility of birth, but also an intellectual superiority, a lofty omniscience based on their distinct ability to locate, dictate, and create wisdom. For most of history following the Iron Age, literacy was acquired only by the elite classes of societies—the theoretic minority living at a station above the mythic minority. So the cognitive changes I am describing were primarily experienced by only a small segment of society. However, these drastic changes in the cognitive experience and perception of a relative few, initiated a powerful top-down effect in the spiritual ideas and practices of the many. While it is often said that "History is written by the victors," a more technically accurate phrase would be: History is written by the *literate*. Since the dawn of history, the collective cultural wisdom of each generation has been passed down not by the masses, but by the literate elite.[58] Before literacy, there was only myth and oral folklore. History itself is a product of literacy; the era of pre-literacy is prehistoric. And so, my discussion of the progression of cognitive abstraction in Western civilization from the 15th century BC in the Eastern Mediterranean and Near East, until the 19th century AD in Europe and America, will focus primarily on the advances in literacy among the relatively few.

In discussing the difference between a preliterate and a literate culture, we are referring to a contrast between an oral tradition and a written tradition, which entails a different experience of language, a different perception of words, and different modes of cognition: mythic as opposed to theoretic. In one of the oldest known oral traditions, the Homeric tradition of ancient Greece, the epic poems about the heroes and gods were sung by the bards directly to the people. In the singing, there was a direct appeal to the *emotions* of the listeners, not to abstract logic and reason. The ancient Hebrew word *Dabar* means both "word" and "event."[59] Words in an oral culture are an event. They happen in a certain moment within a specific context, and generally refer to a specific being, action, or object—as opposed to written language—which could be written by anybody at any time and at any place, and could be read by anyone at any time and any place. Because oral language is connected to a specific time and place, it tends to be more "concrete" and "imagistic"—it evokes ideas that can easily be visualized by the listener—as opposed to written language, which, because it could be read and reread by the reader, and analyzed and scrutinized, tends to be more abstract.[60]

There has been much debate over whether or not abstract thought develops in preliterate cultures. Clearly, since I perceive oral language itself as abstract thought, I hold that preliterate peoples do indeed engage in abstraction. However, I also hold that literacy, by its very own nature, not only promotes abstraction, but builds abstraction as a function of its own acquisition. That is, like a bricklayer who constructs his own scaffolding as he builds a wall, the process of literacy acquisition itself creates a brain that thinks more abstractly, and is thereby more adept at becoming more and more literate. If oral words are generally "context-dependent"—based in the here and now—then the generator of oral words, thought, will also remain "context-dependent." Written words, however, are not "context-dependent." They could refer to anything at anytime and be read by anyone at anytime. It follows that thinking will necessarily become more abstract in literate cultures, because literacy frees words from their specific contexts, thereby detaching thought from its specific context.[61] A 1972 Regional Report on Literacy by UNESCO states that "the illiterate man's thought ... remains concrete. He thinks in images and not in concepts. His thought is, in fact, a series of images, juxtaposed or in sequence, and hence it rarely proceeds by induction or deduction.[62]

A mind that thinks in words that are always in context is a mind that is personally connected to its surroundings. It perceives the world in terms of the direct relation between one being and another, because its focus is on the *person* who is before you, right here and right now. If literacy is theoretic because its constructs are "extra-somatic," then it follows that mythic orality is "somatic"— contained within the body—and expressive of the personal body's place within the context of his environment. Havelock provides a vivid example:

> Oral information is likely to be unfriendly to such a statement as "the angles of a triangle are equal to two right angles." If, however, you said, "The triangle stood firm in battle, astride and posed on its equal legs, fighting resolutely to protect its two right angles against the attack of the enemy" you would be casting Euclid backwards into Homeric dress, you would be giving him preliterate form.[63]

A preliterate mind has difficulty conceiving of things in complete abstraction, because everything he has ever heard or said has been placed within a specific context, and that context is usually the here and now. If a concept that is not here and now is to be understood, it must be told animistically[64]—the concept must be visualized, contextualized, personalized, somaticized—turned into a real person, like a character in a story. By giving the triangle a body, he is animated, made to be alive and personal. This is what all good teachers and writers do when trying to explain an abstract concept to an audience that is not fluent in abstraction. Even Copernicus, writing at the dawn of the Print Age in the early 16th century, when describing his new empirical theory of the sun's position in relation to the planets, used mythic animistic phraseology to get his point across to an audience still accustomed to learning through lecture and discussion, rather than book reading:

> In the middle of all sits the sun enthroned. How could we place this luminary in any better position in this most beautiful temple from which to illuminate the whole at once? ... so the Sun sits upon a royal throne ruling his children the planets which circle around him.[65]

In phrasing his model of the heliocentric universe in the terms of a divine king surrounded by his heavenly host, Copernicus was appealing to a sensibility that saw the world as an animated plane—a universe of spiritual entities all existing in personal relation to each other. When the mind tunes its perception to an abstract theoretical model of the universe, in which massive spheres of matter and energy orbit each other in proportion to each orb's gravitational pull, the personal relation is lost. When the personal relation is lost, the sun and moon and planets and stars are de-animated. They lose not only their conscious will to orbit, but they lose the souls inside of them that inspire them to shine. Thus, when the word loses its context, the object that the word denotes loses its context, and then everything that we perceive for some reason has no deeper meaning, no personal reference, no inner purpose, no soul. We look up to the heavens searching for God, but (as Gertrude Stein would say), "there is no *there* there," just a bunch of massive spheres of matter and energy, orbiting each other in proportion to each orb's gravitational pull.

The Age of Disenchantment

> The fate of our times is characterized by rationalization and intellectualization, and, above all, by the "disenchantment of the world."—Max Weber
>
> Isn't it enough to see that a garden is beautiful without having to believe that there are fairies at the bottom of it too?—Douglas Adams[66]

Literacy is a visual mode of perception, orality is an auditory mode. Shifting the sensory mode in which you perceive something changes your entire neurological and psychological experience of that thing. "Sight isolates, sound incorporates."[67] When we look at something, we focus on that one thing to the exclusion of everything around it. This is opposed to hearing, which is always in context. Sight focuses me, prompting me to analyze and dissect what I see. Sound envelopes me, creating a sense of unification between myself and my surroundings. The visual ideal is clarity, distinctness. The auditory ideal is harmony.[68] To see a painting better, I may step back to gain perspective. To hear better, I invariably move closer to the source of the sound. While the auditory experience of the spoken word grounds you in the world, both in terms of the present moment and the present context, it also grounds you in the *personal relation* you share with the speaker or listener. This is opposed to the visual experience of the written word, which draws you out of the external world and drives you inward, into your own private internal world of mental representations and conscious thought, a solitary kingdom in which the connection to the present moment, present context, and present relation are all lost.

There is magic in words. Like the magic number, which was created ex nihilo for the mind by the mind, the word too is such a magical apparition. This is why words carry mystical/spiritual power, why words can summon spirits and speak to gods, why words can be used in magic spells to cure or to curse, and why words can create and destroy worlds. Enchantment comes from the magic of the spoken word: en-chant—to chant the words aloud. The intrinsic magic of enchantment is lost in translation from the oral to the literary form. In a tribal oral culture, where sight is often obscured by the woods or the bush, hearing becomes the primary mode of perception. Sounds are "dynamic things," indicating the presence of a living thing moving in one's vicinity. You must have an alert ear to hear the sound of a rustle or a footfall. By the time you see the tiger or enemy attacking you, it's probably too late. The literate person, living in a world where dense woods and bush have been removed from sight, sees his world rather than hearing it. With vision as his primary sense, he seeks clarity. At the same time, the modern clatter and cacophony of sounds that bombard him—the rumble of traffic, the chatter of crowds, the drone of the radio, the constant background noise of modern life—must be filtered out, in order to save his senses from overload. The relatively recent shift in the balance of sense perception from sound to sight has created a disenchanted—dis-en-*chant*-ed—world of literate people, in which the magic and power of the chanted word has been stripped away, in favor of the analytic and logical focus of the written word. Thus, Weber's "Age of Disenchantment" has as much to do with a change in the balance of sense perception, as it does with a general diminution in spiritual perception.[69]

Anthropologists and ethno-psychologists, especially in Africa, have noted that literacy, when introduced to a preliterate society, produces drastic psychological changes within just one generation.[70] Indeed, just a very little bit of literacy is all that's needed to produce these effects, "some familiarity with written symbols—in reading, writing and arithmetic," is all it takes.[71] The changes are so drastic because they are occurring at the neurological level, and because they effect the most fundamental levels of cognition. The most lucid changes involve the new literate generation's perception of work. While the preliterate Africans were able to toil ceaselessly without questioning the point of their labor, the literate Africans were constantly questioning the reasons for why they must work so hard, making the work itself much more aversive and much more labor intensive, as they now had to "force themselves" to work, rather than just working naturally, without conscious reflection.[72]

The Birth of Monotheism

> But when you pray, go into your room, close the door and pray to your Father, who is *unseen*.—Matthew 6:6

Monotheism spread towards the end of the Iron Age as a consequence of a general cognitive shift from mythic to theoretic culture, causing thought to become ever-increasingly more abstract. As abstract consciousness dominates all thought, spiritual perception becomes more inhibited, more obsolete. Monotheism can only arise as a popularly accepted spiritual premise when the sensory perception of the gods has decreased to the point of imperceptibility and infrequency that it seems that almost nobody has direct contact with the gods anymore. In a society in which everyone perceives gods all the time, monotheism is impossible, because each individual spiritual perception would be unique and peculiar to the perceiver. One guy would see a male god, his wife would see a goddess; their son would see an animal god, his sister would see a tree goddess.... It would be impossible to convince people like this that all of their divergent perceptions of gods were actually just one single god—not *a* god—but *the* "God." Only when the sensory perception of the divine becomes a rare occurrence, experienced only by the uncommon individual, does the premise of monotheism become tenable. Once theophany[73] is relegated to the solitary prophet, then a single integrated image of one God can be shared communally, and the notion of one single God—invisible to everyone and heard only by the solitary prophet, though intuitively felt by everyone—can be conceived. In order for everyone to see the same God, he must first become invisible.

Perhaps this is why when Jews say the holiest prayer in their liturgy, the "Shema," it is required that they cover their eyes. The prayer reads: "Hear O' Israel, our Lord is Our God, our Lord is One." The basic premise of monotheism is repeated in this, the holiest of all prayers, twice daily by all observant Jews. It is the first prayer taught to children, which they are required to recite before they go to sleep each night. And, if at all possible, it is the last words a Jew should utter before he meets his Maker. It is significant that the prayer is called the "Shema"—"Hear"—denoting an oral, rather than a literary or visual experience. The oral experience retrieves the mythic mindset, which retains a stronger sense of spiritual perception than the subsequent theoretic mindset that is experienced in the visual modality. The covering of the eyes during the recitation of the prayer is mandatory and quite significant. The ritual symbolizes the fact that we cannot see God with our external eyes, but only with the inner-eye that gazes inwardly, to perceive the spirit and the soul. Because we cannot physically see God, we can all share an internal image of God that can be collectively shared, while also being individually experienced and personal. This conception of God is what makes monotheism possible. Thus, it is symbolically enacted during the recitation of the prayer which encapsulates, ingrains, and exclaims the monotheistic premise of the Jewish faith. Holding our hand over our closed eyes also forces us to inhibit the visual mode, and retrieve the oral mode of perception.

When one people destroy the idols of another people, they are intentionally killing their enemy's gods. The effect of this form of iconoclasm is catastrophic, but new idols could be forged, gods can be reborn, and new gods can arise. But when a people destroy *its own* idols—auto-iconoclasm—it points to a drastic shift in the experience and understanding of spiritual perception. An idol is revered because it is seen as the receptacle of a god, the physical embodiment of the god's spirit, the interactive medium for the reception of the prayers and sacrifices of its worshipper, and also for the emission of spiritual voices and visions towards the worshipper. When the perception of the god is no longer seen through the medium of an idol, then the idol is no longer a god, nor is it a receptacle for the god; but rather, it is a *symbol* of that god, a metaphorical representation of the god. Once the idol is recognized for what it actually is—a symbol—then the symbol is broken. "A God comprehended is no God."[74] In the Iron Age, as depicted in the latter books of the Old Testament, people began to destroy their own idols; but the idols destroyed by their former worshippers were broken even before they were destroyed, because once a spiritual symbol is recognized conceptually as a symbol, it no longer has its spiritual power. It's an abstract concept, not a sensory perception. *A symbol recognized as a symbol is a broken symbol.*

The Vanishing God

> My soul thirsts for God! For the living God! When shall I come face to face with God?—Psalm 42

In the late Iron Age, we see the beginning of a recurrent theme that will be seen in the religious texts of cultures throughout the ancient Near East. The theme could be summed up and epitomized in the following passage from an ancient Egyptian hymn dedicated to Amun, whose name literally means, "the hidden one."

> Turn back to us, O lord of the plenitude of time!
> You were here when nothing had come into being,

> And you will be here when "they" are at an end.
> You let me see darkness that you give—
> Shine for me that I might see you![75]

The theme of a god who was once physically present on the Earth, but is now gone, is the leitmotif of nearly every psalm, prayer, and hymn of antiquity. At the end of the Iron Age, as modern civilization made its first grand march into recorded history, the gods of antiquity did seem to recede backwards into the hazy mist of forgotten time. The ancients noted this departure frequently, and bemoaned it in the entreaties to their gods, begging for their return. Indeed, at dusk, it does seem that the sun is departing. From our egocentric perspective on the surface of the Earth, it's impossible to discern that, in actuality, it is *we* who are turning away from the sun.

The Scriptural Age

> They wove bright fables in the days of old,
> When reason borrowed fancy's painted wings;
> When truth's clear river flowed o'er sands of gold,
> And told *in song* its high and mystic things!
> —T. K. Harvey

I refer to the period between 500 BC—AD 1600, the time between the beginning of the widespread usage of the phonetic alphabet in the Near East and Eastern Mediterranean, through the beginning of the widespread usage of the printing press in Europe, as the "Scriptural Age." During this time, we see the desire to cast divinity into the form of a human representative, e.g., Jesus, as a symptom of a heightened need to personalize God. The advent of literacy and the cognitive changes that ensued resulted in a more abstract conceptualization of God in the mind of the scribes, philosophers, and theologians. The new God had become invisible, imperceptible, and detached from the real world. The resulting reaction to this movement was a distinct desire, especially among the illiterate masses, for something more spiritually concrete, something more perceptible, hence a resurgence of the older tradition of the divine king. This resurgence can be seen not only in the veneration of Jesus himself as the messiah, but in the messianic movement itself, which was rampant in the Near East in the centuries before and after Jesus. Similar forms of human divinization were going on in other parts of the world. The Roman emperor at the time of Jesus, Caesar Augustus, was worshipped throughout the Empire as a living god. The Buddhists and Hindus in India had begun the practice of "bhakti," in which specific Hindu gods, and even the Buddha himself, were revered as divine figures who took human form.[76] St. Paul, in particular, aimed at replacing the veneration of God via the literal word of God, the Torah, with the veneration of God via the physical son of God, Jesus, who was portrayed as the physical embodiment of the holy Word of God.[77] But even as the Western world began to embrace the humanized, personalized, somaticized spirituality of Christianity, the literate elite, becomingly increasingly lost in abstraction, continued to delve inwardly, a conscious-driven introspection that shut off spiritual perception as a sensory experience. The theologian, locked away with his manuscripts of sacred texts and subsequent interpretations, seeks a theoretic God in the abstract letters of the words of the text. As a result, he perceives God, not in an outwardly physical sense,[78] but as an inner sentient presence. "Writing makes possible the great introspective religious traditions such as Buddhism, Judaism, Christianity, and Islam. All these have sacred texts."[79] In the Scriptural Age, the deliberate redirection of spiritual perception inwardly was driven by the scriptural experience itself, which is different from both the preceding oral experience of a preliterate ritual, and the succeeding literate experience of reading a printed book.

The scriptural experience is never silent. The original function of reading carrels in medieval libraries was not to insulate the reader from outside noises, but to *isolate* the reader from other readers, as all of the readers were reading aloud.[80] Reading was therefore more of an oral-auditory experience; as opposed to silent reading, in which the lips do not move and the words are not heard. It should also be noted that the reading practiced by theologians was an exercise closer to prayer than ordinary reading. *Lectio,* "reading," was a "spiritual exercise," as nearly all reading was *lectio divina,* reading the holy scriptures. The purpose of this type of reading was not to attain external knowledge, but to focus inwardly, to meditate upon the scriptures until one finds the inner truth revealed by the sacred words.[81] The goal in studying a sacred script was to internalize it, to make it a part of yourself. Study, like prayer, was a spiritual practice. The fact that the holy scriptures, such as the Torah, Koran, and Vedas, were written in sacred languages—Hebrew, Arabic, and Sanskrit—meant that the words themselves were holy, making the parchment containing the words—the Torah scrolls, Koran scrolls, and Vedic scrolls—sacred, holy articles.

Modern Christians, perhaps, do not fully partake in the scriptural experience, because they do not have a sacred language. Latin, a language that was never spoken as a common language but only used in written form and for ritualistic purposes, is probably the closest thing that Christians have to a sacred language, but very few modern Christians study or pray from the New Testament in Latin, or from a parchment manuscript. And while Jesus himself embodied the Word of God, the actual words of the New Testament, the Gospels, have no sacred aspect because, unlike the Torah, they were not written by God. The words of the New Testament are simply a collection of memoirs about Jesus, written by his disciples. Furthermore, the language the New Testament was written in, Greek, is not considered holy or sacred by anyone.[82] Nevertheless, many Christians believe that it was the "opacity" of Latin, the mysteriousness of its sound and the enigma of its meanings, that created its mystique in the ritual of the Christian Mass.[83] When the words cannot be understood literally, the meaning of the ritual, ironically, is more clearly perceived for what it is ... a metaphor for something that cannot be fully comprehended. Bronisław Malinowski wrote that magic spells and enchantments are typically written in dead languages, because the strange sounding words evoke a "coefficient of weirdness" that adds an archaic, esoteric, cryptic, arcane quality to the words, making the magic in them even more potent. The deathly magical curses, "Abracadabra" or "Avara Kedavra," are much more magically potent than a colloquial, "Drop dead." The same can be said for sacred languages used in ritual and prayer. When the Protestants and then the Vatican allowed Church services to be read in the language of the peoples in the pews, rather than the traditional inscrutable Latin, it had the opposite to the intended effect. Rather than drawing the congregants further into the ritual, because they could now understand the words and follow along in their prayer books, the congregants tended to lose interest in the ritual, because the power of the ritual itself—the symbolic meaning—was lost when the mystery of the sacred language was changed into a secular language, and all of the acts and words now had a literal, secular meaning. The literal understanding of a ritual destroys the symbolism behind it, making the ritual impotent, meaningless, spiritless, dead. Instructing the worshippers that the ritual and the myth associated with it must be understood as symbols is also unhelpful in reviving the power of the ritual. *A symbol recognized as a symbol is a broken symbol.* The point of having a symbol is that it grips you on an unconscious level. The power of the symbol is in its unconscious association with the spiritual plane. This is how symbols evoke the sense of spiritual perception. If a person is consciously analyzing the symbol for spiritual content, he can understand on a theoretic level what the meaning is, but he doesn't *feel* the power of the symbol, because conscious thinking itself inhibits the spiritual feeling. A symbol, to be effective, must be experienced, not construed.

When my children, who are still little (and only half Jewish), ask me on Christmas Eve if Santa Claus is *really* real, I reply, without hesitation: "Yes, he's real!" I'm not bothered by the lie, because it's for a good purpose—the purpose of keeping this beautiful symbol of love and peace and generosity alive in my children's hearts—if only for a few more years. I know better than to plant the seed of conscious doubt by responding with some sort of intellectual rationalization, such as, "He's real if you believe in him," or other claptrap like that. Young children have little-to-no abstract understanding of symbols. Symbolic figures like Santa Claus, or the Tooth Fairy, or the Easter Bunny, or God, in the mind of the child, are either real or not real. One day my children will understand that Santa Claus is a symbol and not a man, and on that day, the symbol will be broken, and Santa will die. I'd like to put that day off for as long as possible.

If we consider the reading of a script as opposed to the reading of a printed book, there are many significant differences. When I attended temple as a boy, I was privy to a scriptural experience that has changed little since the beginning of the Scriptural Age, over 2,600 years ago. First of all, the scripture, the Torah scroll, is revered as a holy object itself, as it contains the magical sacred words of Yehovah. The Torah itself is a parchment made of animal skin that is treated with the utmost reverence and care. It is sheathed in an embroidered velvet cover, draped with amulets of silver and gold, and housed in a sacred ark. In every way, the Torah scroll and its ark is a direct re-embodiment of the original stone tablets written with the finger of God, delivered to Moses, and housed in the Ark of the Covenant, from which arose God's own voice. If a Torah is torn or destroyed, the congregation mourns for it as if a real person was injured or killed. Indeed, the Torah is treated far better than the way most *people* are treated. As the Torah is removed from the ark and brought forth towards the pulpit, the congregation flocks to it as if it were God himself. They reach towards it, trying to touch it and kiss it, with intense passion, devotion, and love.

When the cantor reads from the Torah, he sings the words aloud—an *oral* experience. Oftentimes, the cantor is so familiar with the verses in the Torah that he closes his eyes in reverence. Hence, he is not actually reading, he is reciting from memory. The task of memorizing sections or even the entirety of the Torah is held as a standard for Torah scholars and cantors alike, and it recalls the stress placed on the memorization of words that was universal in preliterate oral societies, and retained in scriptural societies. The memorization of the Koran by Muslims and the Bible by Christians is similarly held in high regard as an act of scholarly piety. The Latin term, *"meditatio,"* refers to the medieval practice of monks whose method of Bible study focused on memorization of the text itself. "It is what inscribes, so to speak, the sacred text in the body and in the soul."[84] The memorization of the text, the interiorization of the mythos revealed in the text, recalls the earlier oral tradition, in which the illiterate bards and storytellers had no choice but to memorize their epic tales. They were walking scriptures!

As the congregation listens to the cantor, the perception is through the ear rather than the eye. Anyone who has ever attended a poetry reading knows the difference between the somewhat distanced and cold experience of reading a poet's words on the printed page, and actually hearing the poet himself recite his words aloud. The latter phenomenon is a visceral, personal, emotional experience, as it creates a feeling of personal relation with the poet and his words. Similarly, the act of reading a story to your child at bedtime is inherently personal, emotional, intimate. The child could experience the story by reading it silently to himself, but the *relation* and intimacy of the experience is completely lost, even if you, the parent, are still physically present.

The cantor *sings* the verses of the Torah. It is a *musical* experience. Most of what we could call reading in the Scriptural Age was actually a singing performance by religious scholars, monks, rabbis, and priests, who were incanting verses from holy books. "*The medieval monks' reading carrel was indeed a singing booth.*"[85] As the cantor sings out to the congregation, the congregation sings back, as a chorus, interposing the cantor's solo performance with choral refrains and bridges. Music and singing not only represent a much more primal mode of communication, they also provide a much more intensely emotional experience. Music, more so than any other form of art or expression, has the most direct, immediate, and visceral effect on our emotions, as the processing of auditory stimuli is so direct and immediate, while the visual tends to be more abstract and distant. "*All art constantly aspires towards the condition of music.*"[86] The singing of the script also recalls the mode of oral transmission in preliterate societies, when traveling bards would transmit the mythos of their culture to villagers via musical verse, poetry, and song. Indeed, all poetry has its root in song[87]—as music and song are primary functions, processed in the right hemisphere—while reading is a secondary function, processed in the left. The effect of the mythos transmitted musically was not only a personal oral-auditory experience, it was a deeply *emotional* experience as well. "Music has charms to soothe the savage breast."[88]

There is a similar oral-auditory scriptural experience among Muslims, who hear the Koran sung aloud when they attend mosque; and by Christians (especially the more traditional Orthodox Christians of Eastern Europe), when they hear the Bible recited in Church, and even more so when the choir and congregation engage in communal singing of carols and hymns. Indeed, the most effective method of invigorating church rituals in the past century has been to jazz up the musical experience of the church meeting, such as the use of gospel music in Baptist churches, bluegrass music in Evangelical churches, and most recently, Christian Rock. The contemporary unreligious person may only come across something like a scriptural experience in certain proscribed occasions and settings: the personal space of a parent reading a bedtime story to his small child, the intimate emotional space of a poet reciting his innermost feelings aloud ... but for people living in the scriptural age, *all experiences of the written word were scriptural experiences*.

In Roman times, the author of a text would make his words known by performing a public recitation of his work. This public recitation provided the origin of the term "publication."[89] Several points can be drawn from this historical artifact. (1) Most of the public was illiterate, hence the need for public recitations. (2) Knowledge in Roman times, even literary knowledge, was still primarily transmitted though an oral medium. (3) Manuscripts, unlike books, were not products of mass consumption. To the contrary, manuscripts were typically considered exceedingly rare and exceedingly valuable. This is why the destruction of the ancient library in Alexandria is considered to be one of the greatest calamities of all time. The manuscripts lost were invaluable because they were rare, many of the scrolls being the only copies in existence. The rarity and importance of the scripts in the Scriptural Age, the sacredness of the words and the text, and the fact that so few people could actually read and write, made the scriptural experience of literacy much more emotionally significant than the experience of literacy subsequent to the invention of print technology.

The script is also a highly tactile product.[90] Parchment has a much more visceral tactile quality than modern paper, and the profession of the scribe could hardly be associated with the profession of a writer. As I write these words, typing them into my computer, my focus is only on the words as they appear on the screen. They essentially have no material substance. How these words will eventually be transformed into printed matter is none of my concern ... it will all be done by machines. It's also possible that the digital words will never be transcribed onto paper, if this manuscript is published as an e-book. The scribe, however, is intrinsically involved in the physical act of transcription. He must purchase the hide of an animal from a butcher, clean and cure the hide, stretch it and dry it. He must also mix his own ink and prepare his own quills. If the script will be that of a holy scroll such as a Torah, which was usually the case, a myriad of laws and rituals must be abided at every stage of script production. The act of writing itself was a holy act, a sacred ritual, which must be performed with the utmost reverence and scrupulosity. While writing, the scribe must wear a prayer shawl and phylacteries, as the writing of a Torah is, like prayer, a spiritual process. The scribe writes with his own hand, creating text in his own handwriting, which is completely particular to him. In the end, though the words he wrote and the order in which they were written may be identical to the words in other scripts, the manuscript itself is completely unique. The parchment comes from one particular animal who was ritually slaughtered and whose life was sacrificed for the honor of creating the holy scroll. The words are written in one man's handwriting, which is unique and singular, and which also (as forensic psychologists know), imparts certain elements of the writer's personal feelings and personality, embedded within the swirls and marks of the scrivener's script. Thus, every scripture is perceived to be singular, just like a person, with a life and soul of its own. This is why a Torah or Koran scroll is revered and adored as if it were alive, and why the congregants mourn after the destruction of a holy scroll, just as if a real person died. It would be impossible to convey the same sort of feeling for a printed book, which was mass produced by a machine. What is the feeling then for a digital book, which has no true substance or matter at all?

The Print Age

> Literature accelerates the advance of thought at a rate which leaves the slow progress of opinion by word of mouth at an immeasurable distance behind. Two or three generations of literature may do more to change thought than two or three thousand years of traditional life.—Sir James George Frazer, *The Golden Bough*

Gutenberg invented the printing press in 1440. It was the greatest technological advent in the sphere of literacy since the invention of the alphabet. As with previous inventions that affected literacy, it took awhile for the effects of this technology to spread and take hold; but certainly by the time that Martin Luther posted his Ninety-Five Theses on the church door in Wittenberg in 1517, the influence of the press was well underway. It's ironic that the Gutenberg Bible was the first book ever printed on a press, because the printing press would go on to become one of the greatest influences on religion in history, opening the door for books other than the Bible to be printed—even books that criticized and denounced religion itself. Furthermore, the printing press made possible the "democratization of knowledge,"[91] as it fostered the spread of information, cheaply and quickly, via newspapers and pamphlets. Mass communication through the press sparked a sharp increase in literacy in the Middle Ages. At the level of the literate elite, new theories and discoveries could now be dispersed far and wide at a pace that would have seemed lighting fast in those days. The printing press, indeed, was the internet of its age. The Enlightenment and the Scientific Revolution followed on the heels of the printing press, paradigm shifting episodes in history made possible by advances in literacy, which in turn resulted in advances in abstract thinking.

In the three years following Luther's posting of his Ninety-Five Theses, Luther's tracts were distributed in 300,000 prints. Just a few decades earlier, that would have been an inconceivable number of copies.[92] Luther soon became, along with Erasmus, one of the first bestsellers of written material. The Reformation inspired by Luther was the first religious revolution that was driven primarily by the *printed* word, as opposed to the oral word or the written word. As such, it could be considered as much of a *literacy revolution* as it was a religious revolution. The new phenomenon of literacy existing among a growing minority of the population, rather than a tiny fraction of a percentage of the population, made it possible for laypeople to read the Bible and other religious literature on their own. A layperson reading a religious text? That had never happened before! Driven by a new population of literate, independently thinking, and critically minded people, the Protestant Reformation expressed the desire for laymen to have direct access to the spiritual world through religious ritual; which, at the time, was dominated by the clergy of the Roman Catholic Church, who held an unrivaled monopoly over all aspects of religious doctrine, service, and ritual. What exactly was wrong with Catholicism, according to the Protestants? Well, despite the more obvious complaints about corruption, greed, nepotism, political despotism, and the like, the primary points that the Protestants were protesting about were also derived from a mode of thinking that arose out of a mindset created by (you guessed it), literacy....

Literacy Breeds Literalism

> Nothing may be changed that disagrees with the Latin edition of the Vulgate,[93] be it a single period, single little conclusion or a single clause, a single word of expression, a single syllable or one iota.—Leon of Castro, Spanish Inquisitor, 1576[94]

In his book, *Arguments and Icons* (2000), Whitehouse delineates two different modes of religiosity: the "Imagistic mode," in which symbols that have multiple meanings are expressed in rituals that are highly emotionally charged; and the "Doctrinal mode," in which symbols that have one meaning are expressed through liturgy and recited in rituals that are less emotionally charged. The Doctrinal mode is found in literate societies, because the written format lends itself to singular, literal meanings. In the literate society, written religious ideas become formalized into doctrine and dogma, and the symbols take on a literal quality. During the period of the Second Temple in ancient Judaea, starting from the second century BC through the destruction of the Temple in 70 AD, there was a religious and political rift between the Sadducees and the Pharisees. The Sadducees rejected the validity of the Oral Law, citing the Written Torah as the sole manifestation of divinity. The Pharisees upheld the validity of the Oral Law. An oral tradition is inherently more flexible than a written tradition, as it is open to interpretation, not written in stone. Hence, the Pharisees were accused of bending Jewish tradition in order to accommodate the new customs and conventions of their Greek and Roman governors, by providing interpretations of Jewish law that allowed for a certain amount of acceptance and tolerance of non–Jewish traditions. The Sadducees, however, accepted only a literal interpretation of the Torah. Their denunciation of all non-scriptural based customs and laws promoted intolerance, zealotry, and a very strict and rigid approach to the practice of ritual and worship—an approach in which the focus was on precise conformity to the details of the ritual—rather than the spiritual meaning of the act of worship itself. Thus, in the case of the Sadducees, the existence of a holy book and the ability to read it, literacy, bred a literalistic or doctrinal approach to religion.

The psychological term, "graphocentrism," refers to a bias in the reader towards placing precedence on the written word over the spoken word. When words are put into print, they take on the aura of being more "real" than words that are spoken, even if the printed word is factually untrue. Putting a word into print makes it visible, solid, concrete ... a cold hard fact. With mass printed books came catechisms and textbooks, literature that projected the aura of incontrovertible fact in the way that handwritten manuscripts and oral lectures could not.[95] Print takes the word out of the metaphysical auditory plane, which changes from moment to moment, and places it squarely into the physical visual plane, which can be held down and analyzed, because it doesn't change. Even the look and feel of a book, as opposed to the rather sloppy and inconsistent look and feel of a handmade script, purveys a sense of standardized and mechanized precision, the unnatural uniformity that imparts flawless perfection and absolute truth.[96] The spoken word blows away with the breeze, while the printed word stands firm like a solid brick. Because it seems permanent and immutable, the printed word appears more real. All purveyors of yellow journalism, propaganda, libel, and tabloid gossip are aware of this fact.[97] Lenin's famous saying—"A lie told often enough becomes truth"—only became famous because it was *printed*. In actuality, Lenin probably only *said* it once, but it was *printed* a billion times. A propagandist's lie is not particularly effective if it is simply *said*. In order for the lie to be told enough times, it must be *printed*. Only then can it reach the requisite number of eyes to become truth, and only then does the lie attain the aura of truth, which arises from the printed format itself. As Benjamin Franklin, himself a printer, famously wrote: "Believe none of what you *hear,* and half of what you *see*." The believing half is an artifact of the print bias.

When the print bias is merged with an already strong belief in the spiritual validity of a holy book, the effect is a religious brand of literalism that is quite profound. "It was as if print, uniform and repeatable commodity that it was, had the power of creating a new hypnotic superstition of the book as independent of and uncontaminated by human agency."[98] The sanctification of the text itself is a central tenet of the script based religions, and the Holy Scriptures they each hold sacrosanct: the Torah, Bible, and Koran. Because the written words themselves are holy, the message they convey is equally holy, and therefore must be scrupulously and literally upheld. Because the text can never be refuted in the way that a speaker can be, the text must always be right. And while a speaker takes his life in his hand when he claims to speak for God, the extra-somatic printed text has no qualms regarding this risk.[99] The "vatic" quality of sacred texts therefore breeds a form of religious literalism that is born out in an obsessive-compulsive focus on exactness and scrupulosity, on being absolutely certain that every aspect of a religious ritual is being performed precisely "as it is written," "to the letter," "word for word," and "quite literally," "by the book."

Literalism Breeds Fundamentalism

<blockquote>The heretic is the discourser without end.—George Steiner</blockquote>

When the priestly class of noble accessories to the divine king first arose in the Neolithic Age, the religious guild grasped its first monopoly on spiritual practice and spiritual theory. They were the masters of ritual and myth. In the Scriptural Age, when the priest-scribes transformed their oral mythos into written scripture and gospel, the priests, rabbis, and theologians locked up spiritual perception in a book, and then closed the book. They took control of the experience of God, the perception of God, the knowledge of God, by taking possession of the Word of God, which was achieved by writing the Word down. Once written down, the Word is in the grasp of Man, under his control. Fundamentalism, in essence, is about control—religious control—and how this control can be used to govern the relations between humans, and the human perception of their God.

The irony of print, especially in the early days of the Print Age, is that while literacy is typically associated with the opening of the mind to new ideas, the technology of print itself had the effect of closing the mind, at least in reference to the specific printed book that is interiorized, the Bible. Paradoxicality, once seen as an essential quality of God's nature, became in the Print Age a sign of erroneous thinking, because of its illogicality, its lack of clarity, its indistinctiveness. Thus, the desire to rid theology of paradoxicality led to a literal approach towards scriptural interpretation that, ironically, only brought more paradoxes to the surface.

The literal approach to scripture, when applied outwardly towards people—Protestants, Catholics, Jews, Muslims, African and South American "heathens," and other assorted "heretics"—led to the fundamentalist doctrines of persuasion and conversion through torture, warfare, and extermination, that so marked the dark and violent eras of Reformation, Inquisition, and Colonization. But fundamentalism is never one-sided. In the Middle Ages, both Catholics and Protestants were guilty of fundamentalist doctrines; just as in the Modern Age, much political strife is inspired not only by Islamic Fundamentalism, but by Christian Fundamentalism and Jewish Fundamentalism as well. The Catholic

Church was essentially right in perceiving some of the Protestants' desires for reform as changes that would dilute the essence of Christian spirituality.[100] When religion is made more theoretic, it moves further away from its mythic origins, and though the aim of the reformers was to bring people closer to God, the effect was to make God even more imperceptible. The Catholic Church's extreme reaction to the Protestants was based in a fear of schism, a very true fear that the Church was losing its monopoly over Christian ritual and myth.[101] "Fundamentalism ... nearly always begins as a defensive movement; it is usually a response to a campaign of coreligionists or fellow countrymen that is experienced as inimical and invasive."[102] A similar fear of change and a loss of control can be seen in modern fundamentalist movements. "In the twentieth century ... the turning of many to orthodox faith was, at least in part, a response to how cold and frightening our times had become. This phenomenon looks like a grasp for hope—precisely in the face of the sensation of the hiddenness of God, precisely as an expression of the fear with which the absence of God leaves us."[103]

Fundamentalism Breeds Iconoclasm

> In their desire to produce a wholly rational, scientific faith that abolished *mythos* in favor of *logos*, Christian fundamentalists have interpreted scripture with a literalism that is unparalleled in the history of religion.—Karen Armstrong[104]

Catholic fundamentalism provoked the revolt of Protestant fundamentalism, and Protestant fundamentalism expressed itself in iconoclasm—the rejection and destruction of the "idols" and "graven images" of the Catholic Church.[105] Iconoclasm, as per the 2nd Commandment prohibiting "graven images," is depicted in many biblical scenes in which the idols and images of "strange gods" are destroyed. The Protestants recapitulated the biblical iconoclasms with their own version of religious literalism. "Luther's reliance on 'scripture alone' would lead to a theology that was more dependent than hitherto on the word.... The word would now replace the image and the icon in people's thinking."[106] The Protestants intended to "cleanse" the Church of all non-literal aspects of Christian worship.[107] Along with the graven images, the Trinity itself went out the window.[108] The notion that one God could be three was inimical to the literal mind. The paradox, accepted by a mind stationed in a mythic mindset, becomes a contradiction to the mind stationed in a theoretic mindset. Furthermore, the rituals of the old Catholic Church that were centered around the *act* of worship and the *sensory experience* of worship, were gutted by the Protestants and their single-minded focus on the Word. But as the mind and body move away from the primacy of the physical act and sensory experience towards the abstraction of the conceptual word, the deed of the rite loses its visceral power. The shift in the focal attention of congregants in the Protestant and, more recently, Catholic churches, demonstrates that the focus is now more on the word than on the deed.

The focal point of churches in the past has always been the altar, the place where the ritual or deed was performed, the place where the sensory experience of God was perceived. The altar retained its connection with the primal ritual—the sacrifice—a visceral, sensory, violent, emotional gesture written in blood, flesh, smoke, and fire. The post-literate focal point became the pulpit, the place where the priest leads the word of prayer, and the place where the word of the sermon is delivered. Worship then becomes focused on words rather than deeds. But the word divorced from the deed becomes an empty experience, a repetitive service, a meaningless ceremony.[109]

For example, the notion of the "transubstantiation" of the communal bread and wine into the flesh and blood of Jesus is conceived in the 12th century AD, only after a millennium of Christian ritual. Prior to the Middle Ages, it was understood intuitively that the bread and wine, once consecrated, were divine objects that partook of the divine host, and thus became divine themselves. So the worshippers in ancient times ate and drank the bread and wine and believed that they truly were tasting and consuming the flesh and blood of Jesus, because not only is it possible for objects such as bread and wine to partake of the divine and thus become divine, it is also possible for mortals to partake of the divine sacrament and thus become divine themselves.

However, once a theoretic literalism takes hold of the mind's perception of reality, it becomes nearly impossible to truly believe that the bread and wine are flesh and blood. That would be paradoxical, and paradoxicality is unacceptable to a rational mind. Thus, if the ritual is to be saved, it must be rationalized and literalized, so that it makes some sort of logical sense. Thus, the doctrine of transubstantiation is created in the 12th century by Catholic theologians as a rationalization of a pre-existing ritual. But when the even more literal mind perceives the same ritual in the Print Age, and this literal mind is now independent and skeptical of the old traditions, transubstantiation is rejected once again as a paradox. The rejection of the idea that the communal bread and wine were truly the flesh and blood of Jesus was a clear sign that "Christians in Europe were losing the older habits of thought."[110] The movement of much of Christendom away from Catholicism and towards Protestantism was marked by a rejection of the metaphorical in favor of the literal, a rejection of the paradoxical in favor of the logical, a rejection of the deed in favor of the word, and a rejection of the mythic in favor of the theoretic.[111]

The Electronic Age

> We are the primitives of a new culture.—Umberto Boccioni, 1911

The new wave of Protestantism in the late 19th and 20th Centuries was propelled by advances in electronic media. Microphones, public address systems, telegraphs, telephones, radio, film, and television all served to spread the Word far and wide. The effect of this new media was profound. While books change the mind, books can be shut or never opened. The eyes can turn away from the written word, but in the case of auditory mass media such as radio, "we simply are not equipped with earlids."[112]

We are all the captive victims of sound. In the age of electronic media, no one is immune to the pervasive and invasive power of mass media. The residents of the electronic community hear and see the same messages repeatedly, regardless of their willingness or consent. These messages invade our mind and change our thinking, not just through their content, but as a function of the *medium* itself. So while print created a public of individuals, mass media created a mass audience.[113]

Electronic mass media "retribalizes" society by connecting individuals together through common experiences, common knowledge, and common reactions to common events.[114] For example—the bombing of Pearl Harbor, the Kennedy assassination and funeral, the terrorist attacks on September 11th, 2011—these events were communally experienced by the American people, the American "tribe," and thus had the effect of creating communal meanings and communal responses.

While electronic mass media enhances communication by delivering it widely, quickly, and cheaply, it obsolesces the sense of individuality that was enhanced by literacy. Mass media retrieves the mythic sense of communally shared images and stories, and flips our focused theoretic attention on the written word into a more generally focused mythic and episodic attention to visual images and oral messages.[115]

The Digital Age

> Great God! I'd rather be
> A Pagan suckled in a creed outworn;
> So might I, standing on this pleasant lea,
> Have glimpses that would make me less forlorn;
> Have sight of Proteus rising from the sea;
> Or hear old Triton blow his wreathed horn.
> —Wordsworth, from
> "The World Is Too Much with Us," 1802

> No! let me gaze, not on some sea far reaching
> Nor star-sprent sky,
> But on a Face in which mine own, beseeching,
> May read reply.
> —F.W. Newman, 1870[116]

As we look forward towards the vertical slope of technology in the Digital Age, it is impossible to see the road ahead of us, because the incline of technological change is too sudden and too steep. Whereas the rearview mirror of the recent past has always given humankind a perspective on the future, a rearview mirror is useless when one is travelling at the speed of light.[117] Nevertheless, it is useful to note that while media, the technology that communicates thought, has formed, shaped, and inhibited spiritual perception, it has never eliminated it. Rather than going away, it is more likely that our perception of God and the divine will evolve along with digital media, and that our perception will reflect the changes in cognition that digital media create.

Not since the invention of the printing press in 1440 has a new invention changed communication so fundamentally that it has changed the way that we way we think, the way we perceive, and the way we understand the world. Digital technology has re-invented humanity. The computer's approach to the world is to focus on details and specifics rather than interpreting meaning or perceiving the whole within its context. As we become more integrated with computers, as we spend more and more time "connected," "online," our noses glued to the screens of computers, laptops, Iphones, and Ipads, and as our children grow up being even more integrated with computer technology, the mind will inevitably become more computer-like. Clearly, humans are destined to become cognitively intertwined with artificial intelligence. But will we remain merely the creators of computers that process intellectual functions, or will our minds become the *products* of computer processed intelligence? Just as the hand with its opposable thumb is a byproduct of millennia of interactivity with the hand-tool, the mind is in the process of molding itself into a byproduct of digital media.

The archaic human was intimately connected with his surroundings, seeing spirit in every one and every thing, animating his environment and interacting with everything in it in a personal way, ever mindful of the spiritual essence within everything all around him. Compare this to the modern human, so engrossed in his digital device that he barely notices any thing or any one around him. His mindful focus and consideration is on the digitalized information dispersed in the stratospheric ether, not on the person sitting right across from him at the table. He is not so much blind to his immediate environment, but indifferent towards its. To apply Buber's philosophy, the archaic human related to everyone and everything as a "Thou," while the modern human relates to everyone and everything as an "It." Digital humanity lives in a de-animated world, in which the digital is replacing the real, and the real is being displaced into the shadow world of meaningless specters. Digital gadgets and the software and websites that run on them become extensions of the consciousness that employs them. The internet tool is an "I-tool"—both an internet gadget and an ego gadget—an extension of our sense of "I." The I-tool extends our inner language by connecting it both receptively and expressively to the internet, which is limitless. It extends our personal sense of identity by projecting our personas into the ether via social networking. Its grapho-visual functions extend our eyes via digital cameras and digital imagery. Its auditory-oral functions extend our ears and mouths to hear and speak at speeds that far exceed the speed of sound. Its informational functions extend our consciousness into the range of infinite potentialities. In doing so, we unwittingly digitalize ourselves. Our sense of self, our "I," is diminished into a virtual "i," which is just a small "i" in a world of "its."

New cognitive faculties develop as a consequence of newly introduced technologies. As a result, older faculties necessarily become less useful or obsolete. In order for the cognitive faculties of reason and logic to have evolved, the older faculties of instinct and intuition had to be inhibited and subdued. Writing and reading caused a decrease in the ability to memorize, because literacy makes memorization unnecessary, and therefore obsolete. Facility with calculators causes a decrease in the ability to calculate figures in one's head. The use of GPS navigators results in a decreased ability to navigate manually. Word processing software results in a general decline in penmanship, grammar, and spelling. Speedy modes of transportation and instantaneous means of accessing commodities and information eliminate the need for patience. As we dive headlong into the foggy ether of digitalized everything, developing new mental faculties that are specially adapted for the world of digital interface, it would behoove us to be mindful of what faculties we are making obsolete.[118] If language and literacy have altered or inhibited the mental faculties that enable spiritual perception, then what effect might digitalization have on the same faculties?

Digital media, with its appeal to multisensory and multimodal forms of cognition and perception, is likely to continue the cognitive trend initiated by the electronic media of the 20th century. We will see the retrieval of oral (mythic) and imagistic (episodic) modes of perception and cognition. In the area of religion, the movement in digitally enhanced spiritual perception will be aimed at providing a visceral and sensory experience of God. Romantic poets of the 19th century such as Wordsworth and Newman (quoted above), bemoaned the state of modern literate man, who could no longer see the face of God, hear His voice, or touch His presence. The desire to experience God on a more direct sensory level was also expressed in the revivalist Christian movements of the 19th and

20th Centuries, such as the Evangelicals and Pentecostals, as well as the Hasidic Jewish movement in Eastern Europe. In the 1960's, the "Hippy" counterculture used psychedelic drugs and music, and explored Eastern spiritual practices such as yoga, meditation, and chanting, to attain a sense of transcendence and spiritual unity. In trying to explain the meaning of his hit song, "My Sweet Lord," George Harrison said:

> If there's a God, I want to see Him. It's pointless to believe in something without proof, and Krishna consciousness and meditation are methods where you can actually obtain God perception.... When you become real pure by chanting, you can actually see God like that, I mean personally. But there's no doubt you can feel His presence and know that He's there when you're chanting.[119]

Harrison's contemporary in the 1960's counterculture, Timothy Leary, advocated the use of psychedelic drugs to attain a heightened sensation of God's presence:

> Like every great religion of the past we seek to find the divinity within and to express this revelation in a life of glorification and the worship of God. These ancient goals we define in the metaphor of the present—turn on, tune in, drop out.[120]

Though Leary never gave up his own use of psychedelics in his private spiritual practices, he admitted that the pharmaceutical route of entry was less than ideal for most people for many reasons. Shortly before he died, he declared that the personal computer was the "LSD of the 1990s," and advised people that rather than looking for God in a drug, that they should "turn on, boot up, jack in"—that is, they should explore the "cyberdelic" route to spirituality—"cyberdelic" being a combination of the words "cybernetic" and "psychedelic." In essence, Leary was stating that the future of spirituality will involve the merging of spiritual practices with digital media and virtual reality immersion technology, thus predating my own ideas on the topic by over two decades!

The Digital Idol

> Their idols are silver and gold, the work of human hands. They have mouths, but do not speak; eyes, but do not see. They have ears, but do not hear; noses, but do not smell. They have hands, but do not feel; feet, but do not walk; and they do not make a sound in their throat. Those who make them become like them; so do all who trust in them.—Psalm 115

An ongoing leitmotif in the history of religion is the notion of idolatry.[121] In its most basic form, idolatry is the materialization of God into a physical form, so that he may be experienced with the physical senses. When literacy and the abstractness that came with it made God invisible and banished him to the Heavens, the new monotheism banned idolatry in the physical form. God was now spirit, not substance; yet his spirit was manifest in the physical words of the Holy Scriptures. Christians revived the substance of God by giving him a physical Son; but then just as quickly withdrew the Son. Nevertheless, the substance of God was manifest in the words of the Son, embodied in the Gospels, and in the artifacts and icons of the Catholic Church. The Protestants denounced the artifacts and icons as "idols." Like the Jews, they insisted that the spirit cannot be depicted in "graven images," and that the spirit is manifest only in the words of the Bible. In the 20th century, in the wake of rising atheism and secularism, theologians denounced as "idolatry" the conceptualization of God in any "real" or "physical" or "personal" sense. This, according to Paul Tillich, is making an "idol" of God, even if the idol is made of thoughts and feelings. Instead, Tillich conceived of God as the "ground of being,"[122] an abstract idea that provides real comfort to nobody. Even Tillich's completely abstract conceptualization of God could be subject to his own critiques, because Reason itself can be conceived as an idol.[123] In the end, even Tillich, like Kierkegaard and most other profound religious thinkers, admits that true belief begins with an "acceptance" that is purely experiential, an "ecstasy" that provides a sense of transcendence beyond the rational.

The history of cognition laid out in this chapter traces the evolution of thought from preverbal images to oral words to written words to printed words to electronically recorded and then electronically broadcasted words, sounds and images; and finally, to digitally transmitted words, sounds, and images. The last stage allows us to return to the primordial images that existed before we began thinking in words, and the experience of the environment before we became detached from it. Immersive virtual reality technology and digital media can create any environment imaginable, and it can also give us the very real sense of being in that environment. Neurological electro-stimulation technology can evoke the unconscious images and sensations that have been hidden in the deep recesses of our minds for millennia, but inhibited from conscious expression, existing only in the netherworld of dreams.

It seems that there was a time not so long ago in human history when idolatry was a nearly ubiquitous phenomenon. People needed a physical sensory experience of the divine, and that need was fulfilled when the idols they worshipped evoked real images and interactions with their gods. To recall Julian Jaynes' concept of the "hallucinogenic function" of the idol, perhaps the human brain was hardwired to experience these forms of perceptions. The Talmudic sages provide a complementary notion, that deep within the human heart is a desire and a capacity to see and hear God, but that capacity has been inhibited. Ancient Jews considered Christianity—the worship of a man as a god, and the worship of the Cross—as a form of idolatry. Luther and his Protestant followers considered the iconography of the Catholic Church as a form of idolatry. Modern theologians often refer to the worship of money and material possessions, the worship of political figures or of power, the worship of celebrities and fame, the worship of sexual attraction and sex itself, and the worship of technology and technological gadgets, as contemporary forms of idolatry. Clearly, there is something about the human mind that craves an object of devotion, something outside of the self to worship, and there is a drive to give this thing a physical form. In the Digital Age, new idols will be forged that will retrieve this drive, and enhance this inhibited form of perception.

The Digital Idol will be perceived in the virtual dimension within our own minds. Its form will be different for everyone, just as the Bronze Age idols of old, the "Teraphim," were different for each household and for each person. We will conjure our own visions of God, our own "graven images," molded out of digital information and neural processing. The hardware of the idols—the plastic remotes, the fiber optic cables, the copper plugs, and silicon microchips—will only be the physical manifestations of the God. His true essence, his spirit, will be inside the idol, somewhere in the metaphysical ether of digital and neural information as it crosses at the speed of light through integrated circuits and neuronal synapses.

There will doubtlessly be an urge to communalize the digital spiritual experience. To use the connectivity of the internet to share revered divine images of Jesus, Mary, Buddha, Vishnu, etc. It is therefore possible that, as happened in the past, myriads of individual personal gods will merge into one supreme communal god ... a Digital God. However, whereas the monotheistic God that arose in the Bronze Age became invisible, ineffable, unspeaking, and imperceptible, the Digital God will be defined by exactly the opposite qualities. Through the portal of an interactive media system, the digital idols will be visible, audible, tangible, visceral—they will not only have eyes, ears, mouths, and feet—but they will also see, hear, speak, walk, and even touch. And through the limitless data processing potential of the Digital Age, the Digital God, no matter if it is worshipped by billions, will always be completely interactive on a personal level with each individual user. The "hallucinogenic function" of the idol—the inclination for the human mind to project words and images into the mouth and eyes of the idol, that were then reflected back towards the worshipper—will be retrieved by the digital idols. Through them, our unconscious thoughts and wishes will be revealed to us, as though they were a revelation from God. Our spiritual perception will be flipped from the theoretic to the episodic mindset. In the Digital Age, as in the Palelolithic Age, each man will be a prophet, each woman an oracle, and each individual will behold a perception of his own personal Digital God.

Chapter Five

The Psychology of Spiritual Perception and the Digital Peak

> There is no doubt, it seems to me, that there have been profound changes in the experience of man in the last thousand years. In some ways this is more evident than changes in the patterns of his behavior. There is everything to suggest that man experienced God. Faith was never a matter of believing. He existed, but of trusting, in the presence that was experienced and known to exist as a self-validating datum. It seems likely that far more people in our time experience neither the presence of God, nor the presence of his absence, but the absence of his presence.—R. D. Laing[1]
>
> Psychology: from the Greek words *psyche*—"soul"—and, *logos*—[to study with] "words."—Psychology: "the study of the soul."

Prior to the 19th century, the word "psyche" was always used in a spiritual context. For most of human history, what are now called "mental disorders" were presumed to be spiritual problems, caused by troublesome demons or spirits, or arising as a result of an individual's improper relationship with the spiritual world. In 1694, Steven Blankaart used the word *"psychology"* for the first time in an English text, *The Physical Dictionary,* defining the field as the branch of medicine "which treats of the Soul."[2] Centuries later, "psychology" was co-opted by the social sciences as a field of research quite separate from its spiritual roots. It was re-chartered as the "scientific study of behavior." The roots of psychology, though submerged, have never been lost. The great psychological thinkers: William James, Freud and Jung, Fromm and May, Erikson and Maslow ... have always kept the field grounded in an appreciation for the conjectural nature of what psychology, in essence, really is: a process of "soul searching." Though the word "soul" has been more-or-less banished from psychological discourse, the essence of psychology, the study of the soul, has never been completely forgotten. Furthermore, the ancient assumption that psychological health and spiritual health are indivisible is born out by modern psychological research, which shows that a strong sense of spirituality is directly related to high measures of happiness and satisfaction, and low measures of depression and anxiety.[3] A famous study of priests has shown that a "strong relationship with God" and regularly practiced spiritual rituals are predictive of an abiding sense of "inner peace" and a sense of "personal happiness."[4] The same results have been found among spiritual and religious people across cultures, races, nationalities, and faiths.

In this chapter, the study of the soul will be momentarily "reborn," as we explore various psychological theories about spirituality. In particular, I will be focusing on psychological theories about the nature of the unconscious mind, the experience of dreaming, and the perception of the spiritual dimension of life, and how all three of these psychological constructs are inextricably tied together.

Tylor's Animism

> Thus she spoke, and I longed to embrace my dead mother's ghost. Thrice I tried to clasp her image, and thrice it slipped through my hands, like a shadow, like a dream.—Homer, *The Odyssey*

E.B. Tylor, a foundational figure in the field of anthropology, believed that the experience of dreaming was a pivotal element in the evolution of spiritual beliefs. According to Tylor, the belief that a person's "ghost-soul" wanders away from his body while he sleeps, is a universal explanation of the dreaming process, both among preliterate people in his day (the 19th century), and among preliterate people in the Stone Age.[5] The ghost-soul belief is a wonderfully parsimonious theory for the believer, because it solves two puzzles simultaneously:

1. What is happening to me, i.e., consciousness, whilst I am dreaming?
ANSWER: My ghost-soul is wandering.
2. What happens to me after I die?
ANSWER: My ghost-soul moves on to another being or another place.

Furthermore, if the ghost-soul belief is projected onto other people and other things, it solves countless other problems as well, such as:

What happened to my beloved mother when she died?
ANSWER: Her ghost-soul lives on.
Will I ever see my deceased mother again?
ANSWER: Yes, you will see her ghost, you will encounter her soul in your dreams, and when you die, your soul will be with hers.

What was that rustling noise behind the bushes? I looked but I didn't see anything.
ANSWER: That was the ghost-soul of the bush, or the ghost-soul of your mother, or the ghost-soul of a lion, etc.

"Animism" is the term coined by Tylor to represent the belief in the existence of souls and spirits. Tylor believed that animistic thought is the universal basis of religion, that it was the first religion among prehistoric peoples, that it is the common religion among preliterate peoples, and that it is still at the root of modern religious thought. Tylor also believed that animism, as a mode of thought and perception, was a direct result of consciousness, as the answers animism provided were only necessary once human beings began to think critically about their own existence.[6]

James' Mystical State of Consciousness

> Neither shall they say, Lo here! or, lo there! For, behold, the kingdom of God is within you.—Jesus of Nazareth, Luke 17:21

In 1902, William James, premier American psychologist of the late 19th and early 20th centuries, published what is arguably the most significant and influential book on the psychology of religion ever written: *The Varieties of Religious Experience*. In the book, James explores the notion of a "mystical state of consciousness."

> ...our normal waking consciousness, rational consciousness as we call it, is but one special type of consciousness, whilst all about it, parted from it by the filmiest of screens, there lie potential forms of consciousness entirely different. We may go through life without suspecting their existence; but apply the requisite stimulus, and at a touch they are there in all their completeness, definite types of mentality which probably somewhere have their field of application and adaptation.[7]

The experience of a particular alternate state of consciousness—the "mystical state of consciousness"—is completely subjective, and most often encountered in the form of waking dreams, or hallucinations.

> It is as if there were in the human consciousness a *sense of reality, a feeling of objective presence, a perception* of what we may call "something there," more deep and more general than any of the special and particular "senses" by which the current psychology supposes existent realities to be originally revealed.... The most curious of the existence of such an undifferentiated reality as this are found in hallucination.[8]

For the most part, James believed that the mystical state of consciousness was experienced by people who, for reasons yet unknown, were more psychologically predisposed to "automatisms," which are acts performed unconsciously, or subjective perceptions of non-objective stimuli.[9] These people with "exalted sensibilities" saw visions and heard voices that both established and strengthened their faith in God. The crux of James' thesis, and the part that resonates most strongly with my own thoughts on the subject, is that a deep and true sense of spirituality is *only* acquired through a directly personal and *sensory* experience of a sentient, spiritual "other."[10]

> In persons deep in the religious life, as we have now abundantly seen—and this is my conclusion—the door into this region seems unusually wide open; at any rate, experiences making their entrance through that door have had emphatic influence in shaping religious history.[11]

James observed and documented hundreds of experiences of the mystical, summarizing his observations by delineating four essential qualities of the mystical state of consciousness:

1. It is *ineffable*—it cannot be expressed rationally, but rather, it is a direct experience of the divine or eternal that transcends rational thought or logical analysis.
2. It is *noetic* communication—the experience relates an authoritative statement about one's life that has the quality of seeming incontrovertibly true, as if the source was a higher power of ultimate authority.
3. It is *transient*—the experience of elevated consciousness cannot be sustained for very long.
4. It is *passive*—the person feels that he is the recipient of a message rather than the conveyor; he is passively listening while some external higher power is revealing its message to him.[12]

The ineffability of the mystical experience is a key feature in my theory, as spiritual perception—James' "mystical state of consciousness"—is only accessible when its cognitive inhibitor—language based consciousness—is turned off. Hence, a mystical experience is ineffable by default, as the lack of analytic language is a precondition for the occurrence of the experience itself. Nevertheless, this does not mean that the experience is always completely bereft of words, or that words cannot be used at all to approximate a sense of the experience, as Maslow explains:

> ...the word "ineffable" means "not communicable by words that are analytic, abstract, linear, rational, exact, etc." Poetic and metaphorical language, physiognomic and synesthetic language, primary process language of the kind found in dreams, reveries, free associations and fantasies ... are more efficacious in communicating certain aspects of the ineffable.[13]

The noetic quality of the mystical experience, according to James, is related to his observation that the state is usually precipitated by an inner conflict—a sense of psychological discontent or emotional uneasiness—which is in some way eased or resolved by the mystical experience. The knowledge imparted to the individual is a deeper knowledge of the self, a knowledge that pertains to and comes from within; but a knowledge that imparts a more profound and authoritative sense of wisdom, as it is experienced as coming from without. Because it resonates so strongly with the individual on both the objective and subjective levels of perception and cognition, it is not subject to critique or doubt through the process of reason. It is pre-filtered perception, as it comes from within rather than from without, therefore bypassing the analytical mode of consciousness that censors normal perception. One could say that it sneaks through the door of perception, while the doorman is asleep at his post. But since the perception itself is sensed as coming from both within and without, it purveys a "noetic" sense of authoritative wisdom that surpasses any externally derived knowledge, as well as any internally derived deduction. A quote from James' book by a certain Professor Starbuck provides an example of mystical noeticism:

> God is more real to me that any thought or thing or person. I feel his presence positively, and the more as I live in closer harmony with his laws as written in my body and mind. I feel him in the sunshine or rain; and awe mingled with a delicious restfulness most nearly describes my feelings. I talk to him as to a companion in prayer and praise, and our communion is delightful. He answers me again and again, often in words so clearly spoken that it seems my outer ear must have carried the tone, but generally in strong mental impressions. Usually a text of scripture, unfolding some new view of him and his love for me, and care for my safety. I could give hundreds of instances, in school matters, social problems, financial difficulties, etc. That he is mine and I am his never leaves me, it is an abiding joy. Without it life would be a blank, a desert, a shoreless, trackless waste.[14]

James did not consider Professor Starbuck's description of his own sense of spirituality to be abnormal in any way, other than the level of eloquence with which it was expressed. James believed that the subtle experience of God's constant presence, the "once-born," punctuated intermittently with powerful moments of mystical awareness, the "twice-born," was the normative spiritual pattern of the average religious person's life. I don't believe the experience of spirituality has changed much since James' day, though the proportion of self-described "spiritual" or "religious" people has certainly gone down, at least in the Western world. According to a Gallup Poll conducted in 1976, 50 million adult Americans, over 1/3 of the adult population, have reported at least one "born again" experience in their lives.[15]

In James' perspective, the common direct experience of "higher spiritual agencies" presupposes the "possession of a subconscious region which alone should yield access to them."[16] In my view, this "subconscious region"—this "exalted sensibility"—is the sense of self that is normally inhibited by language based consciousness. The personal spiritual experience, the state of mystical consciousness, is an experience of one's "subliminal self," in which the limitations of ordinary consciousness are transcended, and a truer, deeper, more essential sense of the self is achieved ... but all in relation to a spiritual sensation that is perceived as an outer presence.[17]

Freud's Illusion

> Am I to believe every absurdity?—Sigmund Freud, 1927[18]

Freud's first book, *The Interpretation of Dreams* (1900), posits dreaming as a "primary process," in which "the free indulgence of the psyche in the play of its faculties is reproduced ... as the non-interference of the preconscious activity within the dream." That is, the dream experience is the free expression of the psyche when it is not controlled or dominated by consciousness. In the dream, there is a "return to the embryonal standpoint of psychic life."[19] As a completely unconscious process, dreams represent *"an archaic world of vast emotions and imperfect thoughts,"*[20] they are expressions of *"primitive* modes of operations that are suppressed during the day."[21] Dream imagery and the experience of dreams are "primal," representative of older and more primitive modes of perception. On this point—that dream cognition represents an unconscious, episodic, preliterate, primitive, primordial, and irrational mode of perception—I agree with Freud completely. Freud never explored the spiritual nature of dreams, which is unsurprising, considering Freud's atheistic bent.

In *Totem and Taboo* (1913), Freud psychoanalyzes the origins of religion, pointing to "totemism" as the most primitive form of spiritual belief. Freud believed that the totem animal was worshipped as an ancestral spirit because, on an unconscious level, the totem was connected with the father figure: "Psychoanalysis has revealed to us that the totem animal is really a substitute for the father..."[22] The tendency to project spirit or consciousness into non-human beings and objects is referred to by Freud as the "animistic mode of perception," a tendency that I believe is an ancestral precondition for spiritual perception.[23] According to Freud, the animal that was sacrificed in the primitive ritual was a totem, a symbol or substitute for the father, who was revered and worshipped via the sacrificial rite.[24] Rather than being an atonement with the spirit of the animal itself (as I suggested previously), Freud argued that the sacrificial rite was a symbolic act of atonement with the spirit of the *father*, who at one point in evolutionary history was murdered by his sons, in a primordial act of oedipal violence. Thus the totem sacrifice becomes the origin of all subsequent religious ritual and thought.[25]

In *The Future of an Illusion* (1927), Freud interprets God as an "illusion"—a mental image conjured by "wish fulfillment"—like the hallucinatory images in dreams. Beliefs in gods and spirits are "fulfillments of the oldest, strongest and most urgent wishes of mankind. The secret of their strength lies in the strength of those wishes." In particular, these wishes relate to:

> ...man's helplessness and along with it his longing for his father, and the gods. The gods retain their threefold task: they must exorcize the terrors of nature, they must

> reconcile men to the cruelty of Fate, particularly as it is shown in death, and they must compensate them for the sufferings and privations which a civilized life in common has imposed on them.[26]

Freud chose the word "illusion" very carefully, as an illusion is a belief that one wishes to be true; as opposed to a delusion, which is a belief that everyone knows to be untrue.

> Thus we call a belief an illusion when a wish-fulfillment is a prominent factor in its motivation, and in doing so we disregard its relations to reality, just as the illusion itself sets no store by verification.[27]

Despite the fact that Freud was one of the greatest iconoclasts of all time, he may have been a bit wary of coming straight out and saying that everyone who believes in God is delusional. By saying God is an "illusion," he allows himself the retreat of saying that he is not commenting on the nature of the existence of God himself, just on the psychological experience of God.

Richard Dawkins, nearly a century later, would have no qualms about naming his book, *The God Delusion*. Dawkins states that everyone who believes in God is "delusional." As for people who consider themselves "agnostic," people who believe that, while there is no proof of God's existence, there also exists in this eternal and infinite universe the possibility of anything.... Dawkins argues that if the agnostic were forced to state his case in the form of statistical probability (the language of science), he would have to admit that the possibility of the existence of God is so statistically improbable, as to make it statistically insignificant, and therefore not worth the supposition of actually being true. Hence, most agnostics are just wishy-washy atheists, unwilling to make definitive statements that may offend people (like Freud in 1927). Dawkins' argument, however, requires the individual to assume a state of mind towards God that is purely logical, rational, mathematical, scientific, abstract, and free of emotion or sentiment. Such a state of mind, I argue, in-and-of-itself inhibits spiritual perception, and drowns out the sense of the spiritual in a person's mind. The theoretic and abstract manner of thinking required by Dawkins to calculate one's own belief in God is a manner of thinking that will *inhibit* any sense of God. Therefore, the conclusion comes about as a direct result of the thought process invoked. An argument in which one must assume a perspective that inherently supports the desired conclusion is not so much an argument, but a one-sided observation, a circular hypothesis. In a sense, it is similar to the opposing position of the theist: "In order to believe in God, one must *feel* His presence." The state of mind the person must invoke in order to feel God, spiritual perception, requires belief in order to experience it, and will in-and-of-itself result in a specific conclusion, belief. Both arguments are similarly one-sided. Dawkins' argument, however, has more power behind it, at least in our modern society—because while nearly every literate person can assume a position of logical, rational, mathematical, abstract thinking—a great many people simply cannot assume a position of spiritual perception, because it is inhibited by the literal mode of thinking itself. Nevertheless, when reading Freud, it is quite clear that Freud himself believed that religious people are deluding themselves in their false belief in the "illusion" of God.

According to Freud, God is such a powerful psychological force because he is both an illusion created by wish fulfillment, and a projection of an inner need for Father. The father, at the resolution of the Oedipus Complex, is "internalized" or projected inwardly by the son as an internal authority figure, the "superego." This internal moral authority inflicts psychological pain and punishment upon the ego in the form of guilt. In this sense, the "inner father" or superego retains a bit of the ambivalence felt towards the real father in the oedipal stage of development, as the inner father is both loved and feared, a source of both comfort and pain. When the father dies, he is externally projected as a spiritual or divine father ... God. This external projection, since prehistoric times, has been preassembled by society—a strong, caring, judgmental, rule obsessed, occasionally angry father figure—already established and ready to be feared, loved, and obeyed. Freud pointed out that the tendency for gods to be perceived as hostile, jealous, spiteful, aggressive, moody, and destructive, is a vestige of the ambivalence of the son's feelings towards the father in the oedipal stage, when the father was perceived as a rival for mother and as a potentially castrating antagonist. Furthermore, since in a religious society, faith is considered a virtue and spiritual doubt is considered a sin, doubting the existence of God results in guilt, which is the psychological product of the internalized image of the Father/God. Hence, belief in God becomes self-perpetuating, as any sense of disbelief results in guilt and anxiety, which feels bad, while any sense of belief results in guilt or anxiety relief, which feels good.

Freud also famously labeled religion as a "mass obsessional neurosis," a collectively agreed upon means of dealing with existential anxiety. "Devout believers" are "safeguarded" from anxiety and neurosis, because "their acceptance of the universal neurosis spares them the task of constructing a personal one."[28] God, in this view, is the cultural antibiotic for the curse of consciousness, whose bacteria manifests itself in existential anxiety. In a potentially meaningless universe punctuated with inevitable death, God fills the void of meaninglessness with spiritual values. One must either accept the "universal neurosis" of an omnipresent, omniscient, and omnipotent God—or one must be cursed with the individual neurosis of living in a random, meaningless, purposeless universe.

In *Civilization and Its Discontents* (1930), Freud inferred that the feeling of spirituality must be something like "a sensation of 'eternity,' a feeling as of something limitless, unbounded—as it were, 'oceanic.'" He admits openly, "I cannot discover this 'oceanic' feeling in myself." Nevertheless, he insists that the feeling is a wish fulfillment, an illusion, a physical longing for the father projected into a psychical longing for God. In a previous chapter, I proposed a theory of spiritual development that begins before birth, a time when this "oceanic feeling" of spiritual unity with everything—a feeling of deep connection with something eternal and infinite, something that is both within and without of ourselves—was the only sense we had. We seek this womblike "oceanic feeling" in our spiritual lives. The psychological return to a primary state, the re-experience of an "embryonic standpoint of psychic life," as Freud called the dream state, is the basic feeling of spiritual perception that we once felt all the time, and now (as rational post-literate adults), feel rarely, if ever.

In his last book, *Moses and Monotheism* (1939), Freud proposes a radical revisionist version of religious history, which, for the most part, is irrelevant to the topic of spiritual perception, with the exception of one point that he makes near his conclusion. After suggesting that the "early Israelite scribes of Moses had a hand in the invention of the first alphabet,"[29] Freud points to the 2nd of the Ten Commandments as a precept that would have profound implications:

> It is the prohibition against making an image of God, which means the compulsion to worship an invisible God ... [that] signified subordinating sense perception to an abstract idea; it was a triumph of spirituality over the senses....[30]

By outlawing "graven images" of any kind, monotheistic Judaism created a hidden, invisible god, a god that could only be experienced on an abstract, non-sensory level of perception. Freud relates this re-focusing of the spiritual from the sensory to the theoretic to a "belief in the omnipotence of thoughts ... an overestimation of the influence which our mental faculties—the intellectual ones in this case—can exert on the outer world by changing it." This belief came about, Freud argued, as a direct result of Literacy, which represented for mankind a level of mastery over language and thought that it had never experienced before.[31] Literacy promoted an abstract, dematerialized concept of God—an invisible God—while at the same time it promoted a consecration of the literary aspect of God, the Holy Scriptures.[32] Freud believed that monotheism was the product of this "advance in intellectuality."

Freud concluded that one should view religions as artifacts of past mentalities, "neurotic relics" that should be replaced by "the rational operation of the intellect."[33] As for faith and belief, Freud called these attributes "senseless." He contrasted the rather obscure and antiquated Christian "doctrine of absurdity"—"I believe because it is absurd"—to the more modern view of the "absurd"—that which could be considered "nonsense."[34] The old Christian view used the term "absurd" to refer to the spiritual—that which cannot be sensed—because it is metaphysical. The newer Freudian view uses the term "absurd" to refer to the nonsensical, meaning that anything that cannot be sensed, does not exist.

> *Am I to believe every absurdity?*
> ...If the truth of religious doctrines is dependent on an inner experience which bears witness to that truth, what is one to do about the many people who do not have this rare experience?[35]

According to Freud, as society moves more and more towards the deification of pure reason, the absolute belief in that which is "sensible" and that which can be proved to be scientifically, rationally, and observably true, the tolerance for spiritual "absurdity" will precipitously wane.[36] I would like to point out that what Freud refers to as a "rare experience," the inner experience of spiritual perception, is not particularly rare at all. Freud's claim that society was destined to turn away from religion is nearly 90-years-old. If he was right, the "process of growth" towards this "fatal inevitability" is certainly taking its time.

Jung's Spiritual Drive

> It is the role of religion to give a meaning to the life of man.—
> Carl Jung[37]

In terms of the psychology of spirituality, there can be no greater contrast to Freud's theory than the theory of his greatest disciple, Jung. When asked in a 1959 BBC television interview if he believed in God, Carl Jung replied simply: "I don't believe: I know." Jung knew that there was a spiritual dimension to our existence, that it was real (though sometimes he called it "psychologically real"), and that the connection to this dimension was through our own unconscious minds. Dreams, for Jung, rather than being just primordial expressions of animalistic drives and desires, were spiritual expressions of divine significance. The symbols in dreams—the archetypes—were of divine origin, in that they represented the symbolic link between the unconscious mind and the spiritual dimension. The archetypes, far from being regressive, were transcendent; they pointed our minds upwards beyond the ground of our self-centered egos.[38] Nevertheless, while the symbols in dreams allow us to transcend ordinary consciousness, they have their roots in a more primitive, animistic mode of perception, a preliterate mode that has been both abandoned and repressed by modern conscious thought.[39]

Jung believed that the personal sensory experience of God was the only true psychological religious experience, everything else was merely conformity and social engagement. Jung's own personal experiences of God, through dreams and vivid hallucinations, established not only his firm belief, but also his conviction that faith alone was not sufficient to satisfy the "spiritual drive"—the unconscious desire to commune with divinity—which he believed was even more potent than the libido. Though Jung indicated that he did believe in an external metaphysical spirituality, he also stated that this belief was not a necessary or required component of his psychological theory of religion. For Jung, gods are archetypes that dwell in the collective unconscious of every human being, even in the minds of atheists. Archetypes, when they appear in dreams and visions, serve the psychological function of expressing and satisfying the spiritual drive of divine communion and atonement. They represent "the whole spiritual heritage of mankind's evolution, born anew in the brain structure of every individual."[40] Because unconscious archetypes come to us from the figures we perceive in myths, legends, stories, and art, the archetypes inhabit a virtual world that Jung called the "collective unconscious," the unconscious mind's vast storehouse of symbolic images that we share with all humanity.

The archetypal dream or vision has a "transcendent function," in that it allows the individual to transcend his own individual psyche and receive guidance or edification from his own unconscious representation of the divine. Throughout this book, I suggest that digital media and neuro-technology may provide a means of facilitating this transcendent function, by consciously accessing one's own spiritual archetypes—the symbolic images within the unconscious mind—that are typically only experienced while dreaming, and during rare moments of spiritual perception. If this is possible, then digital media could also open up one's unconscious mind to spiritual archetypes from other cultures, from other's people's unconscious minds, and from the "ancestral history" of symbolic imagery that goes back to the Paleolithic cave paintings and beyond. Indeed, digital media could facilitate a true "collective unconscious" of symbolic images—a shared virtual space where unconscious archetypes from around the world and throughout history are encountered and integrated—an ethereal cathedral filled with living spiritual symbols, entered through the cave-like tunnel of the dreaming mind.

Jung insisted that true religious experience is a personal sensory experience, a spiritual encounter with an archetypal image or perception, made possible by the transcendent function. Every other aspect of religion is part of a religious "creed," a "codified and dogmatized form of original religious experience." So, while Jesus had a true religious experience, many of his followers, Christians, have not. If they don't actually see God, or Jesus, or Mary, or any other archetype of the divine, then they are only experiencing the creed of Christianity. While most religious people believe that their faiths provide a medium, structure, or vehicle through which a religious experience can be attained, Jung believed that creeds impose a barrier to psychologically real religious experiences. It is the function of the archetype to break through the barrier of religion, in order to provide a true sensory experience of the spiritual.

Fromm's Forgotten Language

> The language of the universal symbol is the one common tongue developed by the human race, a language which it forgot before it succeeded in developing a universal conventional language.—Erich Fromm[41]

Erich Fromm was one of the first psychoanalysts to focus specifically on existential anxiety. He believed that the average human life is filled with existential "dilemmas," the primary one being the "Human Dilemma." The advent of conscious self-awareness in humans precipitated an existential crisis, because the self-conscious human can no longer live a purely instinctual life, as he did when he was a preconscious beast. The state of "original harmony with nature" experienced by animals is no longer available to humanity. The end of the instinctual life and the dawn of the conscious life means that the human "has to live his life, he is not lived by it. He is in nature, yet he transcends nature."[42] The leap forward into consciousness was followed by a sense of exile from Nature, a theme that was interpreted by Fromm as a graceful allegory in the Biblical tale of the Garden of Eden. When Adam and Eve ate the forbidden fruit, "the eyes of both of them were unclosed, and they knew that they were naked" (Genesis 3:7). They had become consciously self-aware, a revelation that stripped away both their sense of security in existence, and their inherent connection with Nature, hence their exile from Eden.

The anxiety evoked by the Human Dilemma gives rise to a variety of "Existential Needs," such as the need for "Relatedness," a drive for union with others, so that the self-conscious ego doesn't feel alone and isolated in his private inner world of solipsistic mind-space, his interior "kingdom of mind." Another existential need results in the drive towards "Transcendence," the desire to rise above ordinary passive existence in order to regain a sense of connection with something that is bigger than ourselves, the need to regain what was lost when self-conscious awareness cut ourselves off from Nature. There is also a need for a "Frame of Orientation," a personal philosophy or guiding theory. Self-conscious awareness gives rise to the notion that there needs to be a reason to live, a meaning to life. Solipsistic awareness—I exist because I exist, and nothing more—is insufficient to quench the thirst for meaning induced by existential anxiety. An "object of devotion," something outside of ourselves, is needed as a focal point, something that gives us a source of meaning in life, a channel for getting in touch with that which is meaningful, and a goal for our projection of meaning, a target that receives our outpouring of devotion. Fromm believed that an inherent "spiritual drive" has the capacity to satisfy all of these existential needs. It pushes us towards relation to others, even spiritual others. It prompts us to transcend ourselves, giving us a sense of unity or oneness with the divine. It frames our existence within a mantel of spiritual meaning that offers a sense of security, safety, belongingness, and oneness with an entity that is perceived as external, eternal, and infinite; yet also loving, embracing, nurturing, and intrinsically connected with ourselves.

In his book, *The Forgotten Language* (1951), Fromm focuses on the "universal symbols" found in dreams, fairytales, and myths. Like Jung, Fromm saw the connecting principle behind these shared symbols in the premise that the unconscious mind speaks in a symbolic language that precedes verbal language, both historically and neurologically.

> The dreams of ancient and modern man are written in the same language as the myths whose authors lived in the dawn of history.... Symbolic language is a language in which inner experiences, feelings and thoughts are expressed as if they were sensory experiences, events in the outer world.... It is the one universal language the human race has ever developed, the same for all cultures and throughout history.[43]

Like Jung, Fromm linked the function of the "forgotten language" to the "spiritual drive." There is an inherently spiritual core to dreams and myths, one that is sensed rather than construed.[44]

Frankl's Spiritual Unconscious

> The fundamental anthropological truth [is] that self-transcendence is one of the basic features of human existence.—Viktor E. Frankl[45]

In his book, *The Unconscious God* (1975), Viktor Frankl delineated three dimensions of human nature: the physical, the psychological, and the spiritual. He distinguished between the psychological and the spiritual by asserting that spirituality resided in a special part of the unconscious mind—the "spiritual unconscious"—whose function was to inspire existential meaning in a person's life. A survivor of the Holocaust, Frankl observed first-hand what true suffering was. In the concentration camp, he saw men fall into "despair," which he defined as "suffering without meaning."[46] The men who fell into despair soon withered and died. The men who could somehow find meaning in their existence, even within the living Hell of the concentration camp, retained the strength and resilience to live. The meaning they found, which was always spiritual in nature, allowed them to transcend their suffering and their horrific surroundings. According to Frankl, life without a deep sense of meaning is an "existential vacuum,"[47] which can never be filled with purely physical pleasures and distractions. Only the deep sense of meaning attained through a connection with one's own spiritual unconscious can fill up the existential vacuum. In Frankl's view, the "will to meaning," the instinct to search for and find meaning in one's life, regardless of the circumstances, is the source of, the means to, and the endpoint of spirituality.[48]

Maslow's Peak Experience

> The intrinsic core, the essence, the universal nucleus of every known high religion, has been the private, lonely, personal illumination, revelation or ecstasy of some acutely sensitive prophet or seer.—Abraham Maslow[49]

Abraham Maslow delineated two two types of religious personalities: the "peaker" and the "non-peaker." Peak experiences are mystical experiences that are indicated by the same qualities as William James' mystical state of consciousness. These experiences are passive, receptive experiences that convey a sense of transcendence as well as an awe inspiring feeling of unity or connection with a "God-like" entity. While the peak experience is a direct and personal revelation of some higher truth, the experience itself is ineffable.[50] As for the "non-peaker," his truth is the acceptance and obedience to the structure inspired by another person's peak experience. He is not open to peak experiences, because he fears the loss of control associated with it—he's unwilling or unable to dive deep into the dark waters in order to experience the "oceanic" feeling of cosmic unity—and he is resistant to being swept up by the waves of "irrational emotions," which are the hallmark of a peak experience. Maslow found that non-peakers tended to be "ultra-scientific."[51] Perhaps the difference between the religious personalities is not necessarily a question of "type," but of choice. One must be open to the possibility of a new experience and open to the potential of a new perception in order to have the experience. If one is not open to the possibility of perceiving life in a new way, then the cognitive door to that form of perception is shut.[52]

Maslow is most famous for his model of the "hierarchy of needs," visually framed as the "pyramid of needs." Though Maslow didn't directly apply his pyramid model to peak experiences, I think the two theories are relatable. As peoples' needs change, their perception of God changes. At the base of the pyramid, when physiological needs are dominant, we see a practical god—a god who could be summoned directly for specific purposes—such as the falling of rain for the crops, the appearance of game for the hunter, or the growth of corn for the harvest. In preliterate societies, where subsistence living is the norm, every aspect of survival is controlled by the spirits. People in these societies can directly control the natural forces that they depend upon for survival, because they have direct access to the spirits that either control or embody the natural forces.

At the next level of Maslow's pyramid, when physiological needs are consistently satisfied but safety needs are dominant, we see a more detached god, who is only called upon intermittently, in times of need. God is supplicated to cure the ill, destroy the enemy, or to grant favor or good fortune in times of uncertainty. Thus we see the phenomenon of religiosity surging in times of crisis. "There are no atheists in foxholes." The fear of death can evoke the spiritual side of the most secular of thinkers. On September 11th, 2001, after witnessing the Twin Towers fall from a viewpoint in downtown Manhattan, my wife—a devout atheist—expressed the desperate need to go to church. This was, I assure you, a very rare regression to her Irish Catholic childhood.

Once we feel consistently safe and sound, we rise to the next level of Maslow's hierarchy, where belongingness needs dominate. At this level, God is equated with Love, and is therefore expressed and experienced as Love. *The Cloud of Unknowing,* a Middle Age text of Christian mysticism, expressed the notion that God can only be felt through Love:

> For He can well be loved, but he cannot be thought.
> By love he can be grasped and held, but by thought, neither grasped nor held.

The God of Love is an interpersonal God. He teaches us to love our neighbors and our family, to love and accept ourselves, and to share our lives, our traditions, and our bounty with others around us. Even if you are alone, "Jesus loves you." If you are lost, "Mother Mary will show you the way home." If you are empty, commune with God, atone with God, and He will fill you up with love. The God of Love is all about community, family, and tradition. He is the interpersonal connection that fills churches and temples, and assures us that the "family who prays together, stays together."

At the next level of the hierarchy of needs, there are esteem and self-actualization needs. These needs are not easily channeled into external drives, because they involve the manner in which the ego regards itself. Esteem involves feeling proud of oneself, while self-actualization is the process of reaching one's own true potential, which typically involves finding a meaningful purpose in life. The abstract self-relatedness of these "higher order needs" involve meta-self-consciousness, reflection on one's self from a 3rd person perspective. A peak experience, in essence, provides that moment of meta-self-conscious reflection, through the encounter and integration of a spiritual "other," which is essentially a perception of a deeper sense of self. This moment of meta-self-conscious reflection, however, can only occur as an intuitive experience, not through deliberate intellectual reasoning. Rational conscious reflection, according to my theory, would be inhibitive to spiritual perception, i.e., the "peak experience." Hence, the peak experience provides the peaker with the same sense of esteem and self-actualization that non-peakers must sweat and toil over for years to achieve deliberately. The sense of personal fulfillment that the peak experience affords: the sense that God loves you, that you are intrinsically connected with him, that God has a special plan for you, that he has chosen to grace you with his presence because you are special, that you have firsthand knowledge of a universal truth that few people have been offered ... are feelings that would certainly enhance someone's sense of esteem, and make them feel "self-actualized" to the highest degree. This sense of having an inherent and unquestionable meaning to one's existence—the lack of which, for non-peakers, is the primary barrier to self-actualization—comes to peakers without the slightest effort at all (and with no psychiatrist bill either).

The Digital Peak

> When we are well and healthy and adequately fulfilling the concept "human being," then experiences of transcendence should in principle be commonplace.—Abraham Maslow

The common thread between all of the theories discussed in this chapter is that spirituality does not serve purely communal or practical purposes—it is born of experience—and seems to fulfill a basic human need to transcend our normal existence and encounter something beyond ourselves. However, many people cannot experience spiritual perception, because, for them, the door to this mode of perception has been closed. Belief in the spiritual can mold our perceptions, pulling open the door of spiritual perception. However, many people have no sense of belief in the spiritual, leaving them stranded on the closed side of the perceptual door, with no way of opening it. Digital technology, however, may provide the key to this door. Digital media combined with neuropsychological stimulation can elicit a real perception of a virtual god, thereby overcoming the inhibition of spiritual perception due to both cognitive constraints and the lack of spiritual belief. In the Digital Age, when everyone expects everything instantaneously, few people are willing or able to climb the "peak" of spiritual practice and discipline that leads to an experience of spiritual insight. And in the days of managed healthcare insurance, few people will be able to pay for years of psychoanalysis or psychotherapy in search of personal "self-actualization." The healthcare system in the 21st century will be stretched beyond its limits caring for the skyrocketing population of elderly people. It's projected that the number of elderly Americans suffering from Alzheimer's Disease alone will reach 14 million by the year 2050. So, unless you're diagnosed with a clinical psychiatric disorder or substance abuse problem, ongoing high quality mental healthcare in the future will only be affordable to the rich. A Digital Peak, however, could be accessed instantly, without requiring years of meditation, disciplined self-abnegation, spiritual study, psychotherapy, or psychoanalysis. The Digital Age will be the age of virtual psychiatry, on-demand religion, and instant God.

But what will be accessed or retrieved via this on-demand digital system of religious experience? The same content that has always been delivered through the medium of spirituality ... the archetypes of the unconscious mind. Jung, Fromm, Joseph Campbell, Mircea Eliade, and dozens of others envisioned archetypes as a "picture language" of the soul, a language of visual symbols that precede verbal thought both cognitively and evolutionarily. The archetypes are expressed unconsciously in our dreams, and are consciously reflected back to us through the largely unconscious mirror of myth, poetry, art, story, and song. "Myths are the collective dream, just as dreams are the individual myths."[53] According to Jung, the encounter and integration of the archetype in the dream performs a "transcendent function," by allowing us to bypass the conscious word of thought, in order to get straight to the internal image that unifies us with our own selves, typically through a symbol of the divine. The vision of the archetype in the dream state is a moment of cognitive-perceptual unity, because the symbol is not analyzed with words, but simultaneously perceived and understood as a spiritual message. "The archetype is a retrieved awareness or consciousness.... It represents or personifies certain instinctive data of the dark primitive psyche; the real, the invisible *roots of consciousness.*"[54]

The virtual peak experience achieved via digital media will allow the user to simultaneously create and revere his own virtual archetypes. After initiating a state of semi-conscious awareness, the system will provide a virtual reality environment in which archetypes are encountered. The form and function of the archetypes are up to the user. It could be an object of devotion, a figure that evokes respect, admiration, love, or fear, a holy image, an inspiring message ... anything! If desired, archetypal images or religious icons that reside in the collective unconscious of a common religion could be prompted to appear in the Digital Peak. This could be done in a number of ways.

On a simple level, prerecorded archetypal images and icons could simply be projected by the digital media system through the helmet, to be perceived by the user. Less simply, archetypal images and icons that exist within the dreamer's own unconscious mind could be elicited through mental associations that evoke the symbols from the memory and imagination of the dreamer himself. This method works according to the "associative" process of unconscious memory, which is not necessarily logical or linear. Consider psychoanalytic techniques like "free association" or the Rorshach tests used by psychoanalysts. One random word or ambiguous ink blot evokes an idea or image, and then another random word or ambiguous image leads to another idea or image, and so on. Because the words and images being used to elicit the associations are random and ambiguous, it is really the unconscious mind that is filling in the blanks, projecting its own content into the ambiguous stimuli, and unintentionally making the mental connections between the associations. Soon, the psychoanalyst will see a "pattern" in the associations, pointing to a repressed feeling or neurotic issue. Incidentally, many people tend to see spiritual images in ambiguous stimuli, such as the image of Mary on a potato chip, Jesus on a piece of toast, or Elvis on a Pop-Tart.

In the Digital Peak, the system itself will fulfill the role of the psychoanalyst. The system will begin by projecting random or ambiguous images to elicit mental images in the user, "associations." As the process continues, the system will gauge the user's brain waves, his autonomic responses, and the areas of the brain that are being activated, while it simultaneously keeps track of the images that are being perceived by the user. In this way, the digital psychiatrist can attain a very accurate sense of archetypal themes or "patterns" in the associations, it can tell which association patterns evoke strong spiritual feelings, and it can tailor the images and the entire virtual environment towards a meaningful spiritual encounter. Using its data bank of limitless images, and its infinite processing potential, the system will trace and follow the patterns of associations, providing images that are increasingly evocative of the user's spiritual perception. Advanced systems will be able to record the actual mental images inside the user's mind, add those images to its bank, and use them in the process of associations. The more the user engages in this process, the more data the system has on the users association patterns, and the more images it has in its data bank to guide the association process towards a peak spiritual experience.

At the optimal moment in the process, a specific archetypal image would be projected by the media system, just as a strong sense of spiritual perception is triggered in the mind of the user, using electro-neural stimulation of specific areas of the brain. A moment of intense spiritual awareness will occur. This is the "peak phase" of the experience. Prerecorded sounds, music, or verbal messages may be especially effective at this moment, particularly if the user is in a lucid dream state, as hearing is not inhibited during the dream state, while external vision (because the eyes tend to close), usually is inhibited. If desired, the user could program the media to synchronize the entire experience to a specific piece of music; or he could program the media to project a specific verbal message to him at the peak moment in his dream.

In many ways, the Digital Peak would be doing the job of the traditional psychoanalyst or psychotherapist. Benefits of this form of digital psychoanalysis are that no appointments are necessary, sessions could be done at your own home, there are no worries about insurance reimbursement, no limits on the number of sessions that the user can engage in, no set time limit or "50-minute hour" as there is with a real psychoanalyst, and most importantly, no fee! In addition, there's no fear that the analyst will judge or ridicule the user, allowing the user to release his inner feelings with complete freedom and abandon.

Indeed, because the user is in a semi-conscious state, the inhibition of conscious thought would be primarily overcome by the process itself.

Beyond the notion of just getting in touch with one's inner feelings, repressed memories, and suppressed anxieties, the transcendent function of the Digital Peak will enable the user to transcend his own personal ego, to encounter a spiritual aspect of his own psyche. The Digital Peak can also perform the self-actualizing function of Maslow's conceptual peak experience. The user will go beyond his "ordinary state of consciousness" in order to experience a moment of "creative self consciousness,"[55] a moment in which the user is creating his own sense of existential meaning. The user will experience an "ecstasy"—an "ec-sta-sis"—a "stepping out" of his normal state of existence, in order to get a glimpse of the "higher order" issues in his life. The Digital Peak can help the user get in touch with his own spiritual self, and help him define his identity in a way that gives substance and direction to his existence. If desired, it will also enable him to transcend his own personal mind—to encounter the archetypes of other people's spiritual unconscious—within the virtual cathedral of the digitalized mind.

CHAPTER SIX

The Philosophy of Spiritual Perception and Spiritual Networking

> By the meaningless sign linked to the meaningless sound we have built the shape and meaning of Western man.—Marshall McLuhan[1]

In *The Origin and Goal of History* (1949), Karl Jaspers coined the term "Axial Age" within the following context: "the axis of history is to be found in the period around 500 BC, in the spiritual process that occurred between 800 and 200 BC.... Man, as we know him today, came into being."[2] What Jaspers was referring to was a "revolution" in thinking that occurred at around the same time in many different places around the world, that drastically changed forever the way we constructed our cognitive models of the world. What changes in human society could have brought about such a significant revolution?[3] In human history, revolutions—changes in *kind* rather than *degree*—come about only as a result of the introduction of a game changing new force in the field. The breakthroughs of the Axial Age came about as a result of a new *kind* of thinking, not as a result of a higher *degree* of thinking.[4] In this case, the game changer was Literacy.

Philosophy as a discipline of thought comes of age with literacy. When we think of philosophy, our tendency might be to think of philosophers such as Socrates, who engaged in oral arguments with students or anyone else who happened to be around. However, the type of thinking that is required for philosophical thought *demands* literacy as a prerequisite. Only when words are written down can they be clearly separated, analyzed logically, and manipulated in order to develop syllogisms.[5] Although we may be able to think logically and speak logically, these abilities come about as natural tendencies of thought, only *after* our minds have been programmed to "see" our thoughts clearly, linearly, and sequentially. Before we can think logically our brains have to be configured to "see" logical symbols such as words in our minds' eye. Literacy creates the possibility of objectivity because it turns words into objects which can be seen, held down, grasped, and inspected within the confines of a page.[6]

The Via Negativa

> We do not know what God is.
> God Himself does not know what He is because He is not anything.
> Literally God *is not*, because He transcends being.
> —John Scotus Erigena, 9th century BC

In the centuries following the life and death of Jesus, the movement of the mind towards the outer limits of abstraction among the most literate of the literate elite, resulted in a "God of the Theologians," who was almost entirely abstract, and who would have been completely anathema to the masses, if only they could have understood what the theologians were writing about. As medieval theologians struggled to comprehend and define a God that was neither seen nor heard, neither tasted nor smelt—who was only vaguely felt, though not in a physical, tactile sense—they came upon a new path to Him, the "Via Negativa."[7] This inward path of introspective spirituality led theologians straight into nothing....

The "negative way" is not a path of denial. To the contrary, it is an attempt to categorically affirm the existence of a God who could not be perceived via the positive experience of the senses. However, as a first step, the path assumes that God cannot be known on any objective physical level. God is purely spiritual, purely metaphysical, purely transcendent of the earthly plane. As a consequence, it is not only impossible to have a direct experience of God—it is impossible to have any concrete *knowledge* of God. All that we experience is that we cannot directly experience Him, all that we perceive is that we cannot directly perceive Him, all that we know is that we cannot know Him. Hence, in defining God, all we are left with are the negative qualities, that which we do not know.

The Via Negativa has dominated the more cerebral areas of theology from early Greek philosophers all the way down to modern existentialists, such as Paul Tillich. The problem is, in negating the know-ability of God, we negate the possibility of experiencing God on any meaningful level other than as a purely abstract, intellectual concept. Once God becomes nothing more than a concept—"nothing"—he ceases to exist on the perceptual level, becoming "nothing." Though God could still be understood as a symbol, a symbol that is understood as a symbol is a broken symbol. It no longer has any spiritual power. So, while the theologians who tread the Via Negativa did so with the intention of affirming God's existence, the path itself does not lead to God, it leads nowhere.

While the elite of the literate elite travelled the dead end of the Via Negativa, the common Christian continued worshipping a personal God in ways that were not so different from his prehistoric ancestors. As the pagan sacrificial and orgiastic rites were slowly but steadily subdued and syncretized[8] by the Roman Catholic Church, the Christian worshipper was provided a sensory-emotional spiritual experience that rivaled any pre–Christian ritual. To begin with, the cathedrals being constructed were tantamount in workmanship and sheer monumental power as the Iron Age monolithic structures assembled for the divine kings of old. For a peasant living in a village in which no manmade structure was much higher than the head of a tall man, the massive cathedral in-and-of-itself was a spiritual sight to behold, a living testament to the majesty of God, and to the reverence with which God was held amongst his people. Once inside, the gothic architecture soaring upwards to the heavens, the rich tapestries, the shimmering stained glass panels, created a sense of mystery and awe that rivaled the holy spaces of any Paleolithic cavern or Iron Age tomb. The vivid iconography in the frescoes and sculptures all revealed an elaborate and deeply meaningful mythos that was quite necessary for the congregants, who were illiterate. Let Basil and Aquinas scrawl their manuscripts on their concepts of an unknowable, un-seeable God—99 percent of the people living in their age couldn't read their scripts—and 99 percent of the people who could read probably had no idea what the hell the negative theologians were talking about. But for the common Christian, God was right there, in the cathedral, anthropomorphically represented in stained glass and painted on the walls. In God's house, enveloped by the angelic harmonies of the choir and the mesmerizing fugal labyrinths of the organ, immersed in the enchanting aromas of the incense and candles, surrounded by the awe-inspiring images of God himself, drawn physically upwards by the architecture and spiritually inwards by the esoteric enigma of the Latin prayers and hymns, intoxicated by the taste of God's blood-wine and overwhelmed by the communal force of devotion and zeal.... How could one *not* see and hear God?

The Birth of Atheism

The statues have become stone corpses from which the living soul has flown....
The actual life-world in which they exist is no longer there....
Georg Wilhelm Friedrich Hegel, 1807[9]

Before the Enlightenment, true atheism was an impossibility.[10] Every aspect of life was draped in religious obligation, every moment of life was lived under the shadow of the Church, and under the eye of an all-knowing God. Language itself, the fabric of conscious thought, did not allow for the notion of atheism until quite recently. "Such words as "absolute," "relative," "causality," "concept," and "intuition" were not yet in use."[11] In the 16th, 17th, and 18th Centuries, the term "atheist" was used as a sort of religious insult, referring to anyone who transgressed moral/religious norms, had divergent moral/religious ideas, or in any way disagreed, in word or by action, with another person's idea of what godliness is supposed to be. "Nobody would have dreamed of calling *himself* an atheist."[12] Below, Karen Armstrong quotes a typical use of the word "atheist" in the late 16th century:

> ...the hypocrite is an Atheist; the loose wicked man is an open Atheist, the secure, bold and proud transgressor is an Atheist: he that will not be taught or reformed is an Atheist.[13]

Prior to the 19th century, it seems that the only thing the term "atheist" did *not* refer to was a person who did not believe in God. That sort of person simply could not yet exist at that time. An atheist in the 16th century would have been like a mathematical genius in the early Neolithic Age, before math as a subject was invented. Without the language of math (numerals, logical symbols, abstract representations), mathematical thinking is impossible. Similarly, without the language of reason—literacy—atheistic thinking is impossible.

Not surprisingly, it was a mathematical genius, Blaise Pascal (1623–1662), who first published some thoughts on atheism as a feasible mindset, remarking that in an age where logical deductions about our world are based on observable data, the belief in the existence of God may be no more than a matter of personal choice. However, it is no small irony that Pascal himself underwent an extremely vivid and intense spiritual experience at the age of 31, in which he realized that the god that was meaningful and certain was not the god "of philosophers." On November 23, 1654, Pascal experienced a revelatory vision, which he called his "night of fire."

> From about half-past 10:00 in the evening until about half-past 12:00.
> FIRE.
> The God of Abraham, the God of Isaac, the God of Jacob.
> Not of the philosophers and intellectuals.
> Certitude, certitude, feeling, joy, peace.

This revelation was, perhaps, a sort of psychological abreaction towards his own feelings of guilt for having atheistic thoughts. A gift of certainty to a mind plagued by doubt. There's usually a price to be paid for thinking ahead of one's time. For Galileo, the price was paid in prison. For Pascal, the price was paid with guilt and psychological torment, recorded in his theological writings, the *Pensées*, in which he divulges a wager that he, and by abstraction, all reasonable minds, must make. Pascal's famous wager is this:

> You must wager on the answer to a question.
> You have no choice, you must wager.
> You are wagering your entire life on the outcome.
> There are only 2 choices and 1 outcome.
> The question will never be answered in your lifetime, you will only find out the true answer after you die.
> The question is this: "Does God exist?"
> If you say "yes," God does exist, then you win infinite peace and happiness.
> If you say "no," God does not exist, then you lose everything that is potentially meaningful in life.
> What will you choose?

According to Pascal, any "reasonable" person would choose "yes," even if there's no observable or logical proof to support that answer, because there's everything to gain and nothing to lose. Thus, the existence of God is supported (somewhat), by reason.

The Enlightenment was based on a vision, a shared ideal among educated literate people about a world governed by reason, rather than superstition, fear, and delusion. Such a world had never existed until that time, and it could be argued that such a world has yet to exist. But the "scientific spirit" of the day promised a brave new world of enlightened thinking. Enlightenment did *not* mean the abandonment of God. It meant a different view of God, a reasonable, logical view. The Bible, when read as a literal narrative, makes little sense. Thus, the God of the Bible would have to go.[14] The new God would be "Deus," and his religion was called "Deism." Deus was not anthropomorphic like the Biblical god. Deus was the embodiment of reason upon which the governing principles of the universe were created, he was more of a concept than a being. He was "impersonal," detached, and disinterested in human affairs.[15] The universe was "intelligently designed" by Deus, but whatever Deus was, he is no longer physically present.[16] Nevertheless, his intellect is manifest in the fruits of his creation.... Nature, and the immutable Laws of Nature. So, if this is the case, then any form of ritual, such as prayer, is pointless, because there's no God there to hear one's prayers. And what happens if one abandons ritual and prayer? Religion divorced from ritual becomes an empty vessel of dogma and beliefs, because without the spiritual perception that is evoked through ritual—without the *experience* of God—there might as well be no God at all.[17]

Although he wasn't appreciated in his time, Baruch Spinoza, in retrospect, was arguably the most advanced philosopher in the early years of the Enlightenment. Perhaps because he was a Jew living in a Christian world, Spinoza was used to being an outsider, and was therefore less afraid of expressing heretical views.

(Spinoza was excommunicated by his Jewish community, and his books were banned by the Catholic Church.) Spinoza believed that God was not necessarily the creator of the physical laws of the universe, but rather he was "inherent and immanent in all things—material and spiritual." Hence: "If God cannot be separated from anything else, it is impossible to say that "He" exists in any ordinary sense."[18] If God is not perceived as an "other," if He is part of everything, than what exactly is He? How can we point to any distinct thing that could be experienced as God? Spinoza's philosophy brings us to the brink of atheism, the level of abstraction in which there is nothing other than a purely conceptual God, a concept that does not exist as a specific being or entity in any physical or spiritual sense.

To refer to the religion of medieval Jews and Christians as 'monotheism' is preposterous. These people lived in a world filled with spirits of every sort and variety. Demons who invaded your dreams or killed your baby in his sleep, trolls and fairies who inhabited your gardens and fields, imps and elves who disturbed your livestock, ghosts in houses and graveyards, angels in the heavens and also at your crossroads ... a plethora of spiritual beings that were everywhere all the time. The spirit world (inclusive of God and angels), was the cause of every sickness and every cure, the reason behind every disaster and the force behind every boon, the life force behind every birth and the death force behind every grim reaping. In the symbolism of the Trinity, in particular, we see the massive rift between the abstract perception of God among the theologians, and the concrete perception of God among the people. For the theologian, writing in the library of his secluded monastery or university, the Trinity was a metaphor for the ultimate un-know-ability of God.[19] To the people, however, the Trinity represented nothing short of three divine figures—all with *personal* personalities—real *beings* who could all be related to individually. God the Father: Protector, Creator, powerful Master of the Universe. Jesus the Son: Hero, Mentor, the guiding light in the darkness. And Mother Mary: Comforter, Nurturer, Healer of all wounds. It's no wonder that, amongst these three, Mary was the divine figure that was by far seen the most, heard the most, and prayed to the most, when the common Christian needed divine help. What the theologians had begun to call "idolatry," was simply the only way that the common Christian could conceive of God. If God was not physical, if God could not be seen or heard, felt as a real presence, then God did not exist. Indeed, if God could not be real in the sense that you could experience him directly and that his presence could have a direct impact on your life, then what was the purpose of his existence in the first place? If God was not really real in the physical sense, then he was not real at all, and might as well not exist. On the other hand, intellectual concepts, to the illiterate peasant, were *not real*, because for the most part, they were inconceivable. Intellectual distinctions between monotheism and polytheism, Christianity and paganism, idolatry and negative theology, was just so much mumbo-jumbo. What the people wanted and needed was living, breathing, seeable, hearable, knowable gods.

Oral cultures, "tribal cultures," survive by the total commitment of each self to the collective agency of the group. Individuality is not frowned upon, it's *impossible*. The person who commits all acts within a group context, who speaks and hears all words within the context of a group, who thinks all thoughts within the "groupthink" of a collective, can harbor no true concept of an individual self. The fabric of tribal society, the Mythos of symbolic words and acts, is only meaningful within the context of a unified group. The thinking required to accept unwaveringly the effectiveness of religious rituals and the absolute truth of religious beliefs—groupthink—begins to unravel when the technology of individualism transforms thinking itself. Literacy and, in particular, print technology, make true individualism possible.[20] Individualistic thinking becomes like a loose strand in the fabric of collective thought. When pulled, the loose strand begins to unravel the whole fabric. Print technology weaves in this loose strand. It formalizes the distinction between an oral culture and a literate culture, as the technology itself serves to internalize and therefore "individualize" the mind of the reader, detaching or "detribalizing" the mind from a collective mentality.[21]

The portability of the book also promotes detachment from the group: physically, socially, and intellectually. At the same time, it promotes detachment from the self.[22] The literate mode of thinking requires deep focus in a singular modality—focusing solely on these words on the page—to the exclusion of other modes of perception and other aspects of awareness. The result is a split in the psyche, caused by the active inhibition of all modes of conscious awareness other than language based consciousness. The literate individual capable of this form of cerebral detachment begins to perceive his world through the dissecting lens of secularism. He recognizes the spiritual not as a physical phenomenon that really exists, but as a metaphysical symbol which represents something that really doesn't exist. At the societal level, a growing population of split-minded individuals creates a rift between the segment of society that wants to remain faithful to its spiritual, political, moral, and cultural traditions, and the segment that chooses to abandon old traditions and demand individual rights and freedoms.

At the same time that literacy-bred individualism was sparking atheistic and secularist movements across Europe, various movements arose in the 19th and 20th centuries to revive Christianity by preaching and practicing more personal, visceral, intuitive, and hands-on forms of religious belief and service. Mormonism, Pentecostalism, Christian Science, and Evangelicalism are but a few of these movements. A God conceptualized in completely abstract form is of no use to an average person, whose theological needs require a physical sense of comfort in the sensed presence of a spiritual being.[23] The new revivalist movements in Christianity, as well as the contemporary Hasidic movement in Judaism, satisfied this need. The new movements also read the Holy Scriptures with an "unprecedented literalism."[24] By placing God firmly in the "book," and then deifying the book to the level of God himself, the new literalized God was made more real and present in the lives and churches of his worshippers.

The Birth of the Unconscious

> Most of us have consigned to the unconscious all the fantastic psychic associations that every object or idea possesses.—Carl Jung

> The unconscious is a direct creation of print technology, the ever-mounting slag-heap of rejected awareness.—Marshall McLuhan

Consciousness—the awareness of one's own thoughts—is a very tiny part of cognition. Nevertheless, consciousness, no matter how small it may be, is *everything*. That is, consciousness is the only thing that we are truly aware of. In that sense, though consciousness is small in size—like the 1 percent of Americans who control over 90 percent of America's wealth—it is immensely powerful. Consciousness conveys our sense of existence to ourselves, and all that is unconscious is more-or-less non-existent to the conscious mind.

An example may be helpful here.... Say you are driving a car. What are you doing as a driver? Your eyes watch the road, your hand rests on the wheel, and your foot controls the brake and gas. You are "driving," but who is controlling all of the myriad other functions that are going on in order for the car to operate? Who is churning the transmission? Who is spinning the driveshaft? Who is channeling the will of the steering wheel to the wheels of the car? Who is channeling the volition of the gas pedal to the engine and then to the tires? Who is channeling the will of the brake pedal to the brake pads? Who is monitoring the engine temperature, the gasoline level, the engine oil level, the tire inflation level, etc? Well, the car is doing all of that. The auto-mobile functions autonomously. You, the driver, are blissfully unaware of these myriad of functions, unless an unwelcome red light flashes on the dashboard, and then, suddenly, consciousness is drawn in to awareness of the hitherto unconscious inner functioning of the automobile.

To extend this analogy one more level, other than driving, what are you actually doing? How much consciousness is actually involved in driving? Your eyes are aware of the road, but only as much as necessary for safe driving. Your hand on the wheel and your foot on the pedal, in most experienced drivers, function more-or-less autonomously. All drivers have had the experience of "absentmindedly" missing an exit on the highway while driving home, or of arriving home without even being aware of the time spent driving. Some people, especially under the influence of Ambien, even drive while asleep! Where is consciousness when we are driving? Typically, it is busy in conversation with a passenger, or (illegally) on the phone, or in conversation with itself, or it is listening to the radio, or it is thinking about the nature of consciousness, etc. Far from being asleep at the wheel, the driver's *usual state* is unconsciousness. The conscious mind is off somewhere else. Oftentimes it is not even in the car.

So what is meant by "the birth of the unconscious?" It begins with an increasing awareness of one's own conscious thoughts, not just as passing fancies, but as real concrete concepts that could be plucked from the mind like fruit and written down on paper. The visualization of thought objectifies consciousness. Literacy turns ideas into visual objects, making them concrete, because the thoughts themselves could be seen in the mind, extracted from the mind, written down, and then seen as objective realities on the page.[25] In the Print Age, our thoughts in word format became real objects. At the same time, the conscious mind detached itself from non-literal modes of awareness (thoughts that are not in word format). These "unconscious" thoughts suddenly become unlike objects. They were "nonobjective." They seem surreal, "unreal." What were previously experienced as intuitive perceptions—the sense of being at one with Nature, the sense of being metaphysically connected with other animals and humans, the sense of being in the presence of the spiritual—all become "unconscious," because the conscious mind has detached itself from these modes of awareness. And what the conscious is detached from, what the conscious is unaware of, by default becomes "unconscious."[26]

What McLuhan refers to as the "slag-heap of rejected awareness" is actually the essence of spirituality! The unconscious was never born. It existed eons before consciousness. But when consciousness grasped the reigns of cognition and perception and detached itself from intuition, that which was not conscious—the "unconscious"—was then perceived as something other than our conscious selves ... the stranger in our dreams, the shadow in the corner of our awareness, the sense of a spiritual presence—our mystifying interior doppelganger—the sentient other.

Thus we reach a stage of cognitive abstraction, a point of detachment from our own perceptual intuition, where it becomes necessary to call attention to the very existence of the unconscious to our conscious minds. This task of introspection, first taken on by poets, novelists, and artists, was eventually seized upon by psychologists such as Sigmund Freud and Carl Jung. It is at this age, when the literally oriented conscious mind has been driven to the extremes of abstraction by literacy, that we find a sudden self-awareness of a sense of disconnection from the spiritual. For some intellectuals in the "Age of Enlightenment," this sense of disconnection led to a denial of the spiritual as just another bit of "rejected awareness" to be thrown onto the "slag-heap." For others, it led to a reconsideration of spirituality, and a reaffirmation of what spirituality means to human beings.

The Birth of Faith

> You cannot tread the path of spirituality and the path of reason; you must choose between them.—E. O. Wilson

Faith as a religious phenomenon began as a direct result of the Enlightenment, otherwise known as the "Age of Reason." The English word "reason" is derived from the French word "raison" which is a translation of the Latin word "ratio" which is a translation of the Greek word "logos." The Age of Reason quite literally refers to the age in which the mentality of Logos finally succeeded in subduing the archaic mentality of Mythos. Reason, *Logos*, is objective; as opposed to *Mythos*, which is a more subjective way of looking at the world, based on personal beliefs. Objectivism begins with a reliance on sense perception: "Seeing is believing." Ironically, this rudimentary form of reason is quite open to spiritual perception, because sense perception is heavily influenced by our beliefs. Though we are not aware of it, we see what we believe, because vision is created in the mind, not the eyes, and our mind is extremely creative in its interpretation of sensory input. However, as reasoning becomes more abstract, it realizes that sense perception is faulty, because it is prone to illusion, delusion, hallucination, dreams, and all other sorts of false impressions. For instance, though our eyes tell us that the world is flat, a reasonable person will tell you that the world is actually round. Your eyes are wrong: Seeing is *not* believing. And, if you happen to be flying a plane over the ocean in very bad weather, and you can either believe your eyes, that perceive the horizon in front of you, or you can believe your instruments, that tell you that you are flying straight down into the ocean, you had better believe your instruments and not your eyes, or a watery grave will soon be your fate![27]

A higher order of reasoning aims to detach itself from irrational sense perception, relying instead on principles of logical deduction: "Deducing is believing." This conscious movement away from the senses and towards abstract reasoning results in even more inhibition of spiritual perception. When there is a direct connection between sense perception and cognition, our mind's interpretation of sensory input is derived to a large degree by our expectations and beliefs. There is cognitive-perceptual unity. Hence, if you look up at the heavens believing in God, wanting to see God, and expecting to see God, you are very likely to perceive God. But when perception and cognition are detached by a process of logical deduction, the perception becomes rationalized into nonexistence: "It was just a coincidence," "It was an optical illusion," "It was just a *voice* in the wind," "It was just a *face* in the clouds," "It was just my imagination," "It was just a dream..."

An abstract God, divorced from the senses, detached from perception, is accessible only through a reason-based concept. This concept, as it turns out, is Faith. However, as reason stretches forward in abstraction, becoming more self-reflective and analyzing its own reasoning process, it realizes that faith, as a concept, is illogical and unreasonable. Faith, in the modern sense, is non-evidence based belief—belief *without* reason. At that point, one must choose between Faith and Reason. If the path of Reason is chosen, God as both a perceived experience and a believed concept becomes inaccessible. Un-menacing as it may seem, it is in this way that the voice of Reason murdered the voice of God.

If the path of Faith is chosen, a conscious commitment to spiritual belief must be made. This idea of "choosing to believe" was another historical first. Prior to the Enlightenment, the word "belief" was an emotional term, related to the German word "lieben"—"to love." To believe in something meant to love that thing. Belief was originally in the heart, not in the head. It was a feeling we experience for another being, not a thought that we have about an object or idea. Belief was an interpersonal emotion, a relation. But during the Enlightenment, the meaning of the word changed to describe something conceptual. Belief became an attitude held towards a concept, towards an impersonal, objective thing.[28] As Martin Buber would say, the original belief was felt between an "I" and a "Thou." After the Enlightenment, belief was a concept held by an "I" about an "It."

In the realm of Science and Reason, we believe something to be true if we can test or measure its nature, and objectively observe the results. In religion, testing God is expressly forbidden—not because testing is relevant—but because testing is too relevant to be allowed.[29] The Abrahamic religions expressly forbid the testing of Faith, as in Jesus' reply to the Devil's 2nd Temptation: "You shall not put the Lord, your God, to the test'"(Mark 4:7). This prohibition, however, clearly does not apply to God himself, as God is seen testing Abraham and Job and Jesus and others, quite relentlessly, throughout the Old and New Testaments. The point is, Faith or belief is a shared feeling, an emotional reciprocity that is inherently personal and subjective. Unlike an object that exists in the real world—an "It"—Faith and the God it is directed upon cannot be tested. Once the notion of testing God is even entertained, Faith is gone, and the test itself just becomes a self-fulfilling prophecy, a question for which the answer is predetermined.

The Three Nails

> Where has God gone.... We have killed him—you and I! We are all his murderers!—Friedrich Nietzsche[30]

Faith is the first nail in God's coffin; the second is Doubt, and the third is Certainty.

True knowledge of God comes from experience, from perception. This is proof of God's existence. Not objective proof, but subjective proof. Knowledge of God comes from the personal experience of a personal God. Faith in God implies the lack of firsthand knowledge. You have faith in something because you do not have firsthand experience of the truth of that thing. Faith, "belief without proof," is only a necessity when true *knowledge* is absent. The perceived necessity of Faith presupposes the fact that a "faithful" person has neither true *knowledge*, which comes from experience, nor does he have *proof*, which comes from direct perception. Faith, therefore, indicates a lack of spiritual perception. If God is not directly experienced, he is not a real presence. He is a concept, an idea to be believed in, rather than an "Other" to be known, felt, heard, and seen. This is why Faith, as a personal virtue, has been deified to a point where it is just as important, if not more important, than God himself. In the absence of knowledge or experience, Faith is the only thing that can affirm the existence of God in the face of all the paradoxes and contradictions that confront us. As Martin Luther explained: "If by any effort of reason I could conceive how God, who shows so much anger and harshness, could be merciful and just, there would be no need of faith."[31]

No objective proof can ever be established for God's existence. Only subjective proof is possible—our own personal feelings, dreams, and experiences. However, this in no way diminishes the significance of subjective proof for the individual. To the contrary, most of the truths that individuals hold dear are known only on a subjective basis. For example, I could say that I know my father loved me. I cannot prove this love objectively to you. My father is dead, so he cannot declare it. He never left behind any written evidence or physical proof of his love for me. I have only my subjective experiences to go on, such as my feelings and dreams. Nevertheless, you cannot claim that I'm wrong, because my own subjective knowledge is all that matters. Such is the case with God. I cannot claim that another person's knowledge of God is untrue, because that person's subjective knowledge is true to them and only them, and I'm in no position to deny it. However, if I never knew my father, my position would be different. If, for example, my father abandoned me or died when I was two-years-old, and I had no memories of him, and he also sent no written letters or presents of any kind, then I would have neither any objective *nor* subjective proof of his love for me. In that case, if I were to say, "I know my father loved me," that statement would be based on Faith—a belief that I have in the absence of any proof, and in the absence of subjective knowledge. Such is also the case with God, for many people. They have Faith as a last resort, because they do not have objective proof, nor do they have subjective knowledge, perception, or direct experience. Faith, for them, is based on the "will to believe." Faith is a man without a life-vest, adrift in a stormy sea, clinging to a piece of driftwood, that is quickly slipping away from his grasp. It is the first nail in God's coffin, because a religion based on faith alone cannot endure.

Doubt is a process of self-reflection upon one's own beliefs. Doubt is the Siren in the kingdom of the conscious mind. It is the inner voice of reason that thinks about our thinking, judging it for veracity and scanning it for errors. Doubt arises as a natural reaction to the realization that our beliefs are not affirmed by our experiences. Hence, for the rational human being, Doubt is the mind's natural reaction to Faith—you cannot have one without the other—and still be rational. Hence, Paul Tillich's point: "Doubt isn't the opposite of faith; it is an element of faith." While Doubt is born out of Faith, it is also subdued by Faith. When the man confesses to his priest, "I have Doubt," what can the priest say, other than, "You must have Faith." And so the carousel goes round and round. Faith triggers Doubt which is allayed by even more Faith, which naturally arouses more Doubt. A "crisis of Faith" might create so much Doubt that Faith is finally lost and abandoned. However, a crisis of Faith, or some other experience, might evoke a revelation, a moment of clarity, an epiphany—a direct sensory experience of God—a moment of spiritual perception. It is at this moment that the "twice born" individual declares, "I have found Faith in the Lord," although technically, semantically, this is not true. What this lucky soul discovered was *knowledge* of the Lord, subjective *experience* of God, not Faith, per se. What most people refer to as "the gift of faith" is not faith at all; it is a moment of perception, a sensory experience, a feeling of presence, a knowledge of God. Most spiritual people are really not faithful, they're just perceptive (spiritually perceptive).

Doubt is the second nail in God's coffin, because for many people in the modern world, it is the force within the mind that pulls us away from Faith, and towards the nothingness beyond it. Doubt is the Siren call of conceptual oblivion. In a sudden wave of Doubt, the sea-tossed man may lose hold of the driftwood, and then find himself hopelessly—faithlessly—adrift in a sea of Doubt. But just as Doubt is the natural response to Faith, Certainty is the natural response to Doubt. For the man adrift in a sea of Doubt, Certainty is the lighthouse he sees in the distance. It is the fundamental desire for the conscious mind to reach a place of Certainty. It is home base, the meeting of all ends, the harmonic resolution of the cognitive dissonance of Faith and Doubt. For the man who loses Faith in the wave of Doubt, the feeling may be one of relief rather than despair. Certainty may come out of this loss. Atheism is a state of Certainty in the belief that there is no God, nor spirit, nor soul, nor Heaven, nor Hell. To be relieved of the burden of Faith and of all the subsidiary burdens of religion that Faith entails feels, ironically, like Heaven, to some. And thus, for many, Certainty is the third nail in God's coffin.

Theism, the opposite of Atheism, is the Certainty of God's existence. Certainty could be based in knowledge, but that knowledge can only be subjective in nature. In the absence of knowledge, there can only be Certainty based on Faith. This form of Certainty is a two-legged stool, wobbly and unstable. It has no firm ground, and cannot stand up to either objective or subjective scrutiny. Certainty based on Faith tries to cover its own insecurity by blustering and confabulating, using flawed arguments about Creationism and Intelligent Design to create the façade of objective validity, and pointing towards any lack of Certainty by anyone else as a sign of a lack of Faith, which is then translated into a deficit of moral character, since Faith itself, amongst the faithful, is held up as a standard of the highest virtue. Certainty based on Faith, since it is inherently insecure, is prone to failure ... it falls into Doubt. What is the antidote to Doubt? More Faith. How much Faith is needed? Faith up unto the point of absolute Certainty. And so the carousel goes round and round....

Rudolf Otto's "Wholly Other"

> God indeed is the best; and I am the worst.—Petrarch, 14th century

Rudolf Otto's theological masterwork, *The Idea of the Holy* (1923), was vastly influential in its day. Rather than focusing on Faith and theological thoughts about God, Otto focused solely on the emotional psychology of the spiritual experience, which he called the "numinous" state of mind. Otto derived the term "numinous" from the Latin term *numen,* which literally means "a nod of the head"; but the term is specifically referring to the experience of being acknowledged by a god who is gracing you with his presence. (The god nods his head reassuringly at you, as if to say: "Yep, that's right, I see you and you see me....") When we find ourselves in the company of a spiritual presence, we feel a number of overwhelming emotions. The primary emotion is what Otto called the "creature-feeling" or "creature-consciousness"—"the emotion of a creature, submerged and overwhelmed by its own nothingness in contrast to that which is supreme above all creatures."[32] Otto cites instances in the Bible, when characters such as Abraham grovel face down in the dirt at the mere sign of God's holy presence. For example: in Genesis, Abraham says to God: "Behold now, I have taken upon me to speak unto the Lord, which am but dust and ashes."[33]

This "creature feeling" may have evolutionary roots that extend well before the existence of humanity. In a sense, domesticated creatures such as dogs, cats, cows, and chickens are human creations. They did not exist in the wild, their bodies and brains have been molded by human domestication for thousands of years. If they were left to return to the wild, they would either devolve into feral creatures quite different from both their original and their current states, or more likely, they would die and become extinct. Does that mean that a creature feeling experienced between a domesticated animal and a human master could be tantamount to the creature feeling felt between a creature and its perceived "Creator"—the feeling felt by a human towards God? Did we, at one point in our evolution, have a creature feeling towards a species that we perceived as being so superior to us that it instilled a sense of dread and awe? Perhaps the Paleolithic cave paintings convey in their mystifying images a sense of the "mysterium tremendum," an awe on the religious scale of these beasts of wonder—the formidable cave bear, the lethal saber-toothed tiger, the colossal wooly mammoths—who instilled both terror and reverence in our primordial forbearers. Does a dog look at his human master with the "mysterium tremendum" of a creature towards its creator? (Cats, most certainly, do not.)

The "mysterium tremendum" is a state of "religious awe" that is felt when we perceive that which is beyond our comprehension. Jane Goodall, in her observations of chimps, noted that when thunderstorms strike suddenly, chimps often respond in the same way that they would to a physical animal threat. "They stamp, hoot, break branches ... and repeatedly charge down hillsides."[34] This animistic perception of the storm—seeing the storm as a personal threat from a physical being—is recapitulated in human behavior, when we name hurricanes and speak of them in anthropomorphic terms.

Ancient religions certainly saw gods in storms. Zeus was the god of thunder and lightning, and the storm was his expression of anger or discontent. Goodall, though hesitant to make direct connections between chimp behavior and religion, suggests that the "awe and wonder, that underlie most religions" might have its root in "such primeval, uncomprehending surges of emotion."[35] When at times we feel in awe of Nature itself; when the thunder terrifies us, the lightning strikes panic in our hearts, and the blizzard, earthquake, hurricane, tornado, or tidal wave threatens to shatter our very existence; or when we are awestruck by the majesty of the rainbow, the grandeur of the Grand Canyon at sundown, the immensity of the ocean, the infinitude of the night sky; or when we are astounded by the roar of a lion, the grace of a seagull, the beauty of a bluebird ... are all these experiences not a sort of mysterium tremendum of the same order (if not the same degree), as our perception of God's divine presence on Earth?

The emotions of creature-consciousness and mysterium tremendum presuppose the fact that the feeling is felt towards "an object outside the self," towards something "numinous," something that is perceived as being "wholly other" than ourselves.[36] The conceptualization of the "wholly other" into a spirit, demon, angel, or god is a "rationalization" of the fundamental experience.[37] The experience itself exists independently of any such rationalization, which, in essence, is an attempt of the conscious mind to interpret or conceptualize a fundamentally unconscious experience. Hence, God is a conceptualization of this sense of the "wholly other," which in-and-of-itself has no direct relation to a concept or thought.

To extend on Otto's premise, we could suppose that the three divine qualities attributed to God—omnipresence, omniscience, and omnipotence—actually have their basis in the primal emotion, the numinous experience of the wholly other. Because the sensed Other comes from within, but is perceived as coming from without, it is both a perception being observed, and an observer perceiving its projector. The sentient Other is aware of both its perceiver, and of the perception of its perceiver, which means that the Other is somehow both inside our mind and outside our mind at the same time. Hence, the Other has the quality of omnipresence, as it exists perpetually inside our own mind, yet it is felt as being eternally present outside of our minds as well. The Other is also omniscient, it knows everything we know, because it is inside our own minds— and what's more—since it has access to our unconscious mind, it knows more about our true selves than we do, as we are only directly aware of our conscious selves. And finally, the Other is also omnipotent, as it wields the power over the mind in any situation; the mind which, over matter, is always superior and overpowering.

The mysterium tremendum has its origins in the more mundane sense of "something uncanny, eerie, or weird."[38] The fact that even the most educated, modern, sophisticated, and intellectually mature individual can still, upon occasion, feel a sense of uncanny dread, accompanied by images of ghostly horror, testifies to the basic and universal experience of the mysterium tremendum. If I watch a scary movie late at night by myself, my dark house—with its spooky reflections in dark windows, and odd movements of unknown shadows in dark corners—for the time being becomes haunted with the creepy sense of dread that I remember distinctly from childhood; and which must have been much more common in adults, in the days before the dark corners of the world were exorcised of their ghosts by the flashlight of analytical consciousness and reason.[39] Kodosh, the Hebrew word typically translated as "holy," is etymologically closer to the term "otherness," that which is separated from or "other-than" the self.[40] In Judaism, things that are "kodosh" must be separated or set apart from the mundane, profane, or worldly order of human affairs. The "other" is holy because it is perceived primarily as something outside of oneself. A prime example would be the Jewish Sabbath, the "Holy Day," which is separated from weekdays by a myriad of customs that distinguish the entire feeling and experience of the Sabbath, so that it's very essence is that it is spiritually elevated over the other days of the week.

Mircea Eliade's Sacred Time

> Man becomes aware of the sacred because it manifests itself, shows itself, as something wholly different from the profane.—Mircea Eliade

Inspired by Rudolf Otto's theory, Eliade believed that the role of religion is to promote individual encounters with the spiritual dimension. He observed that religion in preliterate cultures was aimed at recognizing the intersections between the "sacred" world of gods and the "profane" world of humans. The function of mythology and religious ritual is to facilitate the temporary transcendence of the individual from the profane world to the sacred world. As such, temples were always founded at sites of "hierophany"—a place where a sacred spirit had once appeared.[41] Eliade believed that all mythologies express the universal theme of the "Fall," in which humans were at one time together with the gods, but were then separated from them. The equally universal "Myth of the Eternal Return" is the theme of reconnecting with the gods from whom we were separated. In Eliade's view, the basic feeling of religion is a desperate longing to be reconnected with the gods, just as a baby separated from his mother desperately longs for his return to that sacred state of union. Eliade called this feeling a "nostalgia for Paradise."[42]

Another key idea in Eliade's theory is the importance of symbol in myth in religion. Religion speaks to the individual through symbols, not through rational language. Symbols speak in the "dialectic of the sacred," they inspire and captivate the imagination, and they reside in our dreams and come to us in visions. Eliade's theory of symbols is closely aligned with Jung's theory of archetypes, and the two scholars consulted each other when developing their ideas. For both Jung and Eliade, the spiritual experience is an unconscious experience that speaks to our preliterate mind. It is revealed through great bursts of intuition, in our dreams, and in our imagination, and it is not susceptible to rational thought or the logic of the intellect.[43] Eliade's conception of religious ritual as "sacred time" is similar to Durkheim's concept of "collective effervescence."[44]

The participant in the ritual, powered by the intense group dynamic, experiences a literal feeling of "ecstasy"—a "stepping out" of profane time—and a stepping in to "sacred time." For Eliade, the spiritual experience is a deeply personal one that is enabled by the group ritual, and which has the added benefit of fostering group unity and identification with the common spirit. The principal function, however, is the individual's transcendence from "profane time" into "sacred time," where he personally encounters the spirits and witnesses firsthand the handiwork of the gods. In the ritual, in sacred time, the individual is "living" his tribe's myth, he is partaking in the spiritual creation of his gods.[45] The function of the ritual is to step out of the linear time of the human world and momentarily enter the circular time of the spirit world, where everything that once happened is happening still, and will always continue to reoccur. There is a sense of peace and serenity achieved in that sense of circular time, a safety in the knowledge of the eternal return, which is perhaps why so many rituals involve spinning, dancing, running, marching, swirling, or whirling in circles.

Buber's I and Thou

> Spirit is not in the I, but in the space between I and Thou.—Martin Buber

Martin Buber's long revelatory essay on the nature of man's relationship to others, to God, and to himself, originally published in 1923 as *I and Thou* (*Ich und Du*), was incredibly influential, and has immense implications for the modern world of digitalized social interaction. In his essay, he explains that the experience of a relationship between an individual "I" and an other "Thou," though perceived as being dual, is actually an experience of unity. When two people meet and interact in a meaningful way, they become inextricably connected to each other in such a way that both "I" and "Thou" understand without qualification that they are unified, they are both part of the same whole, they are as one. Buber provided examples, such as the pair of lovers during the act of love, a fetus inside its mother, a baby suckling at its mother's breast, and the person communing on a spiritual level with God. These experiences, while they may involve language, surpass the limitations of language. The personal relationship with God is the essence of what Buber was talking about when he created the notion of the I-Thou experience. Unlike the "I-It" experience, it cannot be objectified. You cannot relate to God as if he were an "It," a thing outside of yourself, a separate being, an other it. You can only relate to God as if he were a part of yourself, an inner Other—a being who is connected to you—but at the same time, a being with whom you can relate to as another being, in the same way that a pregnant mother can relate to the living being inside of her.

Like the experience of love, the personal experience of God does not occur solely in the perception of the individual, but in the *relationship* with the Other. Love does not exist in me, nor in my lover, but in the space in between myself and my lover.[46] As long as we are in the process of trying to figure someone or something out, as long as we are trying to analyze, manipulate, control, or grasp the Other, we are in the process of holding the Other away from us, detachedly, so we can observe the Other and inspect her from a distance. In this sense, even when we are having a dialogue with another person, if we are qualifying the other person by judging her words or analyzing her intent, what we are really doing is transforming the other person into a mental representation, a thought or concept that we have created by ourselves in our own minds. Therefore, that dialogue with another person is actually just a monologue with our own mind, and the person we refer to as a "You" is, in actuality, just an object we are trying to manipulate, analyze, or control ... an "It." The person has become an object of our own thought, rather than a subject with whom we relate. Buber, of course, points out that a personal relationship with God can never be achieved through I-It perception. If we try to think about God objectively, rationally, logically, analytically ... we reduce the Thou to an It, and therefore hinder our ability to relate to the Other in a truly interpersonal way. The I-Thou relationship, therefore, cannot be pursued intellectually. It must come to us. We must experience it naturally, like a baby experiences its world, without preconceptions or logical deductions; only then can the Other-Thou reveal itself as the inner-I.

Buber pointed out that the modern world was fast becoming a place designed for I-It relationships, and that there was very little place for the I-Thou relationship anymore. If he could only see the 21st century, what horror would he have known! When speaking through a telephone rather than speaking in person, we create a buffer between I and Thou that disintegrates the I-Thou connection. When we cannot see the Other's face—see her eyes glance as she thinks, see her lips move as she speaks—we get only a fraction of the I-Thou experience. The conversation machine, which we think is a bridge, is actually a barrier. When we replace the phone with an e-mail, we eliminate the one semblance of humanness left in the interchange, the human voice. We also eliminate the one semblance of the natural world left in the experience, the interaction within real time. E-mails are not read and sent in real time, and so the relationship becomes abstracted and devoid of real feeling. E-mail also translates the spontaneous and inherently personal voice of the oral word into the calculated and inherently impersonal text of the written word. When e-mails are then replaced by text messages, the need to condense written words into shorter messages, often by contracting whole expressions into trite acronyms ("lol," "imho," "ttyl"), reduces what was once an interaction between an I and a Thou into a set of unidirectional transmissions between a pair of unrelated Its. Twitter then removes the sense of personal communication between the two Its. Tweets are neither personal nor exclusive. So now the acronymic unidirectional transmission is directed towards the electromagnetic ether rather than an individual Other or Thou. If the message is addressed to everyone, it is personally meaningful to no-one. The message from an It goes out to a kingdom of its.

And as a final blow (for the moment), digital media even robs us of our own personal reflections. A sunset can no longer be enjoyed privately, personally, as an individual moment of reflection, which in essence is the experience of the I-Thou relationship with oneself, or with Nature, or with God. The sunset must be captured in a digital picture or video and posted on Facebook, Instagram, or Vine. The iphone technology by its mere existence creates a need to use the technology. The technology then becomes the focal point of the experience, rather than the experience itself. When my child sings on stage at her school play, the father in front of me stares at his iphone, which he places between his eyes and the view of his child. The I, when it encounters the Thou—the father when he truly sees his daughter, and when she sees him seeing her—is a relation between two participants. When the father disengages, when he is preoccupied or distracted, so that he looks but doesn't see, the daughter becomes an It. The relation becomes an observation between an observer and the object being observed—an I-It interaction. And when the father inserts a machine in between he and his daughter, he creates a 2nd degree of dissociation between himself and the event. Not a participant, nor an observer, he is a recorder, an extension of his technology. It has become an I-It-It interaction, as the father interacts primarily with his phone, and the digital images on the phone are not present in time, nor in space. (Perhaps the true final blow is that the father will never, *ever*, watch that video.)

Buber's revelation points out explicitly what we all know intuitively: The reality of an experience is not found within the personal experience itself, but within the interpersonal experience—the sharing of the experience—the relation. Personally, I love going out to dinner or going to the movies; but I never do these things by myself. Doing these things alone would be empty experiences. The relation with another is what fills up these experiences, making them feel "real." Similarly, everyone can experience sexual stimulation and orgasm by themselves, auto-erotically, but everyone would agree that a "real" sexual experience is fulfilled through relation with another. Digital media, however, has interjected itself within the sphere of relation, satisfying the same need but in a virtual mode. Eating dinner alone is made "real" by tweeting pics of your Caesar salad. Going to the movies alone is made "real" by posting comments about the film on Facebook with your iphone. Even auto-eroticism is made "real" by digital experiences that mimic the interaction and stimulation of actual sexual encounters: "cybersex," "sexting," internet porn, Skype sex, etc. But is the virtual reality produced by digitality really "real"—or is it just an illusion?

Buber also pointed out that the notion of prayer as a "function" is another way of reducing the I-Thou to an I-It. When one prays to God not to experience the I-God relationship, but to ask for something, then the intention is on the self and not on the Other. The prayer is a monologue, not a dialogue, as it turns God into an outer–It, rather than an inner–Thou. Even if the purpose of our prayer is to pray for others, God is still being approached as an It rather than a Thou, because the focus in the prayer is not the *relation* itself, but the *thing* for which you are asking. What chance have we to truly commune with God, if we in our digital world have lost the ability to truly communicate with each other, and with ourselves?

We experience our world through relationships with others. Our world is constantly changing, but there is a "constant partner," which is the internal sense of "I"—self-conscious awareness.[47] But though the constant partner becomes conscious of its own existence, it can never truly know itself in the way that it can know an external other, a "Thou," because it cannot relate to itself in the same way that it can relate to someone else. Therefore, a "detached self" forms, a part of the self that is unknown and unknowable to the conscious I. And when, at times, there is a "bursting point" and the "bonds are broken," the conscious I is confronted by the "detached self," whom it fails to recognize as himself. And so the conscious I perceives the detached self as a Thou, a separate sentient Other, an entity outside of itself ... a ghost, a spirit, a god. The "constant other," then, for the spiritual person, is God—or rather—the person's *relationship* with God. The relationship is fostered through interaction, through ritual, which for most people in the Western world is performed in the form of prayer, the interpersonal communion that Teresa of Avila referred to as the "conversation between friends."[48] The feeling that God is an "active participant," "a constant partner," a divine Friend, is the feeling aspired to in prayer. Rossetti, a priest and a psychological researcher, has found that time spent in private or silent prayer is a time that fosters our relationships with ourselves, with God, and with others.[49] The place of "spiritual solitude" found in prayer is "beyond loneliness"—it is a place of true relation, in many ways a place of relation more true than most of the "I-It" relations we engage in during our busy day; for the "I-Thou" relation of prayer is focused on the relation itself, the spiritual relation, which is an acknowledgment of both the I *and* the Thou within one's self.

Buber also points out that modern language itself tends to objectify others and our relations to others. When oral language becomes abstracted into written language, it becomes necessary to think of words in a grammatical sense, as components of sentences. A word is not a complete idea in-and-of-itself. When I say "apple," I refer to an object. When I say "eat," I refer to an action. When I say "you," I refer to a subject. Only when I say the complete sentence—"You eat the apple"—is an entire idea expressed. A single word cannot express a complete relation, but only a specific component of a relation. Once words are reduced to sentence components, the words themselves are then functionalized into the different operations of action—subject and object—in order to distinguish between that which is conscious and that which is not conscious.[50] This separation of subject and object represents the primary separation between "I" and everything else that is "not-I," a separation created by language that can no longer be bridged by language.[51] And so language itself becomes the ultimate barrier. It creates the cognitive distance between the I and the Thou, the disconnection between the inner self and the outer world. It then tries to bridge the gap between the inner and outer worlds, but it cannot. The technology upon which we predominantly depend upon to communicate and therefore relate, has turned against us, and now bars the potential for true relation and true unity. It is the flaming sword that God placed at the gates of the Garden of Eden, the sword that turns in every which way, to block all our routes of return. Our struggle now is to learn to "incorporate into the world of the basic word what lies outside language?"[52]

Bergson's Intuition

> It is if a vague and formless being, whom we may call, as we will, *man* or *superman*, had sought to realize himself, and had succeeded only by abandoning a part of himself on the way.—Henri Bergson, 1911

Henri Bergson turned philosophical heads in the early 20th century by calling for a return of the attention towards "intuition," rather than the single minded focus on rational conscious thought that had dominated philosophy since Descartes.[53] Bergson believed that the "spiritual life" was anathema to the rational intellect, and that it was accessible only through intuitive states.[54] Spirituality as an experience (rather than a thought), could only be accessed through intuitive functions; for only then is our awareness and sense perception less affected by the reducing and filtering function of rational consciousness.[55]

Bergson's philosophy preceded a century of psychological and neurological research in perception that all point to the same truth, that the experience of perception is in the brain, not in the senses. Yet Bergson took the point one step further, noting that the basis of perception is not in the senses, nor in the brain, but in the object—that which is perceived. There is a primary connection between the observer and the object he perceives. In our perpetual state of abstract consciousness, we tend to forget this fact; but the "perfect continuity" between object, senses, and perception, remains, though unnoticed.[56] We create what we see in our mind, and what we see creates the neural connections that compose our mind. William Blake put it more simply, and more eloquently: "We become what we behold." That which we perceive is a part of us, because perception is an internal process. There are "mirror neurons" in our brain that fire when we observe an act. The same neurons fire in the exact same way when we perform the same act. This neurological observation gives empirical support to the notion that poets like Blake and philosophers like Bergson pointed out many generations ago: Our minds are mirrors of our environment. Our brains are integrally connected with their surroundings, whether we are aware of it or not. Our surroundings configure our minds.

The primary means of understanding our surroundings, the only way we can "grasp" the infinite world of endless possibilities, is by filtering our sense perceptions and reducing our awareness, narrowing it down to a handful of rational meanings. The penchant for abstract consciousness to sequester itself behind a moat of selective perception, is the function that isolates ourselves in our private "kingdom of mind," a kingdom that ennobles the king but estranges the Lord— for that which cannot be named or numbered in words or digits—cannot cross the drawbridge of reduced awareness.[57]

Paul Tillich's "Ground of Being"

> A symbol points beyond itself to something else....
> It participates in that to which it points....
> It opens up levels of reality which otherwise are closed for us....
> It opens up hidden depths of our own being.
> —Paul Tillich

> The role of the metaphor is the elevation of hidden ground into sensibility.—Marshall McLuhan

Paul Tillich's famous conceptualization of God as "the ground of being," places God above the "content" of the dimension of beings that exist, and establishes God as the "form" of existence itself ... that which gives meaning and structure to being. Tillich's philosophical distinction between "content" and "form" is analogous to the psychological distinction between "figure" and "ground," which is embedded in Tillich's metaphor ("the *ground* of being").[58] Marshall McLuhan used the figure/ground distinction in his approach to media, pointing out that people always focus on the "content" of media (the figure), while not taking into account the even more significant influence of the "form" of media (the ground), which is the medium itself. The ideas of both of these brilliant philosophers can be woven together to elucidate my theory of spiritual perception, in which the perception of the "ground" of spirituality is perpetually inhibited, because of the mind's constant focus on the "figure" of conscious thought.

The raison d'être of conscious awareness in humans is the amazingly advanced ability it gives us to focus on specific details. This ability to analyze, deconstruct, and reconfigure is the cognitive skill that has allowed us humans to master our environments and become the lords of the Earth. Focus, by definition, means directing one's attention onto one specific thing, to the exclusion of everything else from one's focal point of attention. When we focus, we center all of our attention on the "figure" within our field of perception—the thing we are focusing on—resulting in the loss of attention towards the "ground" of our field of awareness, which is everything other than the figure. For example, as you read these words, your attention is focused on the figures of black ink on the page, not on the background of white that is the page itself, the ground. If God is the "ground of being," the thing that is everything, everywhere, and all the time—then the conscious mind is constantly inhibiting the perception of this ground—because the function of the conscious mind is to *ignore* the ground, so it can focus single-mindedly on the figure. So what happens to God, if he cannot be perceived consciously?

Marshall McLuhan used the figure/ground distinction to point out that the ground, while subliminal to conscious awareness, is still an extremely significant force in our psychological experience of any stimulus. The ground is always sensed, even if it is not "perceived." For example, let's say you're shopping at the grocery story, and there's Muzac playing in the background. A sneaky grocery store manager can play a message at a volume that you can hear, but at a level at which it is drowned out by the music. The message may be: "Buy Oreos, Buy Oreos, Buy Oreos..." You hear this message, even if you're not listening to it. It is received by your senses and slips into your mind, even though you're not consciously aware of it. By the time you're standing in the checkout line, you're quite likely to have Oreos in your shopping cart, even if you're not particularly fond of Oreos. This principle of subliminal awareness—that while we are only *consciously* aware of the figure, we are *unconsciously* aware of the subliminal stimuli within the ground—is the basis of much of the advertising business, which is a trillion dollar industry that funds almost all media communications in the world. Thus, McLuhan contends: "The medium is the message." It is the medium itself (the ground), that has the most profound effect on our perception, not the content of the media (the figure).

If we merge McLuhan's and Tillich's ideas, we can imagine a God that is immersed within the "ground" of our perceptual field, so that he is almost never perceived consciously, but can always be potentially sensed unconsciously. Tillich believed that the figure of Jesus as the embodiment of the "Word of God" is a necessary symbol for Christians. Since we don't consciously perceive the "ground" of our being, but only the "figure," than religions require a "figure" that we can focus on. Jesus provides this focal point for Christians. Jesus is the "object of devotion," the figure that points back to the ground. Other religions have similar figures that serve as symbols that point to the "ground." Religious symbols and icons such as the Cross, the Bible, the Koran, and the Buddha, are especially potent because they "participate" in the power of the divine to which they point. The symbols themselves are figures that are directly connected to the ground of God. By focusing on the symbol, we identify with the figure, and then through a process of psychological transference, we ourselves become vicariously connected to the ground, through the medium of the symbolic figure. If we focus deeply enough on the figurative symbol, we may lose sense of our own ground of thought—we may disengage from our own consciousness—and in that way we may open our perception to the true "ground of being" to which the symbol points. Tillich believed that the Christian Incarnation, in which the "Logos became flesh," refers to the "revelation" that God, who has become "estranged" to humanity, can be reacquainted to humanity through the symbol of God, Jesus, who represents the unification of that which participates with God, and that which is estranged from God. This state of unity—achieved through prayer, meditation, dream, and other methods—is an unconscious but *not* an unaware state of unification between the figure and the ground of our perception. It is, in fact, *spiritual* perception.

When travelling at fast speeds, the ground blurs into nonexistence, like the posts on a picket fence seen from a moving car travelling at 100 miles an hour. The fence posts gradually merge into one blurry image, and eventually seem to disappear completely. If the car was travelling at the speed of light, there would be no perception of the fence—or of anything at all—because the light could not catch up to the vehicle speeding past it. This is the situation of the individual mind in the Digital Age. Information is bombarding us so rapidly that we can only perceive the figure of each data point momentarily, before the next point of data dominates our perception. Our information comes to us as all figure with no ground; because, like the picket fence, we are moving too quickly to perceive the ground of our existence, much less comprehend it. However, there is a ground that can be perceived inwardly rather than outwardly … a ground that is constant rather than passing. Paul Tillich believed that, as "the ground of being," God is a constant presence. He is always there, as part of the nature of being, but he is seldom perceived. The mind that conceives the world as a part of his own being, the mind that conceives himself as a connected part of the world, the mind that is an integrated and connected part of Nature, is the mind that is experiencing the essence of God. Consciousness uses words to abstract itself, to detach or disconnect itself from the world of being, the world of Nature. The words that make a conscious human aware of himself as a separate subject create a duality that did not formerly exist. The creation of a separate "I" creates by de facto the assumption of a separate "Thou" or "It"—a separate other. The conscious mind in this mode of language based abstraction is a mind that is not connected to the world as a part of his own being. The conscious mind is *disconnected* from Nature, *disconnected* from being. It is a mind that is inhibited from the experience of the essence of God, because the words of thought that create a sense of abstract detachment are conscious "figures" that draw our attention away from the "ground of being," which is God. Nevertheless, through the figure of a spiritual symbol or metaphor, we can still perceive the presence of that which is hidden in the ground ... the presence of the sentient, spiritual Other.

The Digital Pond

> One thing about which fish know exactly nothing is water, since they have no anti-environment which would enable them to perceive the element they live in.—Marshall McLuhan

In the Digital Age, modern man, self-hypnotically staring into the reflective screen of his i-tool, is truly the 21st century Narcissus. The tool he grasps, made of silicon instead of stone, is himself in extension. If perchance he loses his gadget or it loses power or internet connectivity, he feels tragically lost. Disconnected from his gadget, he is disconnected from his self. In his solitude he hears "phantom rings"[59] calling to him from the ether like Echo to her unrequiting lover. It is the mind conjuring a phantom of its own extension, just as the mind conjures a phantom limb for an amputee, or a phantom husband for a widow. Like Narcissus, Digital Man cannot be drawn away from the reflection of his self-extension. It becomes not only his mirror, but his obsession, his idol, his god—and we become the unwitting "servomechanisms" to these gods—unwitting because our senses are numbed and stultified by the digital media itself.[60]

A fish in a pond cannot perceive the water he is immersed in. It has no "anti-environment" with which to contrast his environment. Therefore, it cannot perceive the ground of its own existence. Similarly, Narcissus cannot perceive that it is himself that he is gazing at when he looks onto the reflective surface of the pond. Like the fish, Narcissus is so immersed in his media that he cannot perceive the effect of the media itself—the ground—he can only perceive the figure that is projected on the glossy surface of the ground.

The name "Narcissus" is derived from the Greek word "narcosis." Narcissus was narcotically numbed by the constant stimulation of his own extension, the reflection of himself, the media that he had become narcotically addicted to.[61] Similarly, we are becoming numb to the constant stimulation of digital media, the extensions and reflections of our own minds. Like Narcissus, our senses have adapted to the constant stimulation of our extensions by numbing themselves, so that we become a "closed system," unable to perceive anything outside of the all-enveloping digital network, and unable to see the effect of the digital network itself on our own minds.[62] Like Narcissus, our extensions have a narcotic effect—we are addicted to our own media—and have no intention of ever not using.

The i-tool is both an extension and a reflection of the self. Holding his i-tool, gazing at his digital reflection in the guise of "selfies" and "re-tweets," Digital Man becomes what he beholds. Like the shadows on the Platonic cave wall, he sees his Facebook profile as his own identity, his Twitter feed becomes his voice, his Instagram his eyes. He is sucked into the virtual world of the internet, which he perceives as being outside of himself; but in actuality, it is a digital hall of mirrors, an endlessly reflecting mirror image of himself. He has become numbed to the virtual world and blind to the real world. As a "closed system," he's only able to reflect upon himself, without even the awareness that what he is gazing at is, in fact, himself. The outside world of real sights and sounds and living physical people now seem to him as foreign and unfamiliar, as distant and indistinct, as the voice of Echo, or the shadows on the Platonic wall. And the illusions, the narcissistic shadows on the wall—the extensions, reflections, and projections—become more real than reality. Narcissus, McLuhan reminds us, fell in love with an image that he did not recognize as himself.[63] The extension, the i-tool, has the same hypnotic power that Nemesis bestowed upon Narcissus' pool. It entrances us with an image that we do not recognize as ourselves. What holds our attention with a narcotic force is the unconscious identification with the uncanny external subject, the being that is simultaneously recognized as "I" and "not-I," resulting in the self-gratifying indulgence of gazing, hour after hour, upon our own reflected image.

The Digital Age places us in a narcissistic hall of mirrors. The more we try to see the Other, the more we merely encounter ourselves in reflection. The more individual uniqueness we try to express, the more we flounder in mass conformation.[64] Until, at last, there is no more Other. There is just the Digital I—the "i"—like Narcissus, capable only of perceiving itself; alone in a de-animated world of "its." If God exists in this kingdom of its, he can only be a Digital God, for the only thing that is truly revered, the only thing that gives the "i" a sense of wonder and awe, a sense of connection with something outside of itself, is the media technology itself—the latest i-tool or videogame—that self-reflecting "it" for which millions will wait days in line for, as men and women did in days of old, when the oracles at Delphi still spoke for Apollo, and the temples still sacrificed to the gods.

Spiritual Networking

> How should we be able to know if some agent could double the speed of *all* events in the world? We could discern a great loss of richness in experience.—Henri Bergson, 1911

Media technology, whether it is the 3,000 year-old phonetic alphabet or a 3G iPhone, changes the perception of the people using it, as the "plastic brain" adapts itself to the new medium. Changes in perception at a population level then change the culture of the population itself, resulting in continued changes in perception, and so forth. And to what effect? The experience of the Other, when abstracted from the context of direct physical perception of the Other, is less rich. The relationship with a friend who is never seen in person but only networked with over the internet is a relationship that is less rich in sensory and emotional experience than the relationship with a friend who is met just as frequently in person. How does one compensate for the loss of richness in interpersonal experience? By multiplying the total number of others. Thus, by this calculus that seems absurd, 500 digital Facebook friends will plug the gap once filled by just a handful of physical face-to-face friends. And what of the loss of richness in other areas of experience? The same absurd calculus would apply ... just increase the number of total experiences, i.e., the quantity of sensory stimulation. So, while the speed of the internet doubles, triples, quadruples the "speed of all events in the world," we do not necessarily note Bergson's "loss of richness in experience," because electronic and digital media simultaneously increase the flow of stimulation, compensating for the loss of richness in experience by multiplying the total amount of experience. Problem solved? Not necessarily....

Spiritual experiences of God are intrinsically different than relational experiences with other people and things. Spiritual perception, unlike other modes of perception, generally comes from a quiet, introspective, inner space. The function of meditation, for instance, is to systematically shut off the external senses, so that one could focus on that which is not conscious, not sensory, and not physical. When people pray, they often shut their eyes. Even in church or temple, the deepest prayer is always a silent prayer. Spiritual perception, unlike other forms of perception, is paradoxical, because it is sensed from within, rather than from without. The modern world, however, is a place that is becoming increasingly overloaded with external sensation, a place that is perpetually flooded with sensory stimulation, a place where everyone is perpetually "online." For many people, being connected to the internet at every moment has become a psychological necessity, an existential lifeline. "Internet addicts" feel the disconnection when temporarily offline as a painful, unbearable experience. At the risk of sacrilege, it could be compared to the agonizing feeling of spiritual disconnection from God expressed in the Psalms. But while disconnection from the internet or from media or even from other people can be remedied by simply increasing the total quantity of digital, sensory, or interpersonal stimulation, a sense of disconnection from God is not so easily remedied. We can't just multiply the quantity of God, or reshape the perceptual experience of God to better fit our digital sensibilities ... or can we?

If spiritual perception is an innate function in humans, then it is likely to adapt to the new environment of digitality. Historically, cognitive changes resulting from new media affect spiritual perception, and oftentimes inhibit it, but they never extinguish it. If internet dependence is perceived as a modern trend rather than a behavioral disorder, perhaps the intrinsic drive towards transcendence can be channeled through the digital media? The internet has already been compared to God. Like the monotheistic God, it is abstract and distant; yet, simultaneously, it can be personalized and contextualized into the present. In its own way, the internet shares with God the same divine qualities of omniscience, omnipresence, and possibly even omnipotence. It is quite possible that the internet will give rise to a new form of spiritual perception ... a Digital God.

In the Digital Age, we are immersed in a sea of media that creates a virtual world around us. We have digital friendships rather than physical friendships, we see digital landscapes on screens rather than physical landscapes, we hear digital music through earphones rather than hearing or making physical acoustic music.... Like McLuhan's fish who cannot conceive of water, we are unaware of our own environment, because we are immersed in it so completely. We unwittingly isolate ourselves within our own perceptual prisons. We unknowingly drown ourselves in our own virtual sea of media. But we cannot just remove ourselves from the virtual prison, just as the fish cannot remove himself from the water. We, like the fish, have become absolutely dependent on our digital environment for our survival. We would suffocate without it. However, the new environment of spiritual networking may help to free us from these prisons.

My main argument in this chapter has been that the relationship with God that is purely conceptual and symbolic is less rich in sensory and emotional experience than the relationship with God that is based on personal meetings with God, in which God's presence is felt as a real sensory experience. Digital media did not create our inhibition in the ability to perceive a "real" God, rather than just conceiving of a conceptual God. This inhibition was created by the media of verbal language, and in particular, by literacy. Digital media, however, can reverse this trend. God is a virtual other. Spiritual perception is the experience of a relationship with this virtual other. In religious rituals, symbols and symbolic acts are used to facilitate spiritual perception—the sensing of this virtual other. Digital media, similarly, creates a virtual world of virtual others comprised of images, sounds, and symbols that we sense directly and that we use to interact with the presence of virtual others. In this way, it seems that God, spiritual perception, and digitality are perfectly suited to one another. They are all virtual realities.

As life continues to be experienced more-and-more online, spiritual life will also be uploaded into the digital world. If the digital experience of spiritual perception imagined in previous chapters is hooked up to the internet, we can conceive of an interactive virtual world connecting billions of users, a spiritual cyberspace in which people can share their spiritual perceptions with others, and open their minds to the experience of other people's spiritual symbols, images, myths, fantasies, dreams, and beliefs. Like the *World of Warcraft,* virtual spirituality could cross continents and bridge ethnic and religious barriers; but for the purpose of love, peace, and understanding, rather than war, death, and destruction. The Digital God will not have one face, but billions.

Virtual spirituality will begin with a digitally fostered exploration within the individual's mind for the experience of unitive spiritual perception ... the digital dream. The next step will be the projection of mental imagery outwardly from the mind of the individual into a digital media system. (This technology does not exist now, but Ray Kurzweil believes it is possible within the foreseeable future, though it may require neural implants.) Given this technology, the mental images seen in dreams could be recorded and watched later, and then programmed into the media system to be projected into future dreams. The images could even be digitally enhanced or edited. More significantly, the images could be *shared* with others. If this technology is combined with internet gaming technology, then an entire new dimension of the digital dream is opened up. It can be a social experience, an online interactive network, in which people enter into other people's dreamscapes, and encounter and interact with other people's spiritual archetypes. The connective force of the internet can also provide communal spiritual experiences that would be experienced simultaneously as an inner cognitive perception for each individual, as well as an outer social experience—a communal dream of a shared divine myth—all within the virtual realm of a digitally structured spiritual encounter.

The spiritual systems of preliterate "tribal" cultures are based in a mythic mindset. Beliefs in spirits and gods stem from myths about the gods that the people believe in. They don't "literally" believe in the myths, because they are not literate people, hence their minds don't think in a literal way. That is, the myths are not taken "literally," in that they have only one specific meaning. The myths are understood at multiple levels, because oral myths are always understood to have multiple meanings. For example, the biblical story of Abraham sacrificing Isaac, when told orally as a myth, is understood by the listener as a factual story about a man who once almost killed his son; but also as an allegory about a man's obedience to God; and also as a proscriptive tale about how people once sacrificed their children, but now that practice is forbidden by God. All of the levels of meaning are understood at once, and perceived at once.[65] The oral myth must be understood at multiple levels simultaneously, because unlike a book, elements of the oral myth cannot be taken out of context, focused on, deconstructed, analyzed backwards and forwards and sideways with no reference to time or place. When we hear a story, the storyteller controls the content, so the listener must accept the story as a whole, understanding all of the levels of meaning simultaneously.[66]

The spiritual systems of post-literate "modern" cultures are based in a theoretic, literate mindset. When we read a story, *we* control the content, so we can pause, stop, go back, and in other ways direct our focus so as to understand it in a linear sequential fashion, in which each part logically leads to the next. A reader reading the Bible perceives one level of meaning at a time, because such is the nature of "focus," to perceive the singular to the exclusion of the multiple. Hence, the text is more likely to be taken literally, with only one possible meaning. The paradoxical nature of the myth—the story seems to be about a morally ideal man who attempts to murder his own son—is not a problem in the mythic mindset, as simultaneous multiple meanings are understood holistically, even if some of the meanings contradict each other. In the theoretic literate mindset, however, paradoxes and contradictions are problematic, because they belie the "one true meaning" of the text. Hence, the sacred texts of the Abrahamic religions, which were transcriptions of an oral tradition, require volumes and volumes of commentary and interpretation to eliminate paradoxicality, in order to be understood by the logical reader.

The electronic/digital mindset retrieves the multiple processing of the mythic mindset. When a film is viewed, for instance, the experience is more mythic than theoretic. All of the different meanings of the film narratives are processed simultaneously, resulting in the instantaneous and concurrent processing of multiple levels of meaning in the film. By moving the spiritual experience away from the theoretic/literate mindset—by moving it away from the purely literary experience of books like the Bible—and by transferring it into an electronic/

digital medium, we are retrieving a more mythic mindset. The resonant images and sounds, the multiple meanings processed simultaneously, the multiple senses being fully engaged, all create a much more visceral and psychologically powerful experience of the myth. The immense popularity of spiritual films and television shows, such as Mel Gibson's *Passion of the Christ* (2004) and the History Channel's *The Bible* (2013), demonstrate that people in the Digital Age crave a more sensory rich experience of myth and spirituality than the written text can provide. The *mysterium tremendum*—the religious awe that is felt when we perceive the *wholly other*—can only come from a sensory experience. Words in a book are not sufficient for most of us. An unofficial sequel to *Passion of the Christ* is currently in production and is scheduled to be released for Easter 2016. The producers of *The Resurrection of Jesus Christ* plan to use digital media technology to create the most realistic depiction of the resurrection ever seen. They plan to distribute it to audiences all over the world simultaneously in every format and venue available: movie theatres, churches, stadiums, television, internet, you name it! The producers are also developing an online video game along with the film, creating a digital format for people to live through an interactive, communal, virtual reality experience of the resurrection. Clearly, the age of the Digital God is at hand.

The online communal digital experience of God and Myth—"spiritual networking"—will be the church and temple of the Digital Age. Spiritual networking will enhance the spiritual experience by flipping the dry, uni-modal, conceptual, abstract, theoretic mode of perception into a mythic mode of perception, in which multiple levels of meaning and perception—the virtual, the real, the metaphorical, the allegorical, the private, the communal—are all perceived at once. The full feeling of the myth can only be experienced in the mythic mindset, when the narrative is taken not as a single literal message, but as a panoply of interrelated meanings, functioning on a host of different levels of understanding. The digital experience, since it is multisensory and multimodal, will also create a more visceral sensory experience—it will feel "real" rather than conceptual. The user will live the myth, not just read about it in a book.

The oral-auditory senses will be brought into play, as people will speak and hear the spiritual messages. They will hear the words of the prophets, the songs of the angels, and the voice of "God." The visual sense will be enhanced greatly, from a monochromatic focus on the word on a page, to a high-definition, 3-dimensional, moving image of spiritual entities within an interactive virtual world. The mimetic mindset will also be retrieved and enhanced. Ritual re-enactments in the spiritual network will be highly active and physically invigorating, rather than the physically stultifying ritual practices of prayer and meditation that focus exclusively on sitting, broken intermittently with an occasional standing, kneeling, or bowing. The tactile senses will also be engaged in the digitally immersed virtual environment. The user will feel the heat of the "burning bush" as he lives that myth. He'll feel the spray of the salty water as the Red Sea splits before him. He'll feel the physical presence of God as he stands atop Mt. Sinai. The episodic mindset will also be retrieved in the spiritual network, as the experience will be interactive, imagistic, and experienced with the senses in real time with real (virtual) others. Spiritual networking will be about living the real spiritual experience of a myth, and encountering God on a true sensory level.

If you've been vaguely offended by this book so far, I would suggest that you *don't* read the rest of this chapter, as it will *definitely* offend you. Well, you've been warned....

Digital Tantra

> *How beautiful you are and how pleasing, my love, with your delights!*
> *Your stature is like that of the palm, and your breasts like clusters of fruit.*
> *I said, "I will climb the palm tree; I will take hold of its fruit."*
> *May your breasts be like clusters of grapes on the vine,*
> *the fragrance of your breath like apples, and your mouth like the best wine.*
> —Song of Solomon 7: 6–9

Sexuality and spirituality have always been linked. Some of the earliest religious relics ever discovered, dating back to 35,000 years ago, are the idols of fertility goddesses, such as the Venus of Willendorf, that depict overtly sexual images. The fertility rites of preliterate cultures, both ancient and contemporary, are overtly sexual. The earliest myths maintain that sexual congress between mortals and gods was necessary in order for life to go on. An archetypal theme in mythology is the birth of a hero as the result of sex between a god and a woman. According to the Bible: "the sons of the gods saw the daughters of men that they were fair, and they took them wives of all whom they chose" (Genesis 6:2). Perseus was the son of Danaë and Zeus; Hercules the son of Zeus and Alcmene; Jesus the son of Mary and Yehovah, etc. Bronze Age cultures such as Sodom and Gomorrah were condemned by the Bible because their spiritual rites were sexual acts as well. Mythic and archetypal figures such as centaurs and satyrs were associated with spirituo-sexual rites involving bestiality. In the East, tantric sexual rites and the spiritual verses found in the Kama Sutra point to the unification of sexuality and spirituality. Ancient Greek rituals such as the Dionysian rites and Eleusinian mysteries involved sexual acts between worshippers and priests in the role of gods; this ritualistic sex was called the *"Hieros Gamos"*— the sacred marriage. There is an undeniably erotic quality to much of the prayers, psalms, and hymns of antiquity. The "Song of Solomon," as quoted above, is a perfect example.

Certain words, such as "passion" and "ecstasy," are used only in two contexts, the sexual and the spiritual. Other words such as "bliss, "rapture," and "exaltation" have similar dual uages.[67] Nuns in convents since antiquity have reported the feeling of being physically overcome or "possessed" by the physical presence of God or Jesus, in terms that are unmistakably sexual. For example, the following passage was recorded by Jean-Joseph Surin during his interview with a 17th century nun, who felt "Christ's presence" come to her in the night:

> When I was on my bed, I felt something descend over me. I was penetrated, as a sponge would be, by a liquid from heaven that infused everything and gave me an indescribable joy and sweetness. There was such a release of melancholy, about which nothing can be said. Then, in a short-lived moment, it seemed that my soul was in glory.

Nuns, priests, and monks from many different religious traditions take vows of celibacy because they believe that one must choose "either the life of the flesh or the life of the spirit," as the same energy animates both passions. The singularly spiritual life would be diluted by sexuality, just as the singularly sexual life would be diluted by spirituality. But history demonstrates that spirituality and sexuality have more typically been balanced or linked in the lives of people, rather than exorcised, vilified, or rigidly separated, as in most of the modern theoretic traditions. As a reaction to the sexual repression of modern religions, we've seen the reemergence of paganism in Europe and North America in the past few centuries, and the reintroduction of spirituo-sexual rites in manifold forms. The "Great Rite," for example, in the neo-pagan Wiccan tradition, is the act of ritual sex between the high priest and high priestess during the Spring fertility rites of the Beltane (May Day) festival.

If so desired, Spiritual Networking can retrieve the missing link between sex and spirit in a safe, secure, anonymous, confidential, and disease-free virtual environment. We have already seen the beginning of the virtualization of sex. Internet porn, cybersex, Skype-sex, and sexting are just the beginning. Virtual reality immersion technology that can replicate sights, sounds, smells, tastes, and tactile sensations with amazing accuracy already exist. The adaptation of virtual reality media for the sexual marketplace is happening right now, and it's guaranteed to be a trillion dollar industry. When the digitally immersive, virtually interactive, pornographic, online version of *World of Warcraft* hits the market, the industry of prostitution and the institution of dating will both be obsolesced. Kurzweil predicted the advent of a "sensual machine" that will replicate every aspect of the sexual act—sight, sound, taste, touch, and smell—within a virtual environment. At first, virtual partners will be real humans; but in time, digital media will replace the need for real human virtual partners with simulated virtual partners.[68] After all, once the entire experience is virtualized and digitalized, what's the difference between interacting with a real person and a computer anyway? In due time, the entire physical aspect of the experience will be replaced by direct activation of the neurological senses and the parts of the brain that are responsive to sexual stimulation, via neural implants.[69] At this point, the "software" of sexual experience will transcend the "hardware" of the human body, making anything possible. "A man can feel what it is like to be a woman, and vice versa. Indeed, there's no reason why you can't be both at the same time... "[70] Once the vessel and medium of the body is transcended, there is no limit to experience, in either the sexual or the spiritual domains. Indeed, transcendence is really the key overlapping feature between sexuality and spirituality.[71]

Newberg and d'Aquili believe that "the neurological machinery of transcendence may have arisen from the neural circuitry that evolved for mating and sexual experience."[72] The orientation association area (OAA) in the posterior superior parietal lobe of the brain manages our sense of selves in space—what we perceive as "I" and "Not-I" in our environment. Newberg and d'Aquili found that the OAA was deaffentiated during the peak phases of meditation or prayer in their test subjects. When the OAA is not functioning normally, we get a sense of physically transcending ourselves, a feeling that is related to both the spiritual and the sexual experience. This may be why the state of sex is so often described in mystical terms. During sex, your sense of your physical body becomes intermingled with another person's body. The OAA is initially hyper-stimulated, because it is receiving the unusual input of overlapping bodies, the "I" is co-mingling in an extraordinary way with a "Not-I." The bodies in the sexual act have somehow merged into one connected body, Shakespeare's "beast with two backs." Furthermore, the culmination of the sexual act, just like the spiritual ritual, is achieved through "repetitive, rhythmic stimulation"[73]—the exact kind of stimulation that would lead to the deafferentiation of the OAA, the area in the brain that is associated with both the mystical and the sexual experience. Hence, the French euphemism "la petit mort" refers to a brief but potent sense of spiritual transcendence that is sometimes experienced directly after the moment of orgasm. The petite mort merges sex with spirit, for whether one is transcending the self in a union with a lover or in a union with God, the neurological processes are very similar, and in some ways identical.

In sex, we strive for a feeling of "ecstasy," to step out of ourselves in order to experience the "passion" that occurs when two bodies and minds fuse and meld into a state of unity. In the spiritual act, we seek the same sense of transcendence. The ecstasy and passion of the spiritual experience is achieved through the transcendence of self and a unity with the Other. This is why sexuality and spirituality are historically, culturally, mythologically, physiologically, psychologically, and neurologically intertwined. In the modern world, the ability to experience spiritual transcendence has been inhibited by the media of our own linguistic thoughts. Perhaps this is why the Western world has become so hyper-sexualized. There is no escaping the bombardment of sexual imagery that surrounds us. But why? Perhaps in sex, modern humans are seeking the transcendence that they once found in God? But sex as a purely physical act is not transcendent. Only when the emotions of intense love and devotion are combined with sex do we feel the true transcendent experience of "passion." Hence, modern humans are lost. We seek God but find only a hollow symbol. We seek passion but find only meaningless sex.

Spiritual Networking, by retrieving the sexual component of spirituality, enhances both parts of the experience. Passion and ecstasy, the feelings derived from a sense of both physical and psychological unity with an Other, are the common aims of both practices. Spirituality and sexuality are not inherently individual acts, they are inherently communal acts. Just as we have sexual partners, we may have spiritual partners, even if it's just the "constant partner" of God. In the modern world, post-literate humans have turned back into themselves on cognitive, spiritual, and sexual levels. We spend our days immersed in our private kingdoms of the mind, we spend our evenings in private autoerotic fantasy worlds, our exiled spirits spend their nights in private unconscious dream worlds. Digital media can reconnect all these detached aspects of the self, and it can connect us with other people as well. Spirituality does not just have to be about uniting with a purely spiritual figure on a purely spiritual level. It could be about uniting with another person or with a group of people on a variety of levels through the practice of a unifying spirituo-sexual ritual. When the perceptual functions of the mind are transformed by digital media into software rather than hardware, anything will be possible. We can re-experience the feeling of being inside someone, just as we experienced it as a fetus—the feeling of being inside our creator, inside Mother, inside God—absolute physical and spiritual unity. We can feel God or the Goddess as he or she was imagined in the myths and psalms: as a lover whom we can enter, a mother whom we can re-enter, or a partner who can enter us. We can re-experience the feeling of being the creator of our own world, just as the baby in his stroller looks up at the sun and the clouds and controls their movements with the powers of his own mind. In the digital world, we can actively create our own worlds out of the ether of our own imaginations. We can even feel what it is to *be* God.

Conclusion: The God Machine

He who uses machines does all his work like a machine.
He who does work like a machine grows a heart like a machine.
He who carries the heart of a machine in his breast loses his simplicity.
He who has lost his simplicity becomes unsure in the strivings of his soul.—Zhuang Zhou (4th century BC)

We are busy imitating machines.—Iain McGilchrist (2009)[1]

Moore's Law states that the number of transistors on integrated circuits tends to double about every two years.[2] Because this number determines the speed of information processing, Moore's observation predicts that the speed of information will accelerate exponentially as we proceed into the future. The implication of Moore's Law (as Henri Bergson predicted a century ago, without even knowing what a computer or transistor was), is that the speed of *everything* appears to be doubling itself in a never-ending, dizzying trajectory to who-knows-where. Some computer scientists suggest that in the not-too-distant future, we will reach the "technological singularity," the moment in time when technological innovation occurs instantaneously and automatically. What happens then? That may be the moment when technology becomes "smarter" than human beings. But what does that *mean?* Nobody knows what it means because it's impossible to predict! Time is moving so fast that we cannot even see a few years ahead of us. There's no "foreseeable" future, because we cannot foresee the next step on a road, when the road directly in front of us is angled at a vertical slope. We are approaching the future too quickly and with too much change to foresee anything with any accuracy. Even the "rearview mirror" of the past is not instructive, as a rearview mirror is useless when one is moving at the speed of light.[3]

A century ago, Henri Bergson could predict that the speed of everything will continue to double; but at the same time, he couldn't predict what the perpetual doubling would entail: computers, satellites, the internet, Iphones, etc. It took as much as a million years for us to get from mimetic gestures and animalistic grunts to the spoken word, it then took at least 50,000 years to get from the spoken word to the written word, and then another 4,500 years to get from the written word to the printed word; but in the past 175 years alone, we have progressed from the printed word to the telegraphed word to the telephoned word to the radio broadcasted word to the television broadcasted word to the satellite transmitted word to the digitally transmitted word. For us, because Time has been speeding up at an exponential rate, the next century will be here before the next decade. We can predict the change, but we cannot predict what the change will entail. Furthermore, if the change entails a "singularity," we cannot even predict the dimension of change that will occur. It might be stupendous, it might be insignificant. Only God knows!

Some have predicted that the "singularity" will result in an "intelligence explosion." One way in which this could occur would be if our computers become so intelligent that they could create better computers than we can, resulting in computers that are even smarter than their computer creators, and so and so on, and all at the speed of light! Another possibility is that, as a function of the ever-increasing human/computer digital interface, human brains will become so intertwined with computer brains that our minds will evolve into cyber-brains, complete with neural implants wirelessly hooked up to an external computer brain. Digital machines linked by the internet to satellites in space and computers all over the word currently control most of the day-to-day functioning of the world. When the cyber-brain of the post–Singularity takes form, it will be like God: omniscient, omnipresent, and omnipotent. Perhaps our cyber-brains will perceive a Digital God in our own reflected image? Or maybe the computer generated computers will process a Digital God, a Creator created for us by our own creations, who will appear to us as a phantom of the ether, a digital ghost in the machinery of information, who can be accessed online and provide instant virtual comfort in response to infinite spiritual needs. Perhaps the Singularity will result in a Unity between our inner need for God and our ability to project and even create God—a manmade image of God, reflecting the Digital Man in his own image—but perceived as a sentient Other—a Digital God.

The once laughable notion of "global telepathy" becomes eerily possible once we equate human brain processing with digital processing, an equation that will be solved once we reach the Singularity, when information processing potential becomes infinite. At that point, we will see the rise of the true cyber-brain—a digital brain capable of consciousness—that interacts seamlessly with human brains. The only factor we'll need to complete the equation would be some system that could facilitate instant and infinite communication between billions of cyber-brains (oh wait, we already have that ... it's called the "internet"). Global telepathy will come to pass—brought to you by digital media—but the idea of a mystical union of all minds is by no means novel. It is, in fact, one of the oldest ideas in existence. When preliterate tribes enter the "Sacred Time" of a spiritual ritual, they are uniting their consciousnesses with the minds of their gods. When nuns pray, they achieve the "Unio Mystica" with God, Jesus, or Mary. When we dream, according to Jung, we perceive archetypal symbols from the "collective unconscious," a communal frame of mind shared by everyone who ever existed. When a Buddhist meditates, he transcends his individual consciousness to merge with a global consciousness. God, Jesus, Allah, Vishnu or the deity of your choice is an "extension of man," the projection and objectification of our need to transcend ourselves and find unity in a spiritual other. In the end, we may be destined to become our own God, by creating a form of media that allows each individual to transcend his own sense of consciousness and unite his mind with a global consciousness.[4]

The Digital God

> Mysticism is just tomorrow's science dreamed today.—Marshall McLuhan

Detachment as a mode of consciousness, when taken to its fullest potential, is flipped into its antithesis: Integral awareness. Meditation, for example, systematically detaches the sense of self from consciousness until a point of maximum detachment is reached, at which point the process flips back onto itself and the self merges with consciousness into a unified state of integral awareness, an episode of cognitive or spiritual unity. Digital computation is the most detached and abstract form of expression that human beings have ever created. For instance, this is how you say the word "love" in binary code: "011011000110 11110111011001100101." But at the point of infinite processing potential, the technology of ultimate abstraction flips back onto itself by producing for its users the potential for integral awareness. When digital media reaches its fullest potential, it can create a virtual world that feels just as real—*if not more real*— than the "real" world it's fabricating. We are currently on the verge of reaching the point of infinite processing potential. When this occurs, infinite abstraction will facilitate integral awareness. Digital simulation will create super-lucid virtual reality. Technological complexity will create mystical simplicity. The serpent will swallow its own tail.

The Singularity may have an unexpected counter-intuitive effect. Perhaps when humanity grasps the final tool in the shed, he will turn that tool inwardly upon himself. Is it possible that after thousands of years of outward gazing, that Narcissus will one day recognize himself in his reflection, and break free of his hypnotic trance? If so, what will he see, and how might it occur? How will the tool change us? Will we psychically merge with the tool, or will the tool force us to reconsider the utility of tools en toto? Will the Singularity somehow facilitate the unity of self that the mystics seek, or the unity with the eternal infinite of which the spiritualists preach?

Language was the wheel that set the vehicle of consciousness evolution in motion. Literacy was the engine that powered the vehicle forward with ever-increasing velocity. Print was the wing that freed it from the prison of the ground and gave it air to flight. Electronic media was the jet that rocketed the ship upwards at blinding speed. The tumult of the 20th century was the sonic boom. The ship has now broken free of the atmosphere. Unfettered by gravity or air, it shoots headlong into the infinite unknown. Digital media is the nuclear accelerator that doubles our speed at ever-decreasing intervals. What will happen when the ship reaches warp speed? Will there be a light speed equivalent to a sonic boom—a *luminous boom*—a second Enlightenment? Will there be yet another century of unparalleled change, revolution, and tumult? Will history repeat itself; or will history have no precedent upon which to repeat? Will we meet our Maker? Perhaps we will *make our meter* ... at last constructing a "measure of man" that realizes our fullest potential? If digitality is the medium that will push the evolution of consciousness beyond the light barrier, then the spirit beckoning us from the other side of the opaque screen of an unknowable future is truly a Digital God.

Chapter Notes

Introduction

1. Dowling College: A small liberal arts college on the banks of the Connetquot River, on the southern shore of eastern Long Island, New York.
2. Spilka et al., p. 184.
3. Spilka, p. 191.

Chapter One

1. Pinker (2004), p. 46, & Armstrong (1993), p. 398.
2. Hamer (2004), p. 5.
3. Extra-somatic: Outside of the body, or more specifically, outside of the brain.
4. The first form of graphic language, pictograms, are found in ancient Sumer, dating back to 3300 BC. Pictograms provided little more clarity than actual drawings or pictures. Except for when the pictogram that was drawn represented exactly the object it was referring to (a stick picture of a man wearing a crown, representing a king), pictograms were too tied down to the concrete to offer a way of truly transfiguring oral words into graphic symbols. Pictograms gave way to ideograms, schematic diagrams that were more abstract, but still needed to be interpreted. Also, a system of ideograms was limited in terms of the total number of ideograms a scribe could use, which could then be understood or "read" by other scribes. Ideograms gave way to phonograms, which were even more abstract, as the reference in a phonogram was to the *sound* of the word denoting the thing, not the thing itself. This was the first time in which we see ancient writers trying to reproduce the oral word (which in-itself is an abstract symbol), in a graphic form. The Phoenician alphabet arose around 1500 BC. The "phonetic" alphabet is even more abstract, as each letter denotes a specific component of sound, not entire sounds themselves.
5. Donald (1991).
6. McLuhan (1967).
7. Ibid.
8. Donald.
9. Pictograms: Specific images that represent specific objects or actions. Hieroglyphs: Symbols representing a combination of objects or complex actions. Ideograms: Symbols that represent entire ideas. Logograms: Symbols that represent entire words. Phonetic writing: Writing words by combining alphabetic letters that each represents a specific sound.
10. Ray Kurzweil is one of the people who believe that voice recognition technology will replace keyboards, touchpads, and touchscreens—making literacy an oral/auditory task.
11. McLuhan (1962).
12. Coles, p. 168. (This is Coles' recollection from a private conversation with Anna Freud).
13. MacLean, Paul D. (1990). *The Triune Brain in Evolution: Role in Paleocerebral Functions*. New York: Plenum Press.
14. Fromm (1951), p. 33.
15. Sagan, pp. 159–60: "The survival of the early mammals depended on intelligence, daytime unobtrusiveness, and devotion to the young.... Thus, an inhibition center developed below what in humans is the temporal lobe, to turn off much of the functioning of the reptilian brain; and an activation center evolved in the pons to turn on the R-complex, but harmlessly, during sleep. This view, of course,

has some notable points of similarity to Freud's picture of the repression of the id by the super-ego (or of the unconscious by the conscious).... The prevalence of dreams in infants would, in this view, be because in infancy, the analytic part of the neocortex is barely working. The absence of dreams in reptiles would be because there is no repression of the dream state in reptiles, they are, as Aeschylus described our ancestors, "dreaming" in their waking state.... Perhaps the dream state permits, in *our* fantasy and *its* reality, the R-complex to function regularly, as if it were still in control. If this is true, I wonder, after Aeschylus, if the waking state of other mammals is very much like the dream state of humans ... where we encounter vivid sensory and emotional images and active intuitive understanding, but very little rational analysis; where we are unable to perform tasks requiring extensive concentration; where we experience short attention spans and frequent distractions and, most of all, a very feeble sense of individuality or self.... If this is where we have come from, we have come very far."

16. Frazer (1922), p. 211.

17. This observation by the anthropologist R.S. Rattray was cited by the psychoanalyst R. Wood, which was then cited by Fromm (1951), p. 110.

18. Sacks (2013), p. 215: "Given the outlandish quality of some hypnopompic images, their often terrifying emotional resonance, and perhaps the heightened suggestibility that may go with such states, it is very understandable that hypnopompic visions of angels and devils may engender not only wonder or horror but belief in their physical reality. Indeed, one must wonder to what degree the very idea of monsters, ghostly spirits, or phantoms originated with such hallucinations. One can easily imagine that, coupled with a personal or cultural disposition to believe in a disembodied, spiritual realm, these hallucinations, though they have a real physiological basis, might reinforce a belief in the supernatural."

19. Sacks, pp. 216–17.

20. Comings, p. 347–348.

21. Since the brain has no pain receptors, brain surgery can be performed while the patient is completely conscious and responsive.

22. Comings, p. 354: "These perceptions include ... the re-playing of past experiences, thought intrusions, feelings of *déjà vu,* out-of-body sensations, trances or *fugue* states, automatic behaviors, feelings of being in the presence of others, of hearing music, of hearing angelic voices, of intense meaningfulness, of being connected to some force greater than themselves, and of talking to God. A review of the evidence accumulated since Penfield's studies also suggest the temporal lobes and its deep limbic structures, the amygdala, and hippocampus are the site of our spiritual brain."

23. Ibid.: "investigators have shown that deep temporal lobe stimulation in the area around the amygdale and hippocampus of the limbic system produces feelings of intense meaningfulness, of depersonalization, of a connection with God, of cosmic connectedness, of out-of-body experiences, a feeling of not being in this world ... fear, and hallucinations."

24. Persinger (1983).

25. Comings, pp. 376–378.

26. Persinger's "God Helmet" research is controversial, because other researchers have replicated his studies using the same methods but did not have the same results.

27. Comings pp. 377–378.

28. Ibid.

29. Persinger as quoted by Comings, pp. 390–91: "*A biological capacity for God Experience was critical for the survival of the human species.* Without some experiences that could balance the terror of personal extinction, existence of the human phenomena called the "self" could not be maintained. It would have been fragmented by the persistent, gnawing realization that death could come at any time."

30. Newberg & D'Aquilli (2002).

31. Ibid.

32. Oliver Sacks (2013): "Epilepsy affects a substantial minority of the population, occurs in all cultures, and has been recognized since the dawn of recorded history. It was known to Hippocrates as the sacred disease, a disorder of divine inspiration."

33. Sacks, pp. 161–2.

34. Ramachandran (1998), pp. 179–80: "But most remarkable of all are those patients who have deeply moving spiritual experiences, including a feeling of divine presence and the sense that they are in direct communication with God. Everything around them is imbued with cosmic significance. They may say, 'I finally understand what it's all about. This is the moment I've been waiting for all my life. Suddenly it all makes sense.' Or, 'Finally I have insight into the true nature of the cosmos.' I find it ironic that this sense of enlightenment, this absolute conviction that Truth is revealed at last, should derive from limbic structures

concerned with emotions rather than from the thinking, rational parts of the brain that take so much pride in their ability to discern truth and falsehood."

35. Sacks summarizing Geschwind, pp. 162–3.

36. Ramachandran (2011): "I sometimes wonder whether such patients who have temporal lobe epilepsy have access to another dimension of reality, a wormhole of sorts into a parallel universe. But I usually don't say this to my colleagues, lest they doubt my sanity."

37. Persinger: "Mystical and religious experiences are hypothesized to be evoked by transient, electrical microseizures within deep structures of the temporal lobe ... the unusual electrical coherence allows access to infantile memories of parents, a source of good expectations, specific stimulation evokes out-of-body experiences, space-time distortions, intense meaningfulness, and dreamy scenes.... Predisposing factors include any biochemical or genetic factors that produce temporal lobe lability. A variety of precipitating stimuli provoke these experiences, but personal (life) crises and death bed conditions are optimal. These temporal lobe microseizures can be learned as responses to existential trauma because stimulation is of powerful intrinsic reward regions and reduction of death anxiety occurs."

38. Ramachandran (2011): "the repeated electrical bursts inside the patient's brain ... permanently 'facilitate' certain pathways or may even open new channels, much as water from a storm might pour downhill, opening new rivulets, furrows and passages along the hillside. This process, called kindling, might permanently alter—and sometimes enrich— the patient's inner emotional life."

39. The term "Geschwind Syndrome" has also been applied to temporal lobe epileptics with the same personality and behavioral traits.

40. Ramachandran (2011).

41. Ibid., pp. 245–6.

42. Sacks, pp. 158–9.

43. Théophile Alajouanine, as quoted in Sacks, p. 157.

44. Cases of famous visionaries who showed possible symptoms of temporal lobe epilepsy: The Sages noted that Moses would commune with God by falling to his face in the Tabernacle before the Holy Ark, writhing spasmodically on the floor. St. Paul the Apostle (while he was still known as Saul of Tarsus), converted to Christianity subsequent to a vision on the road to Damascus, where he was blinded by a flash of light, and then saw a vision of Jesus and heard His voice (visual hallucinations of light and auditory hallucinations in the form of voices are common experiences during temporal lobe epileptic seizures). Afterwards, Saul was blind for three days (possibly due to neuronal trauma). Siddhartha, the Buddha, was Awakened and Enlightened after meditating under the Boddhi tree for 49 consecutive days. (Recall that Newberg's study demonstrated that deep meditation coincides with high activation of the temporal lobes). In 1200 BC, Zoroaster (a.k.a. Zarathustra) was blinded by a vision of a god, leading to a revelation and the dawn of a new religion. The Pythia, the Apollonian oracles in Delphi, delivered the words of their patron god for nearly a thousand years. When possessed by Apollo, they would tremble and shake, fall to their faces and writhe on the temple floor, before crying and screaming out the words of the god. Saint Constantine the Great, Emperor of Rome, while marching into battle in the midday sun, saw a blinding vision of a sword in the sky, which he took for a sign of the Christian cross. Constantine's subsequent "conversion" and adoption of Christianity was a key factor in the eventual founding of the Catholic Church and the Holy Roman Empire. Mohammed experienced a revelation through a vision of the angel Gabriel, after praying intently, alone in a dark cave, for several weeks. This revelation was the beginning of the Koran and of the Islamic religion. Joan of Arc heard the voice of an angel to her right, which was accompanied by a pure "great light," also coming from her right. This was the voice who told her to lead an army against the English. Martin Luther reported that he frequently altercated with "Satan." His personality certainly embodied the "four H's" of Geschwind Syndrome— Hyperreligiosity, Hyposexuality, Humorlessness, and Hypergraphia —personality traits associated with temporal lobe epilepsy. Joseph Smith, the founder of Mormonism, received his revelations through visions, achieved by staring intently at a pair of "mystical" stones. When Ellen White, one of the co-founders of the Seventh Day Adventists, was a little girl, she experienced severe blunt trauma to the head, after which she became highly religious, and began experiencing vivid revelations, in which she saw spiritual visions. White experienced seizures of different length and intensity, experienced countless revelations, and led

a life marked by extremely high religiosity, and incessant spiritual proselytizing and writing.

45. Kurzweil, pp. 151–52.
46. Donald: "The brain may not have changed recently in its genetic makeup, but its link to an accumulating external memory network affords it cognitive powers that would not have been possible in isolation. This is more than a metaphor; each time the brain carries out an operation in concert with the external symbolic storage system, it becomes part of a network. Its memory structure is temporarily altered; and the locus of cognitive control changes."
47. Luke: 17:21.

Chapter Two

1. Buber (1923), *I and Thou*.
2. Fuglesang, pp. 39–40 & pp. 78–79.
3. Jaynes (1976), *The Origin of Consciousness*.
4. McGilchrist, p. 65.
5. McGilchrist, p. 113.
6. Ramachandran (2011), p. 173.
7. The right hemisphere is particularly important in childhood experience and is preponderant even in *language* development in early childhood.... It is with the right hemisphere that we recall childhood memories, and autobiographical memories of all kinds ... the right hemisphere is more advanced until the second year of life.
8. Especially in Broca's area and Wernicke's area.
9. Ramachandran (2001), p. 182: "an area very close to what we now call Broca's area originally evolved in tandem with the IPL [Inferior Parietal Lobe] for the multimodal and hierarchical subassembly routines of tool use. There was a subsequent duplication of this ancestral area, and one of the two new subareas became further specialized for syntactic structure that is divorced from actual manipulation of physical objects in the world—in other words, it became Broca's area."
10. McGilchrist, p. 111.
11. Ibid.
12. Ibid., p. 277.
13. Ibid., p. 112: "It is not an accident that we talk about 'grasping' what someone is saying. The metaphor of grasp has its roots deep in the way we talk about thinking in most languages ... words such as im*press*ion, ex*press*ion, in*tend*, con*tend*, pre*tend* (from Latin *tendere*, to reach with the hand."

14. Walsh (2005), as quoted in McGilchrist, p. 131: "We tend to assume teleologically, because of our focus on language being that most beautiful thing, that it must be endowed by some special mechanism of the left hemisphere ... in fact, it may just be normally repressed in the right hemisphere and allowed to take place in the left."
15. McCrone, p. 164: "The brain's flexibility is further shown by the way it responds when the whole speech area is wiped out by a stroke. With a lot of training, the right-hand side of the brain can be coaxed into taking over the task of talking, and although the relearned speech is not nearly as fluent as it was with the specialized zones, the brain tissue is still plastic enough to shape itself to new demands."
16. The Greek alphabet arose around 1100 BC. It was derived from the earlier Phoenician alphabet. While Semitic languages (such as modern Hebrew), are written and read in the direction of right to left, Greek literacy changed that direction gradually, and by around 400 BC, all Greek words flowed from left to right rather than right to left. The direction of writing, according to McGilchrist, is significant. The movement of the eyes in the right-to-left direction, as in the writing and reading of Hebrew and Arabic, indicates a "right-hemisphere-determined point of view," because the eye is being driven towards the left by the right-hemisphere, providing preferential communication to the right hemisphere; whereas a left-to-right direction indicates a left-hemisphere-determined point of view. Syllabic languages are written from right to left, while phonemic languages (which consist of independent elements of sound rather than entire syllables), are written left-to-right. The Indo-European languages, from which all Western languages are derived, are phonemic languages. The insertion of vowel letters into alphabets also denotes a shift to the left. Without vowels, the pronunciation and therefore the meaning of individual words (as many words without vowels are written the same way), are derived contextually, which is an unconscious or intuitive strategy. But with vowels, the word's meaning is derived independently of its context, based purely on the sequence of the independent sound elements (letters) that compose the word. In written Hebrew, for example, there are no vowels. It is therefore very difficult to understand many specific Hebrew words if they are taken 'out of context,' because the context, not the spe-

cific word itself, often denotes the specific meaning. The Hebrew word exists primarily within its own context, reflecting a historically older mode of perception, based in an oral tradition, in which words were not completely abstract signs; but rather, they were always directly tied in to a specific event or object within the context of a real time and place. The development of writing—from pictures (cave paintings) to hieroglyphs (symbols) to pictograms (morphemes) to phonemes to alphabets—represents a development from sensory based images to precise abstract marks. Each stage of development marks a further leftward lateralization of language processing, a further abstraction from real objects to symbols and intangible concepts. Historically, humans shifted from singing and speaking ideas in oral symbols to writing down symbols. Over time, we became less of a symbol maker and more of a 'marker' —a recorder of specific abstract marks on a page that have precise and exact meanings— rather than a creator and interpreter of broadly conceived symbolic ideas. This shift is represented in the brain. The left hemisphere literally grasped language away from the right hemisphere through writing. The left hemisphere controlled right hand, so dominant in the utilitarian tasks of tool making and tool using, grasped a writing implement and thus transformed language from a form of communication based on oral symbols, to a form of communication based on precise visual marks of alphabetic characters. (McGilchrist, p 274).

17. McLuhan (1965), p. 27.
18. Fuglesang, pp. 78–9.
19. This is a link to a *60 Minutes* segment on Steven Wiltshire: http://www.cbsnews.com/videos/an-autistic-artist-savant/.
20. This is a link to a *60 Minutes* segment on people with "total recall": http://www.cbsnews.com/news/the-gift-of-endless-memory/.
21. McGilchrist, p. 330: "*Logos* represents, as indeed the left hemisphere does, a closed system which cannot reach outside itself to whatever it is that exists apart from itself."
22. Ramachandran (2011), p. 267.
23. McGilchrist, p.81.
24. Ibid., p. 54.
25. Ibid., p. 60.
26. Ibid., p. 65.
27. Sagan, p. 183.
28. McGilchrist, p. 187.
29. Sperry, as quoted in McGilchrist, p. 220.
30. McGilchrist, p. 220: "Perhaps, then, consciousness is unified at the *lowest* levels, and it is actually only when the process becomes *self*-conscious at the topmost levels, within cognition, that the possibility of separation occurs."
31. Ibid., p. 221: "I like this image of the cerebral 'canopy' because it reminds us that consciousness is not a bird, as it often seems to be in the literature—hovering, detached, coming in at the top level and alighting on the brain somewhere in the frontal lobes—but a tree, its roots deep inside us. It reinforces the nature of consciousness not as an entity, but as a process."
32. Ibid., p. 127: "the left hemisphere ... is more the instrument of our conscious will than the right hemisphere."
33. Ibid.
34. Ibid., p. 216: "it is the will of the left hemisphere, at a more conscious level, that normally inhibits the will of the right."
35. Ibid., p. 218: "The left hemisphere point of view inevitably dominates ... the means of argument—the three Ls, language, logic, and linearity—are all ultimately under left-hemisphere control, so that the cards are heavily stacked in favour of our conscious discourse enforcing the world view re-presented in the hemisphere which speaks, the left hemisphere."
36. Ibid., p. 260 "since the data that we have on hemisphere difference are derived almost exclusively from westerners over the last hundred years or so, we do not know whether the same differences to the same degree have always existed or exist elsewhere in the world."
37. Ibid., p. 83.
38. Ibid., p. 85.
39. Ramachandran (1998).
40. McGilchrist, p. 99: "Whatever lies in the realm of the implicit, or depends on flexibility, whatever can't be brought into focus and fixed, ceases to exist as far as the speaking hemisphere is concerned."
41. Ibid., p. 67: "many important aspects of experience, those that the right hemisphere is particularly well equipped to deal with—our passions ... all religious sense, all imaginative and intuitive processes—are denatured by becoming the object of focused attention, which renders them explicit, therefore mechanical, lifeless."
42. Ibid., p. 54: "Because the right hemisphere sees nothing in the abstract, but always appreciates things in their context, it is interested in the personal, by contrast with the left hemisphere, which has more affinity for the abstract or impersonal. The right hemisphere's

view of the world in general is construed according to what is of concern to it, not according to objective impersonal categories, and therefore has a personal quality."

43. Ibid., p. 98: "The unconscious, while not identical with, is certainly more strongly associated with, the right hemisphere ... as Freud wrote, the unconscious 'is a particular realm of the mind with its own wishful impulses, its own mode of expression and its peculiar mental mechanisms which are not in force elsewhere.'"

44. Ibid., p. 93.

45. Wilhelm von Humboldt: "By the same process whereby he spins language out of his own being, he ensnares himself in it; each language draws a magic circle round the people to which it belongs, a circle from which there is no escape, save by stepping out of it into another."

46. John McCrone (1991).

47. McGilchrist, p. 65: "In fact an extensive body of research now indicates that insight, whether mathematical or verbal, the sort of problem solving that happens when we are, precisely, not concentrating on it, is associated with activation in the right hemisphere...."

48. Kekulé as quoted in Batson (1982), p.77: "I turned my chair to the fire and dozed.... Again the atoms were gamboling before my eyes.... My mental eye, rendered more acute by repeated visions of this kind, could now distinguish larger structures, of manifold conformation; long rows, sometimes more closely fitted together; all twining and twisting in snakelike motion. But look! What was that? One of the snakes had seized hold of its own tail, and the form whirled mockingly before my eyes. As if by a flash of lightning I awoke...."

49. McGilchrist, p. 107.

50. Sagan (1977), p. 189.

51. Ibid., pp. 165–6.

52. McCrone, p. 134–7: "The Truk style of thinking is seen as primitive because the islanders are unable to articulate the rules by which they are maintaining their course. When asked, they shrug and point to where they think the island lies. Early humans must have existed for hundreds of thousands of years with such natural methods of thought, doing what they felt was right from experience or custom. Today we would describe such thinking as intuitive or instinctive, but it is really just allowing our rich nets of knowledge to surface in the conscious plane and then taking heed of the images they present. Modern man has been so trained to trust only thoughts driven along by chains of words that this inner knowledge is treated nervously. We may sometimes act on hunches and gut feelings, but we are happier when we can talk of the logical reasons for doing something. Indeed, we will often find an intuitive answer and then look for logical reasons to back up our decision ... logical or scientific thought ... strips away all the obscuring detail of life so that we can see the bare-bones story of how things work..."; "On close inspection, the rational thinking that is supposed to be the hallmark of modern man is really a rather specialized skill. It is extremely useful for the sort of publicly discussed thought that underpins science, but if we analyze what takes place in our own minds, we will see that even our most abstract thoughts are not dry strings of symbols, in the privacy of our heads we tackle problems with metaphors drawn from everyday life rather than by following computerlike chains of logic."

53. Batson, pp. 77–80.

54. Barrett's research as summarized by Boyer, pp. 88–9.

55. Ibid., p. 142.

56. McGilchrist, p. 82: "The right hemisphere is able to maintain ambiguous mental representations in the face of a tendency to premature over-interpretation by the left hemisphere. The right hemisphere's tolerance of uncertainty is implied everywhere in its subtle ability to use metaphor, irony and humour, all of which depend on not prematurely resolving ambiguities. So, of course, does poetry, which relies on right-hemisphere language capacities."

57. Armstrong (2009), p. 29.

58. McGilchrist, p. 228.

59. Tremlin, pp. 172–174.

60. "Tragedy of the theologians": Pascal Boyer is usually noted as the cognitive psychologist who coined this term.

61. Todd Tremlin (2006): "The real "tragedy of the theologian" is that he or she is shopping second-rate wares. Given the dynamics of dual processing and social cognition, basic representations provide robust computational utility and psychological relevance. Abstract, theological representations can be dispensed with, and often are."

62. Tremlin, pp. 175–182, quoting Chaiken and Trope (1999).

63. McGilchrist, p. 427.

64. McGilchrist, p. 431: "The left hemisphere prefers the impersonal to the personal."

65. Blake (1793), *The Marriage of Heaven and Hell*.

66. Ramachandran (1998), p. 68.

67. Dawkins (2006), as quoted in Bellah, 2011, p. 56: "We live near the centre of a cavernous museum of magnitudes viewing the world with sense organs and nervous systems that are equipped to perceive and understand only a small middle range of sizes, moving at the middle range of speeds. We are at home with objects ranging in size from a few kilometers (the view from a mountaintop) to about a tenth of a millimeter (the point of a pin). Outside this range even our imagination is handicapped, and we need the help of instruments and mathematics—which, fortunately, we can learn to deploy. The range of sizes, distances or speeds with which our imaginations are comfortable is a tiny band, set in the midst of a gigantic range of the possible, from the scale of quantum strangeness at the smaller end to the scale of Einsteinian cosmology at the larger."

68. McCrone, p. 68: "Perception ... is a useful term because it makes the distinction that we are never in direct contact with the real world. Everything we see, hear, touch, taste, or smell has been filtered and distorted by the pathways leading to our conscious experience of life; yet ... despite the fragmentary processing, we feel that we see a whole and intact world, or rather, we gloss over the cracks and believe that we are seeing a 20/20 view of life. This gluing together to create an apparently complete vision is the key to perception."

69. Levine, Chein, & Murphy (1948).

70. McClelland & Atkinson (1948).

71. Bruner & McGinnus (1948).

72. Shermer, p. 5: "Beliefs comes first, explanation for beliefs follow. I call this process belief-dependent realism, where our perceptions about reality are dependent on the beliefs that we hold about them."

73. Ramachandran (1998), pp. 88–90.

74. Ibid., p. 90.

75. As opposed to 'perceptual completion,' the notion that the senses give us a 'complete' picture, Ramachandran points out that our mind actually provides us with 'conceptual completion'—the mind provides us with complete concepts, before, in addition to, or even in lieu of a complete picture derived from the senses.

76. Ramachandran (1998), pp. 110–111: "There's good evidence to suggest that we are actually running our visual machinery in reverse!"

77. Ibid.

78. Ramachandran (2011), pp 249–50.

79. Ibid., pp. 230–31.

80. Ibid., p. 238.

81. The term was coined by Hughlings Jackson, as quoted in Sacks, p. 144.

82. Sacks, p. 144–5.

83. Ibid., p. 152.

84. Like normal consciousness, doubled consciousness could have its evolutionary origin in the adaptive trait of hyperagency detection, our predilection to perceive humanlike agents in our environments, especially during moments of perceived danger, even when no one is present. Add to this the function of Theory of Mind, our tendency to project consciousness onto other beings around us, and we have a pretty efficient mechanism for creating conscious doubles of ourselves.

85. As summarized by Shermer, p. 100.

86. Lindbergh as quoted in Shermer, pp. 100–101.

87. Sacks, pp. 288–89.

88. Ibid.

89. William Law: "What could begin to deny the self, if there were not something in man different from self?"

90. Sacks quoting Simpson, pp. 61–2.

91. Sacks, pp. 62–64.

92. Ibid., pp. 81–8.

93. Ramachandran (1998), p. 84.

94. Sacks, p. 195: "I had long wanted to see 'true' indigo, and thought that drugs might be the way to do this. So one sunny Saturday in 1964, I developed a pharmacologic launchpad consisting of a base of amphetamine (for general arousal), LSD (for hallucinogenic intensity), and a touch of cannabis (for a little added delirium). About twenty minutes after taking this, I faced a white wall and exclaimed, 'I want to see indigo now—*now!*' And then, as if thrown by a giant paintbrush, there appeared a huge, trembling, pear-shaped blob of the purest indigo. Luminous, numinous, it filled me with rapture: It was the color of heaven.... I leaned toward it in a sort of ecstasy. And then it suddenly disappeared, leaving me with an overwhelming sense of loss and sadness that it had been snatched away. But I consoled myself: Yes, indigo *exists*, and it can be conjured up in the brain."

95. Hood, R. W., Jr., and Morris, R. (1981). "Sensory Deprivation and Differential Elicitation of Religious Imagery in Intrinsic and Extrinsic Persons." *Journal for the Scientific Study of Religion, 20,* 261–73. (As summarized by Spilka et al., 1985, p. 161.)

96. Posey & Losch, 1983, as cited by Jaynes (1986), p. 10.
97. Ramachandran (2011), p. 57: "It's as if each of us is hallucinating all the time and what we call perception involves merely selecting the one hallucination that best matches the current input."
98. Sacks, p. 24.
99. Ibid., p. 41.
100. Ramachandran (2011), p. 107.
101. Ibid., pp. 86–87.
102. Sacks, p. 231.
103. Comings p. 392 (quoting Persinger).
104. Sacks, pp. 253–4.
105. Ramachandran (2011), p. 291.
106. Persinger's theory as summarized by Shermer, p. 91.
107. Pew Research Center (2012).
108. McLuhan & Powers (1989), pp. 37–8.
109. Huxley (1944), p. 277.
110. As quoted in Huxley (1944), p. 266.

Chapter Three

1. Bellah (2011).
2. Obviously, the nature of consciousness in the mind of the fetus is a matter of pure conjecture, but these suppositions will be tempered by reasonable arguments from erudite theorists.
3. The terms "dualism" and "adualism" are used by Piaget (1929), but he cites J.M. Baldwin, *Thoughts and Things*, as his source.
4. Piaget (1929), p. 153.
5. Prenatal research indicates that fetuses spend much of their time in REM sleep.
6. Piaget (1929), p. 153.
7. Ibid., p. 152.
8. Ibid., p. 153.
9. Ibid., pp. 153–4.
10. It is perhaps no coincidence that the word "precipitate" means both "to rain," and to "cause something to occur," such as the rain.
11. Piaget (1929), pp. 235–6.
12. Ibid.: "Going back to the starting point in the life of thought we find a protoplasmic consciousness unable to make any distinction between the self and things."
13. Gopnik (2009) as cited in Bellah, pp. 590–1.
14. I'm reminded here of Alexander Pope's couplet, "A little learning is a dang'rous thing; Drink deep, or taste not the Pierian spring," in which learning is equated with the act of drinking.
15. Rossetti, p. 15.
16. Rossetti quoting Hars Urs von Balthasar, p. 149.
17. Rossetti, p. 126.
18. Tremlin, p. 102.
19. Piaget (1929), p. 169.
20. Bettelheim, pp. 45–6, summarizing Piaget's theory of animistic thinking in childhood: "His thinking is animistic. Like all pre-literate and many literate people, 'the child assumes that his relations to the inanimate world are of one pattern with those to the animate world of people: he fondles as he would his mother the pretty thing that pleased him; he strikes the door that has slammed on him.' It should be added that he does the first because he is convinced that this pretty thing loves to be petted as much as he does; and he punishes the door because he is certain that the door slammed deliberately, out of evil intention.... To the eight-year-old (to quote Piaget's examples), the sun is alive because it gives light (and, one may add, it does that because it wants to). To the animistic child's mind, the stone is alive because it can move, as it rolls down a hill. Even a twelve-and-a-half-year-old is convinced that a stream is alive and has a will, because its water is flowing. The sun, stone, and the water are believed to be inhabited by spirits very much like people, so they feel and act like people."
21. Piaget (1929) p. 55: "there is confusion between the sign and the thing signified, the thought and the thing thought of. From this point of view the child cannot distinguish a real house, for example, from the concept or mental image or name of the house."
22. Ibid.
23. Piaget (1929), p. 70: "for these children the name is an essential part of the thing ... the name is therefore in the object, not as a label attached to it but as an invisible quality of the object."
24. In the mouth, not the mind: Very small children do not have "internalized speech," they cannot think silently in words, therefore they speak the words aloud, i.e., they talk to themselves, engaging in "private speech."
25. Ibid., p. 60: "until about 11, to think is to speak—either with the mouth or with a little voice situated in the head—and speaking consists in acting on things themselves by means of words, the words sharing the nature of the things named as well as of the voice producing them."
26. Piaget (1929), p. 39.
27. In my book, *Ancient Symbology* (2012), I discuss nominal realism and the magical/spir-

itual quality of words in much more detail, especially in Chapter 8.

28. Piaget (1929), pp. 248–50: "It is not the child which is moulded by language; but it is the language which is already childish."

"Thought creates language and then passes beyond it, but language turns on thought and seeks to imprison it."

"Adult language provides the very conditions necessary to foster the child's animism and this the more so, since generally speaking, the child takes all metaphors literally—it looks to see a "broken arm" tumble on to the ground, whilst the phrase "go to the devil" constituted, for a child of 9 of our acquaintance, the proof that the devil is not far off."

29. Julian Jaynes (1976): "Abstract words are ancient coins whose concrete images in the busy give-and-take of talk have worn away with use."

30. Guthrie, p. 3.

31. Ibid., p. 6: "Animism is universal in perception. It occurs because perception is interpretive (seeing is 'seeing as'), because interpretation is a choice among possibilities and thus a gamble, and because those interpretive bets that aim highest (by attributing the most organization and hence significance to things and events) have the greatest potential payoffs and lowest risks. For example, it is better for a hiker to mistake a boulder for a bear than to mistake a bear for a boulder."

32. Steiner, p. 212.

33. Xenophanes: Greek philosopher, 570–475 BC.

34. Boyer, pp. 142–3.

35. Tremlin, pp.95–97.

36. Jean-Paul Sartre: "There is a God-shaped hole in the heart of man where the divine used to be."

37. The Old Testament depicts quite clearly the incessant trend of the ancient Hebrews to practice idolatry.

38. Piaget (1929), pp. 105–6: "the images of the dream are regarded as being external to mind and as emanating from external sources wither in the persons and the thing dreamed of or in such substances as the night, the light, etc."

39. Ibid., p. 122: "when the dream is of school the dream is 'at school,' just as when the sun is thought of, the word or name thought are "in the sun." The confusion is thus between the dream and the thing dreamed of."

40. Ibid., p. 161: What the magical stage itself shows, in opposition to the later stages, is precisely that symbols are still conceived as participating in things. Magic is thus the pre-symbolic stage of thought.

41. Boyer, pp. 149–150.

42. Taylor as Summarized by Bellah (2011).

43. Dawkins, pp. 391–3.

44. Ibid., p. 131.

45. Piaget (1929), pp. 129–30, provides a quote from Edmond Gosse, a recollection from early childhood, illustrating the progression towards self-conscious awareness: "But of all the thoughts which rushed upon my savage and undeveloped little brain at this crisis, the most curious was that I had found a companion and a confidant in myself. There was a secret in this world and it belonged to me and to a somebody who lived in the same body with me. There were two of us and we could talk to one another. It is difficult to define impressions so rudimentary, but it is certain that it was in this dual form that the sense of my individuality now suddenly descended upon me and it is equally certain that it was a great solace to me to find a sympathizer in my own breast."

46. Frazer, p. 58: "But if in the most backward state of human society now known to us we find magic thus conspicuously present and religion conspicuously absent, may we not reasonably conjecture that the civilised races of the world have also at some period of their history passed through a similar intellectual phase, that they attempted to force the great powers of nature to do their pleasure before they thought of courting their favour by offerings and prayer—in short that, just as on the material side of human culture there has everywhere been an Age of Stone, so on the intellectual side there has everywhere been an Age of Magic?"

47. The dissimilarity between the modes of thought of literate and preliterate societies has typically been expressed through a dichotomy, in which the former modes "progress" from the latter. The progressive dichotomy has been expressed in numerous ways: of "rationality" from "irrationality" (Wilson 1970), of "logico-empirical" from "mythopeic thinking" (Cassirer 1944), of "logical" from "pre-logical procedures" (Lévy-Brul 1910), of the "domesticated" and "wild" (or "cold" and "hot") thinking of Lévi-Strauss (1962), and the "open" and "closed situations" of Robin Horton (1967), as well as dichotomous distinctions between "abstract" and "concrete" thinking, "scientific" and "magical" thought, "history" and "atemporal myth," as well as "Logos" and "Mythos."

Walter Ong pointed out that in each of these dichotomies, the "primary modeling system" is posed as an anachronistic deviant from the "secondary modeling system" that succeeded it. That is, the preceding stage (preliteracy), is not understood as a perspective with its own benefits and viewpoints, but only as a perspective that is lacking the principle feature of the succeeding stage (literacy). Furthermore, the former stage, which is primary, is perceived as being less valid than the latter stage, which is secondary, simply because it comes earlier, and is in large part replaced. Ong suggested, when referring either to 'preliterate' children or to 'preliterate' societies, both ancient and contemporary, that the terms 'oral' and 'post-oral' might be more appropriate.

48. The shift from an oral tradition to a written tradition in the area of children's literature was marked by two landmark publications. John Newberry's compilation of English rhymes, *Mother Goose's Melody, or, Sonnets for the Cradle*, published in 1765; and the Brother Grimms' collections of traditional European folktales and fairytales, *Kinder und Hausmärchen (Children's and Household Tales)*, published in seven editions between 1812 and 1857. These publications (though certainly not the first and not the last), were the key books in the shift from the tradition of *telling* and *singing* rhymes and stories to children, to *reading* storybooks and picture books to children. This period, the late 18th and early 19th centuries in Europe, coincided with an unprecedented leap forwards in literacy, as the first widespread public education systems were formed in European industrialized nations.

49. "An eye for an ear." This is a famous expression by Marshall McLuhan.

50. Bettelheim, p. 26: "Myths and fairy tales alike attain a definite form only when they are committed to writing and are no longer subject to continuous change. Before being written down, these stories were either condensed or vastly elaborated in the retelling over the centuries; some stories merged with others. All became modified by what the teller thought was of greatest interest to his listeners, by what his concerns of the moment or the special problems of his era were."

51. Huxley (1944), p. 19.
52. Laing (1969), p. 116.
53. Piaget (1929), p. 268.
54. Clyde Nunn (1964).
55. Ibid., p. 378.
56. May (1991).

57. I realize that I'm engaging in the same kind of questioning behavior now, as I write this book, which may be perceived by some people as belittling to God.

58. Paul Tillich.

59. To the man with a hammer in hand, the world is perceived as a series of nails: This concept is popularly known as "Maslow's hammer."

60. Karl Jaspers: "If religion is demythologized, it is no longer religion."

61. As for theists, distinctions have been made that are important to note, and which will be further explored in Chapter Four. Maslow distinguished between "peakers," people who experience moments of spiritual perception, and "non-peakers." Jung made a distinction between the unconscious experience of the spiritual, and the conscious experience of a religious "creed," which is the external dressings of religion (churches, priests, ceremonies, etc.). Gordon Allport also delineated between an "Extrinsic Religious Sentiment," which fulfilled the more peripheral psychosocial needs for cultural and social identity, and an "Intrinsic Religious Sentiment," which addressed the core psychological need for "self-unification," a sense of spiritual connection between the inner self and the outer world, that supports a "unifying philosophy of life."

62. This is a reference to a famous quote from Carl Jung, who, when asked in a BBC interview, if he believed in God, responded: "I don't believe, I *know*."

63. An old saying, quoted by McLuhan (1965).

64. Ricoeur as summarized by Fowler (1981).

65. Fowler, p. 198.

66. Huxley (1961): "The mystical experience ... is the experience in which the subject-object relationship is transcended, in which there is a sense of complete solidarity of the subject with other human beings and with the universe in general."

67. http://science.howstuffworks.com/science-vs-myth/afterlife/science-life-after-death1.htm.

68. See Strassman (2001) for all references to DMT.

69. See Raymond Moody's *Life After Life* (1975) and Kenneth Ring's *Life at Death* (1980) for more information on NDEs.

70. Kurzweil, p. 16.

71. Famous saying, sometimes accredited to Arthur C. Clarke.

Chapter Four

1. McLuhan (1964), p. 79.
2. Kabbalah: The mystical tradition in Judaic scholarship.
3. Scribner & Cole (1981), p. 8.
4. McLuhan (1964), p. 79: "Language does for intelligence what the wheel does for the feet and body. It enables them to move from thing to thing with greater ease and speed and ever less involvement. Language extends and amplifies man but it also divides his faculties. His collective consciousness or intuitive awareness is diminished by this technical extension of consciousness that is speech."
5. McCrone, pp. 160–161: "The physical changed needed for speech show that modern language must be a very recent invention of our ancestors. The high arch in the roof of the mouth that helps with voice production is about the only telltale sign of speech that shows up on a fossil skeleton. This arch did not start to appear until *Homo erectus* arrived about 1.5 million years ago, and even then the arch was slight. Judging from fossils, modern speech came along about 100,000 years ago when the earliest examples of *Homo sapiens* were starting to walk the earth."
6. McGilchrist, p. 101.
7. Upper Paleolithic: Roughly 50,000 to 10,000 years ago.
8. The rapid brain development that occurred in the Paleolithic was primarily in the neocortex (the most recently evolved part of the brain, which accounts for 85 percent of total brain weight). Specifically, the areas of the neocortex involved with language and social organization expanded at an exponential rate during the Paleolithic Age.
9. McCrone, p. 155.
10. Ego: The Latin word for "I." Freud, whose theory is associated with the term "ego," never used the word; but rather, used the German word for "I," "das Ich."
11. Barrett (2004).
12. Tremlin (2006), p. 77: "It's better to have fast device that occasionally gets it wrong than a slow device that is always accurate."
13. Tremlin (2006), p. 80: "Our knowledge of agents links physical causality to *mental* causality. Agents, we intuitively assume, have minds."
14. Sacks (2013), p. 293: "Thus the primal, animal sense of 'the other,' which may have evolved for the detection of threat, can take on a lofty, even transcendent function in human beings, as a biological basis for religious passion and conviction, where the "other," the "presence," becomes the person of God."
15. Feuerbach (1957), as quoted by Guthrie, p. 187
16. *Notes sur la Vie*: "Notes on Life," Alphonse Daudet. Quote taken from James (1902), pp. 164–165.
17. From Freud's famous line: "The ego is not the master in its own house."
18. Sagan (1977), p. 99.
19. "Mortality salience": The term used by psychologists to refer to the awareness of one's own inevitable death.
20. Frazer, in *The Golden Bough*, lists dozens of rituals based on the belief that the soul leaves the body during sleep. The Christian bedtime prayer—"Now I lay me down to sleep, I pray the Lord my soul to keep. If I should die before I wake, I pray the Lord my soul to take"—seems to also point to a basic belief in soul departure during sleep.
21. Ernest Jones (1951) pointed out that the term "nightmare" is probably derived from the term "mara," which means "death" or "departure."
22. Indick (2012).
23. Armstrong (2009), p. 6.
24. Genesis 3:8.
25. Pantheist: A person who perceives the world in the animistic mode.
26. Armstrong (2009), p. 9: "In archaic thinking, there is no concept of the supernatural, no huge gulf separating human and divine. If a priest donned the sacred regalia of an animal pelt to impersonate the Animal Master, he became a temporary manifestation of that divine power."
27. Jung (1936), pp. 262–3: "A primitive chief is not only disguised as the animal; when he appears at initiation rites in full animal disguise, he *is* the animal. Still more, he is an animal spirit, a terrifying demon who performs circumcision. At such moments he incorporates or represents the ancestor of the tribe and the clan, and therefore the primal god himself. He represents, and *is*, the 'totem' animal."
28. Guardian Spirit: I would refer to this sort of figure as a "personal god," while others might equate it with the figure of a "guardian angel."
29. These definitions of "guardian spirit," "vision quest," and the "call" of the spirit, are derived from Bellah's description of Ruth Benedict's (1923) observations. Bellah, p. 164.
30. Clifford Geertz (1966), as quoted in Robert Bellah (2011), p. xvii: "It is direct

encounter with the two figures in the context of the actual performance that the villager comes to know them as, so far as he is concerned, genuine realities. They are, then, not representations of anything, genuine realities. And when the villagers go into trance they become—*nadi*—themselves part of the realm in which those [spiritual] presences exist. To ask, as I once did, a man who has *been* Rangda whether he thinks she is real is to leave oneself open to the suspicion of idiocy."

31. Bellah (2011), p. 162. (Bellah's description of Karl Luckert's (1975) theory).

32. Bellah, p. 202.

33. Bronze Age: 3600–1200 BC in the Near East.

34. Stark, p. 69.

35. Jaynes (1986): "In Mesopotamia the head of state was a wooden statue—wooden so it could be carried about—with jewels in its eyes, perfumed, richly raimented, imbedded in ritual, seated behind a large table (perhaps the origin of our altars) in the *gigunu*, which was a large hall in the bottom of a ziggurat. What we might call the king was really the first steward of this statue god. Cuneiform texts literally describe how people came to the idol-statues, asked them questions, and received directions from them ... the evidence from written texts, personal idols, cylinder seals, and the construction of personal names suggests that every person had a personal god. In Mesopotamia, it was his *ili*, which in Hebrew is perhaps from the same root as Eli and Elohim. In Egypt, the personal god which had the same function was called a *ka*, a word which has been an enigma in Egyptology until now."

36. Jaynes (1976), p. 151

37. Jayne's "bicameral" theory is that the interior voice of consciousness was initially experienced in ancient people as an external voice, i.e., the voice of God. This occurred because the part of the brain that behaved did not recognize the part of the brain that thought in words as the interior voice of his own ego. Hence, the words were perceived as emanating from outside of the mind. When an integrated sense of consciousness was developed, the internal voice of consciousness was recognized as the self, and the external "voices of the gods" were no longer heard.

38. Ibid., p. 169.

39. Lewis-Williams and Pearce, pp. 69–72: "huge globular eyes hypnotically staring out of the unrecorded past of 5000 years ago with defiant authority."

40. Jaynes (1976), p. 169.

41. Ibid., p. 182.

42. Ibid., p. 174

43. Ibid., p. 184.

44. A large amount of conjecture has been written about Teraphim. The Targum Yerushalmi, a medieval rabbinical source, stated that the teraphim were the shrunken heads of the sacrificed first born sons of ancestors, mounted on a golden plate and placed on the "wall of descendants." The ancestral head/idol was a protective spirit for the household; it would also speak, providing oracles. This commentary was taken lightly, until recent archaeological excavations of ancient Canaanite sites discovered that most residences indeed had a special room or specific location, in which ritually treated skulls were stored. See Lewis-Williams and Pearce, pp. 72–77; and also see Jaynes (1976), pp. 151–175.

45. Jaynes (1976), p. 230: "In the Neo-Sumerian period, at the end of the third millennium B.C. ... each individual had his personal god who seemed to intercede with higher gods on the person's behalf."

46. Another Christian theological equivalent to the Yetzer Ha'Ra would be Augustine's concept of "concupiscence," which is "the irrational desire to take pleasure in beings instead of God itself ... experienced most acutely in the sexual act" (Armstrong, 2009, p. 122).

47. The highly televised moment in which a massive statue of Saddam Hussein was toppled by American troops in Baghdad in 2003 comes to mind. The deposed dictator's face was briefly covered with an American flag, symbolizing the replacement of the old authoritarian voice with a new one, before the soldiers were ordered to remove the American flag and replace it with an Iraqi one.

48. Bronze Age Collapse: A period from 1200 and 1150 BCE, when many kingdoms in the Aegean, Eastern Mediterranean, and Near East apparently collapsed, due to reasons cited in the text.

49. Machiavelli: "It is better to be feared than loved."

50. This interpretation of the golden calf as a living idol comes from Rashi's commentary on Exodus XXXII 3–5.

51. Iron Age: 1300–800 BC in the Near East.

52. As cited in Bellah, p. 370.

53. McLuhan (1964), p. 136.

54. McGilchrist, p. 279: "Money has an important function which it shares with writ-

ing: it replaces things with signs or tokens, with representations, the very essence of the activity of the left hemisphere."
55. 1 Timothy 6:10.
56. McGilchrist, p. 275.
57. Sagan (1977) p. 233.
58. Bellah, p. 264: "Whatever aids to reflective thought that the technology of writing supplied were limited to the scribal class. Early literacy has been called craft literacy, because it was a specialized craft that only a few could master. Those few, however, may have been essential for the self-understanding of archaic society and for what was to come."
59. Ong, p. 32.
60. Scribner & Cole, p. 5.
61. Ibid., p. 11: "If one assumes that context-dependent speech is linked with context-dependent thought, and context-dependent thought is the opposite of abstract thought, it follows that abstract thought fails to develop in a nonliterate culture."
62. As quoted by Scribner & Cole, p. 14.
63. Havelock (1978), as quoted by Scribner & Cole, p. 6.
64. Animistic: From the Latin root, "anima," which means, "soul." So, to "animate" means to project a soul into something, to "de-animate" means to remove the soul from something, and "animistic" is the mode of explanation or perception that "animates."
65. Copernicus (1543), as quote in Bellah (2011), pp. 40–41.
66. As quoted by Richard Dawkins in *The God Delusion*.
67. Ong, p. 72: "Sight isolates, sound incorporates.... Vision comes to a human being from one direction at a time: to look at a room or a landscape, I must move my eyes around from one part to another. When I hear, however, I gather sound simultaneously from every direction at once: I am at the center of my auditory world, which envelopes me, establishing me at a kind of core of sensation and existence.... By contrast with vision, the dissecting sense, sound is thus a unifying sense. A typical visual ideal is clarity and distinctness, a taking apart.... The auditory ideal, by contrast, is harmony, a putting together."
68. Ibid.
69. Carothers (1959), pp. 309–310: "Rural Africans live largely in a world of sound—a world loaded with direct personal significance for the hearer—whereas the Western European lives much more in a visual world which is on the whole indifferent to him ... it was only when the written, and still more the printed, word appeared on the scene that the stage was set for words to lose their magic powers.... Sounds are in a sense dynamic things, or at least are always indicators of dynamic things—of movements, events, activities, for which man, when largely unprotected from the hazards of life in the bush or the veldt, must be ever on the alert.... Sounds lose much of this significance in western Europe, where man often develops, and must develop, a remarkable ability to disregard them. Whereas for Europeans, in general, "seeing is believing," for rural Africans reality seems to reside far more in what is heard and what is said.... When words are written, they become, of course, a part of the visual world ... they become static things and lose, as such, the dynamism which is so characteristic of the auditory world in general, and of the spoken word in particular. They lose much of the personal element, in the sense that the heard word is most commonly directed at oneself, whereas the seen word most commonly is not, and can be read or not as whim dictates. They lose those emotional overtones and emphases.... Thus, in general, words, by becoming visible, join a world of relative indifference to the viewer—a world from which the magic 'power' of the word has been abstracted."
70. Diedrich Westermann's observations of rural African cultures in the early 20th century, as quoted in Carothers, p. 318: "The new [literate] generation is completely different, capable of rising to greater heights and of descending to greater depths, they deserve a more sympathetic knowledge of their difficulties and their far greater temptations. African parents need to be taught this before it is too late so that they may realize that they are dealing with finer bits of mechanism than they themselves were."
71. Carothers, p. 309.
72. Alexander Pope's famous verse comes to mind: "A little Learning is a dang'rous Thing; Drink deep, or taste not the Pierian Spring: There shallow Draughts intoxicate the Brain, And drinking largely sobers us again."
73. Theophany: Fancy term for spiritual perception, i.e., the "appearance of a god" to a person.
74. Gerhard Tersteegen (1697–1769).
75. As quoted in Bellah, p. 244.
76. Armstrong (1993), p. 83.
77. Ibid., p. 86.
78. "In separating man and God from the rest of the world, Judaism, Christianity, and

Islam empty nature of human features." (Stewart Guthrie, p. 15).

79. Ong p. 105: "By separating the knower from the known (Havelock 1963), writing makes possible increasingly articulate introspectivity, opening the psyche as never before not only to the external objective world quite distinct from itself but also to the interior self against whom the objective world is set. Writing makes possible the great introspective religious traditions such as Buddhism, Judaism, Christianity, and Islam. All these have sacred texts."

80. McLuhan (1962): "In antiquity and the Middle Ages reading was necessarily reading *aloud*."

81. Armstrong (2009), p. 133: "For the monks of medieval Europe, *lectio* ('reading') was not conducted simply to acquire information but was a spiritual exercise that enabled them to enter their inner world and there confront the truth revealed in scripture ... *lectio divina*, ruminating on the sacred page until it had become an interior reality."

82. Armstrong, 1993, p. 144.

83. Armstrong, 2009, p. x.

84. Dom Jean Leclercq as quoted by McLuhan, p. 89.

85. McLuhan, p. 92.

86. Walter Pater

87. Steiner p. 195: "We know of no cultures where the poet and the singer are not, at the outset, the same. Intuitively, the song is held to have come first. The metrics of the poem, the cadences of our prose, are translations out of music."

88. William Congreve, *The Mourning Bride* (1697).

89. McLuhan, p. 84.

90. McLuhan (1965), p. 111: "For in the highly tactile product of the scribe the reader found no means for splitting off the visual from the audile-tactile complex, such as the sixteenth and seventeenth century reader did."

91. Ibid.

92. Duchesne, Ricardo (2006), "Asia First?," *The Journal of the Historical Society* 6 (1): 83.

93. The Vulgate: St. Jerome's Latin translation of the Bible.

94. Leon of Castro, Spanish Inquisitor (1576), writing in reference to the Vulgate (St. Jerome's Latin translation of the Bible) (as quoted by Armstrong, 1993, p. 289).

95. Ong, p. 134: "Print creates a sense of closure not only in literary works but also in analytic philosophical and scientific works. With print came the catechism and the 'textbook,' less discursive and less disputatious than most previous presentations of a given academic subject. Catechisms and textbooks presented 'facts' or their equivalents: memorizable, flat statements that told straight-forwardly and inclusively how matters stood in a given field. By contrast, the memorable statements of oral cultures and of residually oral manuscript cultures tended to be of a proverbial sort, presenting not 'facts' but rather reflections, often of a gnomic kind, inviting further reflection by the paradoxes they involved."

96. Armstrong, McLuhan, and Ong all mention this idea.

97. It is interesting to note that in the post-print age, the age of digital media, the print bias is fading. Most people do not accept everything they read on the web as being truth or fact, simply because it is printed on the web. Because words on the web are digital, virtual, mutable—like the spoken word—they do not automatically take on the aura of literal truth and fact; but rather, retain some of the uncertainty that we have for the spoken word. Nevertheless, a "digital bias" may be said to exist now, in that people tend to trust the work of computers more than the work of other people. While erring is seen as a human attribute ("to err is human"), inerrability is a quality attributed to computers. Hence, when making a web search, if Google doubts our spelling, asking us, "Did you mean..."—we will usually agree immediately with Google, assuming that in the contest between person and computer, the computer is always right. In this way, the digital computer has taken on the first cardinal virtue of God, omniscience. The second cardinal virtue, omnipresence, is fast becoming a reality for the digital deity; and the third virtue, omnipotence, well ... that remains to be seen.

98. McLuhan (1965), p. 194.

99. Ong, pp. 78–9: "The Delphic oracle was not responsible for her oracular utterances, for they were held to be the voice of the god. Writing, and even more print, has some of this vatic quality. Like the oracle or the prophet, the book relays an utterance from a source, the one who really 'said' or wrote the book. The author might be challenged if only he or she could be reached, but the author cannot be reached in any book. There is no way directly to refute a text. After absolutely total and devastating refutation, it says exactly the same

thing as before. This is one reason why 'the book says' is popularly tantamount to 'it is true.' It is also one reason why books have been burnt."

100. Steiner, p. 45: "The heretic is the discourser without end.... The Roman Catholic warning that interpretation without end, even where it claims to be 'fundamentalist' and textually reductive, will modulate, first, into historical criticism, next into more or less metaphoric deism and, lastly, into agnosticism, is logically and historically valid. Where it is without finiteness, secondary discourse is schismatic."

101. Armstrong (2009), p. 271: "Every single fundamentalist movement that I have studied in Judaism, Christianity, and Islam is rooted in profound fear."

102. Ibid.

103. Friedman, p. 201.

104. Armstrong (2009), p. xv.

105. Ibid., p. 174: "Protestants used the Old Testament ban on images as a mandate to trash statues and frescoes.... Luther believed that all 'heretical' books should be burned, and both Calvin and Zwingli were prepared to execute dissidents."

106. Ibid., p. 171.

107. McGilchrist: p. 444 & p. 315.

108. Armstrong (1993), p. 118.

109. Armstrong (2009), p. xii: "Without ritual, myths make no sense and would remain as opaque as a musical score, which is impenetrable to most of us until interpreted instrumentally."

110. Armstrong (2009), p. 172: "Now the reformers declared that the Eucharist was "only" a symbol and the Mass no longer a symbolic reenactment of Calvary but a simple memorial. They were beginning to speak about the myths of religion as though they were *logoi*, and the alacrity with which people seized upon these new teachings suggests that many Christians in Europe were losing the older habits of thought."

111. Armstrong, 2009, p. 173 and McGilchrist, p. 314.

112. McLuhan (1967), p. 111.

113. Ibid.: "Print technology created the public. Electronic technology created the mass. The public consists of separate individuals walking around with separate fixed points of view. The new technology demands that we abandon the luxury of this posture, this fragmentary outlook."

114. Marshall McLuhan (1964): "Specialist technologies detribalize. The nonspecialist electric technology retribalizes."

115. Ong, pp. 136–7.

116. Newman as quoted in Guthrie, p. 181.

117. McLuhan (1989).

118. Huxley (1944), "There is a very general belief that, where gadgets are concerned, we can get something for nothing can enjoy all the advantages of an elaborate, top-heavy and constantly advancing technology without having to pay for them by any compensating disadvantages."

119. George Harrison, from an interview with Mukunda Goswami, taped at Harrison's home in England on September 4, 1982.

120. From a speech delivered by Timothy Leary at a New York City press conference on September 19, 1966.

121. "the idea that the human mind is a perpetual manufacturer of idols is one of the deepest things which can be said about our thinking of God." Armstrong, 2009, p. 281.

122. Paul Tillich: "The name of this infinite and inexhaustible depth and ground of all being is God."

123. "reason can become an idol that seeks to destroy all other claimants." Armstrong, 2009, p. 309.

Chapter Five

1. R. D. Laing (1969), p. 112.

2. Colman, A. M. (ed.). (2009). *A Dictionary of Psychology*. Oxford: Oxford University Press.

3. Rossetti, p. 143.

4. Ibid., pp. 14–16.

5. Tylor (1871): "It seems as though thinking men, as yet at a low level of culture, were deeply impressed by two groups of biological problems. In the first place, what is it that makes a difference between a living body and a dead one; what causes waking, sleep, trance, disease, death? In the second place, what are those human shapes which appear in dreams and visions? Looking at these two groups of phenomena, the ancient savage philosophers probably made their first step by the obvious inference that every man has two things belonging to him, namely, a life and a phantom as being its image or second self; both, also, are perceived to be things separable from the body.... The second step would seem also easy for savages to make, seeing how extremely difficult civilized men have found it to unmake. It is merely to combine the life and

the phantom ... the result is that well-known conception ... the personal soul, or spirit."

6. Piaget (1929), pp. 238–9: "Tylor has maintained with regard to savages, that it is the discovery of the existence of thought that brings animism into being."

7. James, pp. 378–9.

8. Ibid., p. 58.

9. Ibid., pp. 467–68.

10. William James: "I myself believe that the evidence for God lies primarily in inner personal experiences."

11. Ibid., p. 473.

12. Forsyth, p.124–5.

13. Maslow, p. 85.

14. James, p. 70.

15. Batson (1982), p. 63.

16. James, p. 198.

17. Ibid., p. 129.

18. Freud (1927), p. 35.

19. Freud (1900), Ch.7, Sec. E.

20. Ibid.,(Freud is quoting Havelock Ellis).

21. Ibid.

22. Freud (1913), p. 115.

23. Ibid., p. 132.

24. Freud (1913), p. 44: "God is in every case modeled after the father ... our personal relation to God is dependent upon our relation to our physical father.... God at bottom is nothing but an exalted father."

25. Ibid., p. 25.

26. Freud (1927), p. 22.

27. Ibid., p. 40.

28. Ibid., pp. 71–2: "It has been repeatedly pointed out ... in how great detail the analogy between religion and obsessional neurosis can be followed out, and how many of the peculiarities and vicissitudes in the formation of religion can be understood in that light. And it tallies with this that devout believers are safeguarded in a high degree against the risk of certain neurotic illnesses; their acceptance of the universal neurosis spares them the task of constructing a personal one."

29. Freud (1939), p. 51.

30. Ibid., p. 144.

31. Ibid., p. 145: "We surmise that 'omnipotence of thought' was the expression of the pride mankind took in the development of language, which had brought in its train such an extraordinary increase in the intellectual faculties. There opened then the new realm of spirituality where conceptions, memories, and deductions became of decisive importance, in contrast to the lower physical activity which concerned itself with the immediate perceptions of the sense organs. It was certainly one of the most important stages on the way to becoming human."

32. Ibid., p. 147: "By dematerializing God, a new valuable contribution was made to the secret treasure of the people. The Jews preserved their inclination towards spiritual interests. The political misfortune of the nation taught them to appreciate the only possession they had retained, their written records, as its true value. Immediately after the destruction of the Temple in Jerusalem by Titus, Rabbi Jochanan ben Sakkai asked for permission to open at Jabneh the first school for the study of the Torah. From now on, it was the Holy Book, and the study of it, that kept the scattered people together."

33. Freud (1927), as quoted in Pals, p. 73: "as neurotic relics, and we may now argue that the time has probably come, as it does in an analytic treatment, for replacing the effects of repression by the results of the rational operation of the intellect."

34. Ibid., "The 'Credo quia absurdum' ('I believe because it is absurd') of the early Father of the Church maintains that religious doctrines are outside the jurisdiction of reason — are above reason. Their truth must be held inwardly, and they need not be comprehended...." (Freud attributed this doctrine to Tertullian).

35. Ibid., p. 35.

36. Freud (1927), as quoted in Pals, p. 73: "Religion would thus be the universal obsessional neurosis of humanity; like the obsessional neuroses of children, it arose out of the Oedipus Complex, out of the relation to the father. If this view is right, it is to be supposed that a turning-away from religion is bound to occur with the fatal inevitability of a process of growth, and that we find ourselves at this very juncture in the middle of that phase of development."

37. Jung (1964), p. 89.

38. Jung (1962), p. 45: "the unconscious mind is capable at times of assuming an intelligence and purposiveness which are superior to actual conscious insight ... it is a basic religious phenomenon ... the voice which speaks in our dreams is not our own but comes from a source transcending us."

39. Jung (1964), p. 30: For in our daily experience, we need to state things as accurately as possible, and we have learned to discard the trimmings of fantasy both in our language and in our thoughts—thus losing a

quality that is still characteristic of the primitive mind. Most of us have consigned to the unconscious all the fantastic psychic associations that every object or idea possesses. The primitive, on the other hand, is still aware of these psychic properties; he endows animals, plants, or stones with powers that we find strange and unacceptable."

40. Forsyth, p. 62.
41. Fromm, p. 18.
42. Forsyth p. 143.
43. Fromm, pp. 6–7.
44. Ibid., pp. 5–6: "It is as if friendly, or unfriendly, spirits had visited us and at the break of day had disappeared; we hardly remember that they had been there and how intensely we had been occupied with them."
45. Forsyth, p. 229.
46. Frankl, p. 137.
47. Frankl coined the term "Sunday neurosis," in reference to the existential vacuum many non-religious people feel on Sundays, when they have no purposeful work to do, and so they find themselves fretfully chasing distraction after distraction, in order to avoid the inherent meaninglessness of their existence.
48. "The man who regards his life as meaningless in not merely unhappy, but hardly fit for life." (Albert Einstein, As quoted by Frankl, p. 139).
49. Maslow, p. 19
50. Ibid., p. 24: "The peak-experiences and their experiential reality ordinarily are not transmittable to non-peakers, at least not by words alone, and certainly not by non-peakers. What happens to many people ... is that they simply concretize all of the symbols, all of the words, all of the statues, all of the ceremonies, and by a process of functional autonomy make *them*, rather than the original revelation, into the sacred things and sacred activities."
51. Ibid.
52. Ibid., p. 29: "our findings indicate that all or almost all people have or can have peak experiences."
53. Joseph Campbell (1949).
54. McLuhan (1995), pp. 321–22 (from "From Cliché to Archetype").
55. The terms "ordinary self-consciousness" and "creative self-consciousness" come from Rollo May's theory of existential psychology.

Chapter Six

1. McLuhan (1965), p. 50.
2. Jaspers, as quoted in Bellah, p. 268.

3. Eric Weil suggested that a precondition for the breakthroughs of the Axial Age may have been the breakdown of the power structures that preceded that age, i.e., the Bronze Age Collapse. 'Breakdowns predict breakthroughs,' because times of stress and uncertainty evoke thinking that is analytical, self-critical, and creative—"How did we get into this mess?" "What went wrong?" "How can we do things better?—and so on. This may certainly be true; but as Weil himself noted: "... breakdowns in history are extremely common; breakthroughs extremely rare." (Eric Weil, "What is a Breakthrough in History?" *Daedalus* 104, no. 2 (Spring 1975), as cited by Bellah, p. 282).
4. Eisenstadt argued that the Axial Age saw the emergence of a "new type of intellectual elite," who engaged in a thinking process he called "reflexivity," which is the capacity to reflect on one's own thoughts in a critical way, argue hypothetically with oneself, and engage in completely abstract contemplation about metaphysical ideas. How did this happen? It certainly wasn't magic. Different people point to different causes, but everyone agrees that the invention of *writing* was a key factor. Obviously, my point is that writing was not just *a* key factor, it was *the* key factor, the new tool that humans could grasp—like fire, the Paleolithic hand axe, the wheel, or the word—that would eventually reinvent the intellectual landscape of the world.
5. Goody, p. 11: "Logic, 'our logic,' in the restricted sense of an instrument of analytic procedures ... seemed to be a function of writing, since it was the setting down of speech that enabled man clearly to separate words, to manipulate their order and to develop syllogistic forms of reasoning; these latter were seen as specifically literate rather than oral, even making use of another purely graphic isolate, the letter, as a means of indicating the relationship between the constituent elements."
6. Goody, p. 44: "Writing makes speech 'objective' by turning it into an object of visual as well as aural inspection; it is the shift of the receptor from ear to eye, of the producer from the voice to the hand."
7. Thomas Aquinas, *De Potentia*, 13th century AD: "All that man knows of God is to know that he does not know him, since he knows that what God is surpasses all that we can understand of him."
8. Syncretism, in religion, is when an older tradition, such as the pagan ritual of celebrat-

ing the death and rebirth of the sun on the winter solstice, is transformed into an newer tradition, such as the Christmas holiday. In the first millennium of Christian practice in Europe, many older pagan rituals and beliefs were "syncretized" by the Church into Christian rituals and beliefs.

9. Hegel, as quoted in McGilchrist, pp. 514–515: "The statues have become stone corpses from which the living soul has flown..."

10. Armstrong (1993), p. 286: "full-blown atheism in the sense that we use the word today was impossible."

11. Ibid: "From birth and baptism to death and burial in the churchyard, religion dominated the life of every single man and woman."

12. Ibid., p. 288.

13. John Wingfield, *Atheism Closed and Open Anatomized*, 1597, as quoted in Armstrong, 1993, p. 288.

14. Armstrong, 1993, p. 307: "But once the scientific spirit had become normative for many people, it was difficult for them to read the Gospels in any other way. Western Christians were now committed to a literal understanding of their faith and had taken an irrevocable step back from myth: a story was either factually true or it was a delusion."

15. Ibid., p. 310: "The new religion of reason would be called Deism."

16. Armstrong, 2009, p. 207–8: "In reducing God to a scientific explanation, the scientists and theologians of the seventeenth century were turning God into an idol, a mere human projection.... God was no longer transcendent, no longer beyond the reach of language and concepts."

17. Ibid., p. 189: "Reason alone can produce only an attenuated deism that is easily abandoned, as its God is remote, abstract, and ultimately incredible."

18. Armstrong, 1993, p. 313.

19. Armstrong (2009), p. 115: "The Trinity reminded Christians *not* to think about God as a simple personality and that what we call 'God' was inaccessible to rational analysis. It was a meditative device to counter the idolatrous tendency of people like Arius, who had seen God as a mere being."

20. McLuhan (1965), pp. 206–7: "The portability of the book ... added much to the new cult of individualism.... This very natural inclination towards accessibility and portability went hand in hand with greatly increased reading speeds which were possible with uniform and repeatable type, but not at all with the manuscript."

21. Ibid., p. 158: "Print is the technology of individualism."

22. Campbell (1949), pp. 333–34: "the democratic ideal of the self-determining individual, the invention of the power-driven machine, and the development of the scientific method of research have so transformed human life that the long-inherited, timeless universe of symbols has collapsed. In the fateful, epoch-announcing words of Nietzsche's Zarathustra: 'Dead are all the gods...' The dream-web of myth fell away; the mind opened to full waking consciousness; and modern man emerged from ancient ignorance, like a butterfly from its cocoon, or like the sun at dawn from the womb of mother night....

The problem of mankind today, therefore, is precisely the opposite to that of men in the comparatively stable periods of those great coordinating mythologies which now are known as lies. Then all meaning was in the group, in the great anonymous forms, none in the self-expressive individual; today no meaning is in the group—none in the world: all is in the individual. But there the meaning is absolutely unconscious. One does not know toward what one moves. One does not know by what one is propelled. The lines of communication between the conscious and the unconscious zones of the human psyche have all been cut, and we have been split in two."

23. Tremlin, p. 185: "people use their religion to serve practical rather than intellectual purposes and expect their gods to behave like people.... Religion that becomes detached from daily life or promotes abstract theological concepts and practices will become irrelevant to adherents and undergo either revision or decline."

24. Armstrong (2009), p. 238: "They [Evangelicals] read the scriptures with an unprecedented literalism, because this seemed more rational than the older allegorical exegesis."

25. Ong, pp. 131–32: "By removing words from the world of sound where they had first had their origin in active human interchange and relegating then definitively to visual surface, and by otherwise exploiting visual space for the management of knowledge, print encouraged human beings to think of their own interior conscious and unconscious resources as more and more thing-like, impersonal and religiously neutral. Print encouraged

the mind to sense that its possessions were held in some sort of inert mental space."

26. McLuhan (1965), p. 245: "Paradoxically, then, the first age of print introduced the first age of the unconscious. Since print allowed only a narrow segment of sense to dominate the other senses, the refugees had to discover another home for themselves.... The unconscious is a direct creation of print technology, the ever-mounting slag-heap of rejected awareness."

27. This misperception among pilots, of mistaking the ocean for the horizon, was probably the cause of JFK, Jr.'s tragic death.

28. Armstrong (2009), p. 87–88: "But the word 'belief' has since changed its meaning. In Middle English, *believen* meant 'to prize; to value; to hold dear.' It was related to the German *belieben* ('to love'), *liebe* ('beloved'), and the Latin *libido*."

29. Guthrie, pp. 202–3: "Because religion is an ostensible social relationship, it tends to be non-empirical, since openly testing a relationship (unlike a relation to a car or a computer) undermines it. Testing therefore may be explicitly prohibited ... if gods are tested and do fail, they may, like people, be abandoned. The importance of faith in religion does not mean testing is irrelevant, as often is supposed, but the opposite: it is too relevant to permit."

30. Nietzsche (1882), *Thus Spoke Zarathustra*.

31. Martin Luther as quoted in Huxley, 1944, p. 236: "This is the acme of faith, to believe that God who saves so few and condemns so many, is merciful; that He is just who, at his own pleasure, has made us necessarily doomed to damnation, so that He seems to delight in the torture of the wretched and to be more deserving of hate than love. If by any effort of reason I could conceive how God, who shows so much anger and harshness, could be merciful and just, there would be no need of faith."

32. Otto, p. 10.
33. Ibid., p. 9.
34. Guthrie summarizing Goodall, p. 52.
35. Otto, p. 202.
36. Ibid., p. 11: "For the 'creature-feeling' and the sense of dependence to arise in the mind the 'numen' must be experienced as present, a *numen praesens*, as in the case of Abraham.... The numinous is thus felt as objective and outside the self."
37. Ibid., p. 27.
38. Ibid., p. 15: "Its antecedent stage is 'daemonic dread' (cf. the horror of Pan) with its queer perversion, a sort of abortive offshoot, the 'dread of ghosts.' It first begins to stir in the feeling of 'something uncanny,' 'eerie,' or 'weird.' It is this feeling which, emerging in the mind of primeval man, forms the starting-point for the entire religious development in history. 'Daemons' and 'gods' alike spring from this root, and all the products of 'mythological apperception' or 'fantasy' are nothing but different modes in which it has been objectified. And all ostensible explanations of the origin of religion in terms of animism or magic or folk-psychology are doomed from the outset to wander astray and miss the real goal of their inquiry, unless they recognize this fact of our nature—primary, unique, underivable from anything else—to be the basic factor and the basic impulse underlying the entire process of religious evolution."

39. Ibid., p. 17: "Even when the worship of 'daemons' has long since reached the higher level of worship of 'gods,' these gods still retain as *numina* something of the 'ghost' in the impress they make on the feelings of the worshipper, viz. the peculiar quality of the 'uncanny' and 'awful,' which survives with the quality of exaltedness and sublimity or is symbolized by means of it."

40. Armstrong (1993), p. 41.
41. Eliade (1957).
42. Eliade (1949).
43. Eliade (1958).
44. Bellah (2011), pp. 17–18.
45. Eliade (1963), p. 188: "By knowing the myth one knows the 'origin' of things and hence can control and manipulate them at will; this is not an 'external,' 'abstract' knowledge but a knowledge that one 'experiences' ritually, either by ceremonially recounting the myth or by performing the ritual ... that in one way or another one 'lives' the myth, in the sense that one is seized by the sacred, exalting power of the events recollected or re-enacted. 'Living' a myth, then, implies a genuinely 'religious' experience, since it differs from the ordinary experience of everyday life ... one ceases to exist in the everyday world and enters a transfigured, auroral world impregnated with the Supernaturals' presence. What is involved is not a commemoration of mythical events but a reiteration of them. The protagonists of the myth are made present; one becomes their contemporary. This also implies that one is no longer living in chronological time, but in the primordial Time, the Time when the event *first*

took place. This is why we can use the term the 'strong time' of myth; it is the prodigious, 'sacred' time when something *new, strong*, and *significant* was manifested. To re-experience that time, to re-enact it as often as possible, to witness again the spectacle of the divine works, to meet with the Supernaturals and relearn their creative lesson is the desire that runs like a pattern through all the ritual reiterations of myths."

46. Buber, p. 66: "Feelings dwell in man, but man dwells in his love."

47. Ibid., p. 80: "Man becomes an I through a Thou."

48. Rossetti, p. 160: "A relationship to God ... needs to be fostered from both sides. We know that God is completely active on his part. It is up to us to reciprocate. Prayer is our way of connecting with God. Teresa of Avila called prayer a 'conversation between friends.' In order to strengthen our relationship with our divine Friend, we must pray."

49. Ibid., pp. 173–4: "Those who regularly know an intimacy with God and self in private prayer are thought to be able to connect with others better as well. True prayer moves us beyond loneliness to solitude. In this spiritual solitude we find God and our true selves. Then we are able to connect more deeply with others.... "The priest who prays is not alone. He spends time with someone he loves."

50. Buber, pp. 69–70: "In the beginning is the relation."

51. Ibid., pp. 74–5: "once the sentence 'I see the tree' has been pronounced in such a way that it no longer relates a relation between a human I and a tree Thou, but the perception of the tree object by the human consciousness, it has erected the crucial barrier between subject and object; the basic word I-It, the word of separation, has been spoken."

52. Ibid., pp. 56–7: "But how can we incorporate into the world of the basic word what lies outside language?"

53. Bergson (1911), pp. 291–92: "In the humanity of which we are a part, intuition is, in fact, almost completely sacrificed to the intellect.... Intuition is there, however, but vague and above all discontinuous. It is a lamp almost extinguished, which only glimmers now and then, for a few moments at most. But it glimmers wherever a vital interest is at stake. On our personality, on our liberty, on the place we occupy in the whole of nature, on our origin and perhaps also on our destiny, it throws a light feeble and vacillating, but which none the less pierces the darkness of the night in which the intellect leaves us."

54. Ibid., p. 292: "Thus it is revealed the units of the spiritual life. We recognize it only when we place ourselves in intuition in order to go from intuition to intellect, for from intellect we shall never pass to intuition."

55. C. D. Broad summarizing Bergson, as quoted by Huxley in *The Doors of Perception* (1954): "the function of the brain and nervous system is in the main *eliminative* and not productive.... The function of the brain and nervous system is to protect us from being overwhelmed and confused by this mass of largely useless and irrelevant knowledge, by shutting out most of what we should otherwise perceive or remember at any moment, and leaving only that very small and special selection which is likely to be practically useful."

56. Piaget (1929), pp. 235–6: "Perception is situated in the object as much as in the brain, since there is a perfect continuity between the impulse in the brain and the movements of the object."

57. Huxley (1954) summarizing Bergson: "To formulate and express the contents of this reduced awareness, man has invented and endlessly elaborated those symbol-systems and implicit philosophies which we call languages ... [language] confirms in him the belief that reduced awareness is the only awareness as it bedevils his sense of reality, so that he is all too apt to take his concepts for data, his words for actual things. That which, in the language of religion, is called "this world" is the universe of reduced awareness, expressed, and, as it were, petrified by language.... Most people, most of the time, know only what comes through the reducing valve and is consecrated as genuinely real by the local language. Certain persons, however, seem to be born with a kind of by-pass that circumvents the reducing valve. In others temporary by-passes may be acquired either spontaneously, or as the result of deliberate "spiritual exercises," or through hypnosis, or by means of drugs."

58. The "Figure/Ground" distinction was first observed and studied by Gestalt psychologists in the early 20th century, and was applied primarily to the field of visual perception.

59. Phantom rings: This is a real thing. It is the hallucination of hearing your cellphone ringing when it is not. Many people experience this all the time.

60. McLuhan (1964), p. 46: "To behold,

use or perceive any extension of ourselves in technological form is necessarily to embrace it.... By continuously embracing technologies, we relate ourselves to them as servomechanisms. That is why we must, to use them at all, serve these objects, these extensions of ourselves, as gods or minor religions."

61. Ibid., p. 47: "The principle of numbness comes into play with electric technology, as with any other. We have to numb our central nervous system when it is extended and exposed, or we will die. Thus the age of anxiety and of electric media is also the age of the unconscious and of apathy."

62. Ibid., p. 41: "the word Narcissus ... is from the Greek word *narcosis,* or numbness. The youth Narcissus mistook his own reflection in the water for another person. This extension of himself by mirror numbed his perceptions until he became the servomechanism of his own extended or repeated image. The nymph Echo tried to win his love with fragments of his own speech, but in vain. He was numb. He had adapted to his extension of himself and had become a closed system."

63. Ibid., p. 42: "The wisdom of the Narcissus myth does not convey any idea that Narcissus fell in love with anything he regarded as himself..."

64. Clive Hazell (2009), *Alterity,* p. 97.

65. McLuhan, p 72: "The reason we find myths difficult to grasp is just this fact, that they do not exclude any facet of experience as literate cultures do. All the levels of meaning are simultaneous. Thus natives, when asked Freudian questions about the symbolism of their thoughts or dreams, insist that all the meanings are right there in the verbal statement. The work of Jung and Freud is a laborious translation of non-literate awareness into literary terms, and like any translation distorts and omits."

66. Ibid., p. 110: "For the oral man the literal text contains all possible levels of meaning."

67. Newberg & d'Aquili (2001), p. 125.

68. Kurzweil, pp. 146–49.

69. McLuhan (1995), p. 253, from the *Playboy* interview: "the love machine would appear a natural development in the near future ... a machine whereby ultimate orgasm is achieved by direct mechanical stimulation of the pleasure circuits of the brain."

70. Kurzweil, pp. 148–49.

71. Ibid: "Sexuality and spirituality are two ways that we transcend our everyday physical reality."

72. Newberg and d'Aquli (2001), p. 125

73. Ibid.

Conclusion

1. McGilchrist, p. 256: "In our contemporary world, skills have been downgraded and subverted into algorithms: we are busy imitating machines."

2. Moore's Law: Named after Intel cofounder Gordon E. Moore.

3. The rearview mirror at the speed of light analogy is one of my favorite "McLuhanisms."

4. McLuhan (1995), p. 262: "The computer thus holds out the promise of a technologically engendered state of universal understanding and unity.... Psychic communal integration, made possible at last by the electronic media, could create the universality of consciousness foreseen by Dante when he predicted that men would continue as no more than broken fragments until they were unified into an inclusive consciousness. In a Christian sense, this is merely a new interpretation of the mystical body of Christ; and Christ, after all, is the ultimate extension of man." (Quote taken from a 1969 interview with *Playboy* magazine).

Bibliography

Alexander, Eben. 2012. *Proof of Heaven: A Neurosurgeon's Journey into the Afterlife.* New York: Simon & Schuster.

Armstrong, Karen. 1993. *A History of God: The 4,000-Year Quest of Judaism, Christianity, and Islam.* New York: Ballantine Books.

Armstrong, Karen. 2007. *The Great Transformation: The Beginning of Our Religious Traditions.* New York: Anchor Books.

Armstrong, Karen. 2009. *The Case for God.* New York: Anchor Books.

Barrett, Justin. 2004. *Why Would Anyone Believe in God?* New York: AltaMira Press.

Batson, C.D., and Ventis, W. L. 1982. *The Religious Experience: A Social-Psychological Perspective.* New York: Oxford University Press.

Batson, C.D., Schoenrade, P., and Ventis, W. L. 1993. *Religion and the Individual: A Social-Psychological Perspective.* New York: Oxford University Press.

Beane, W. C., and Doty, W. G. 1976. *Myths, Rites, Symbols: A Mircea Eliade Reader.* New York: Harper Colophon Books.

Bellah, Robert N. 2011. *Religion in Human Evolution: From the Paleolithic to the Axial Age.* Cambridge, MA: Harvard University Press.

Bergson, Henri. 1911. *Creative Evolution.* NY: Henry Holt & Co.

Bergson, Henri. 1935. *The Two Sources of Morality & Religion.* Oxford: Oxford University Press.

Berring, Jesse. 2011. *The Belief Instinct: The Psychology of Souls, Destiny, and the Meaning of Life.* New York: W. W. Norton & Company.

Bettelheim, Bruno. *The Uses of Enchantment: The Meaning and Importance of Fairy Tales.* New York: Alfred A. Knopf, Inc.

Boadt, Lawrence. 1984. *Reading the Old Testament: An Introduction.* New York: Paulist Press.

Boise, A. T. 1936. *The Exploration of the Inner World.* New York: Harper.

Boyer, Pascal. 2001. *Religion Explained: The Evolutionary Origins of Religious Thought.* New York: Basic Books.

Buber, Martin. 1923/1970. *I and Thou.* Walter Kaufman, trans. New York: Charles Scribner's Sons.

Campbell, Joseph. 1949. *The Hero with a Thousand Faces.* Princeton, N.J.: Princeton University Press.

Carothers, J.C. 1959. "Culture, Psychiatry and the Written Word." *Psychiatry*, November 1959, pp. 307–320.

Carter, Jeffrey 2003. *Understanding Religious Sacrifice.* New York: Continuum Books.

Casey, Cheryl. 2006. "Virtual Ritual, Real Faith: The Revirtualization of Religious Ritual in Cyberspace. *Online—Journal of Religions on the Internet.* Vol. 2.1.

Coles, Robert. 1990. *The Spiritual Life of Children.* Boston: Houghton Mifflin Company.

Comings, David E. 2008. *Did Man Create God?* Duarte, CA: Hope Press.

D'Aquili, Eugene, Newberg, Andrew, and Rause, Vince. 2001. *Why God Won't Go Away: Brain Science & the Biology of Belief.* NY: Ballantine Books.

D'Aquili, Eugene, and Newberg, Andrew. 1999. *The Mystical Mind: Probing the Biology of Religious Experience.* Minneapolis, MN: Fortress Press.

Dawkins, Richard. 2008. *The God Delusion.* New York: Houghton Mifflin.

Donald, Merlin. 1991.*Origins of the Modern Mind: Three Stages in the Evolution of Culture and Cognition.* Cambridge, MA: Harvard University Press.

Eliade, Mircea. 1949. *Cosmos and History: The Myth of the Eternal Return.* Translatedby W.R. Trask. Princeton, NJ: Princeton University Press, 1954. Originally published as *Le Mythe de l'eternel retour: archétypes et repetition.*

Eliade, Mircea. 1957. *The Sacred and the Profane: The Nature of Religion.* Translated from French by W.R. Trask London: Harvest/HBJ Publishers.

Eliade, Mircea. 1958. *Patterns in Comparative Religion.* Trans. R. Sheed. London: Sheed and Ward, 1958.

Eliade, Mircea. 1963. *Myth and Reality.* Trans. Willard R. Trask. New York: Harper & Row.

Estabrooks, G.H. 1957. *Hypnotism.* New York: E.P. Dutton & Co., Inc.

Forsyth, James. 2003. *Psychological Theories of Religion.* Upper Saddle River, NJ: Prentice Hall.

Fowler, James W. 1981. *Stages of Faith: The Psychology of Human Development and the Quest for Meaning.* NY: Harper & Row.

Frankl, Viktor. 1975. *The Unconscious God.* New York: Simon & Schuster.

Frazer, Sir James George. 1922. *The Golden Bough: A Study in Magic and Religion.* New York: Touchstone.

Freud, Sigmund. 1900. *The Interpretation of Dreams.* In *The Complete Psychological Works: Standard Edition,* Volumes 4 & 5. London: Hogarth Press.

Freud, Sigmund. 1913. *Totem and Taboo: Some Points of Agreement Between the Mental Lives of Savages and Neurotics.* New York: Vintage Books.

Freud, Sigmund. 1927. *The Future of an Illusion.* NY: W.W. Norton & Co., Inc.

Freud, Sigmund. 1930. *Civilization and Its Discontents.* London: Penguin.

Freud, Sigmund. 1939. *Moses and Monotheism.* NY: Vintage Books.

Fromm, Erich. 1951. *The Forgotten Language: An Introduction to the Understanding of Dreams, Fairy Tales, and Myths.* New York: Grover Press, Inc.

Fuglesang, Andreas. 1982. *About Understanding: Ideas and Observations on Cross-Cultural Communication.* NY: Decade Media Books.

Goldman, R. 1964. *Religious Thinking from Childhood through Adolescence.* London: Routledge & Kegan Paul.

Goody, Jack. 1977. *The Domestication of the Savage Mind.* Cambridge: Cambridge Universoty Press.

Hamer, D. 2004. *The God Gene: How Faith is Hardwired into Our Genes.* New York: Anchor Books.

Harner, Michael J. 1973. *Hallucinogens and Shamanism.* New York: Oxford University Press.

Huxley, Aldous. 1944. *The Perennial Philosophy.* NY: Harper & Brothers.

Huxley, Aldous. 1954. *The Doors of Perception.* NY: Harper & Row Publishers.

Huxley, Aldous. 1961. "Visionary Experience." A speech delivered at the XIV International Congress of Applied Psychology. Copenhagen, Denmark, 1961. In *The Highest State of Consciousness,* John White (ed.), 1972. New York: Anchor Books.

James, William. 1902. *The Varieties of Religious Experience: A Study in Human Nature.* New York: The Modern Library.

Jaspers, Karl. 1949. *The Origin and Goal of History.* London: Routledge & Kegan Paul.

Jaynes, Julian. 1976. *The Origin of Consciousness in the Breakdown of the Bicameral Mind.* New York: Houghton Mifflin.

Jaynes, Julian. 1986. "Consciousness and the Voices of the Mind." Julian Jaynes's invited Bauer Lecture presented at the 1983 McMaster-Bauer Symposium on Consciousness. First printed in *Canadian Psychology*, April 1986, Vol. 27 (2).

Jones, Ernest. 1951. *On the Nightmare.* New York: Liveright Publishing Corp.

Jung, Carl G. 1936. *Archetypes and the Collective Unconscious.* In *Collected Works*, Vol. 9.

Jung, Carl G. 1939. *The Integration of the Personality.* In *Collected Works*, Vol. 11.

Jung, Carl G. 1951. *Two Essays on Analytical Psychology.* In *Collected Works*, Vol. 7.

Jung, Carl G. 1953. *Collected Works.* H. Read, M. Fordham & G. Adler, eds. Princeton: Princeton University Press.

Jung, Carl G. 1960. *Psychological Aspects of the Mother Archetype.* In *Collected Works*, Vol. 9.

Jung, Carl G. 1961. *Memories, Dreams and Reflections.* New York: Random House.

Jung, Carl G. 1962. *Psychology and Religion.* New Haven: Yale University Press.

Jung, Carl G. 1964. *Man and His Symbols.* New York: Doubleday.

Jung, Carl G. 1971. *The Portable Jung.* Joseph Campbell, Ed.. New York: Viking Penguin, Inc.

Kuijsten, Marcel, ed. 2006. *Reflections on the Dawn of Consciousness: Julian Jaynes's Bicameral Mind Theory Revisited.* Henderson, NV: Julian Jaynes Society.

Laing, R.D. 1969. "Transcendental Experience." In *The Highest State of Consciousness*, John White, ed., 1972. New York: Anchor Books.

Lewis, C.S. 1936. *The Allegory of Love: A Study in Medieval Tradition.* London: Oxford University Press.

Lewis-Williams, D., and Pearce, D. 2005. *Inside the Neolithic Mind.* New York: Thames & Hudson, Inc.

Maslow, Abraham H. 1964. *Religions, Values, and Peak-Experiences.* NY: Penguin Books.

May, Rollo. 1991. *The Cry for Myth.* New York: Norton.

McCrone, John. 1991. *The Ape That Spoke.* New York: Avon Books.

McGilchrist, Iain. 2009. *The Master and His Emissary: The Divided Brain and the Making of the Western World.* New Haven, CT: Yale University Press.

McLuhan, Marshall. 1964. *Understanding Media.* NY: McGraw Hill.

McLuhan, Marshall. 1965. *The Gutenberg Galaxy: The Making of Typographic Man.* Toronto: University of Toronto Press.

McLuhan, Marshall. 1967. *The Medium Is the Message.* NY: Random House, Inc.

McLuhan, Marshall, and Fiore, Quentin. 1968. *War and Peace in the Global Village.* NY: Simon & Schuster, Inc.

McLuhan, Marshall, and Powers, Bruce. 1989. *The Global Village: Transformations in World Life and Media in the 21st Century.* New York: Oxford University Press.

McLuhan, Marshall. 1995. *Essential McLuhan.* Eric McLuhan and Frank Zingrone, eds. New York: Basic Books.

Ong, Walter J. 1982. *Orality and Literacy: The Technologizing of the Word.* NY: Routledge.

Paloutzian, Raymond F. 1996. *Invitation to the Psychology of Religion*, 2nd Ed. Boston: Allyn & Bacon.

Pals, D. L. 1996. *Seven Theories of Religion.* New York: Oxford University Press.

Persinger, M.A. 1983. "Religious and mystical experiences as artifacts of temporal lobe function: a general hypothesis." *Perceptual Motor Skills*, 1983, Dec: 57 (3, pt. 2):1255–62.

Piaget, J. 1929. *The Child's Conception of the World.* London: Kegan Paul, Trench, Trubner and Co.

Piaget, Jean. 1952. *The Origins of Intelligence in Children.* New York: International University Press.

Piaget, Jean. 1962. *Play, Dreams, and Imitation in Childhood.* New York: W.W. Norton & Co., Inc.

Pinker, Steven. 2004. "The Evolutionary Psychology of Religion." An address presented at the annual meeting of the Freedom from Religion Foundation, Madison, Wisconsin, October 29, 2004, on receipt of "The Emperor's New Clothes Award."

Pratt, James Bissett. 2005. *The Religious Consciousness.* New York: Cosimo Classics.

Prince, R., and Savage, C. 1966. "Mystical States and the Concept of Regression. In *The Highest State of Consciousness*. John White, ed. 1972. New York: Anchor Books.

Raglan, Lord. *The Hero: A Study in Tradition, Myth and Drama*. 1956. In *In Quest of the Hero*. 1990. Princeton, NJ: Princeton University Press.

Ramachandran, V.S., and Blakeslee, S. 1998. *Phantoms in the Brain: Probing the Mysteries of the Human Mind*. New York: HarperCollins.

Ramachandran, V.S. 2011. *The Tell-Tale Brain: A Neuroscientist's Quest for What Makes Us Human*. New York: Norton.

Rank, Otto. 1914. *The Myth of the Birth of the Hero*. In, *In Quest of the Hero*. 1990. Princeton, NJ: Princeton University Press.

Rossetti, Stephen. 2011. *Why Priests Are Happy: A Study of the Psychological and Spiritual Health of Priests*. Notre Dame, IN: Ave Maria Press.

Sacks, Oliver. 2013. *Hallucinations*. New York: Vintage Books.

Sagan, Carl. 1977. *The Dragons of Eden: Speculations on the Evolution of Human Intelligence*. New York: Ballantine Books.

Sagan, Carl, and Druyan, Ann. 1992. *Shadows of Forgotten Ancestors: A Search for Who We Are*. New York: Random House.

Schwartz, Howard. 2004. *Tree of Souls: The Mythology of Judaism*. New York: Oxford University Press.

Scribner, S., and Cole, M. 1981. *The Psychology of Literacy*. Cambridge, MA: Harvard University Press.

Shermer, Michael. 2011. *The Believing Brain*. New York: Times Books.

Silber, M. 2007. *Torah with Targum Onkelos and Rashi Commentary: The Book of Deuteronomy*. New York: BN Publishing.

Silber, M. 2007. *Torah with Targum Onkelos and Rashi Commentary: The Book of Exodus*. New York: BN Publishing.

Silber, M. 2007. *Torah with Targum Onkelos and Rashi Commentary: The Book of Genesis*. New York: BN Publishing.

Silber, M. 2007. *Torah with Targum Onkelos and Rashi Commentary: The Book of Leviticus*. New York: BN Publishing.

Silber, M. 2007. *Torah with Targum Onkelos and Rashi Commentary: The Book of Numbers*. New York: BN Publishing.

Smith, M.B. 1978. "Perspectives on Selfhood." *American Psychologist* 33, 1053–1063.

Spilka, B., Wood, R.W., and Gorsuch, R.L. 1985. *The Psychology of Religion: An Empirical Approach*. Englewood Cliffs, NJ: Prentice Hall.

Stark, Rodney. 2007. *Discovering God: The Origins of the Great Religions and the Evolution of Belief*. New York: HarperCollins Publishers.

Steiner, George. 1991. *Real Presences*. Chicago: Chicago University Press.

Strassman, Rick. 2001. *DMT: The Spirit Molecule*. Rochester, VT: Park Street Press.

Tillich, Paul. 1999. *The Essential Tillich*. F. F. Church, ed. Chicago: University of Chicago Press.

Trachtenberg, Joshua. 1939. *Jewish Magic and Superstition: A Study in Folk Religion*. New York: Forgotten Books.

Tremlin, Todd. 2006. *Minds and Gods: The Cognitive Foundations of Religion*. New York: Oxford University Press.

Tylor, E.B. 1974/1871. *Primitive Culture*. New York: Gordon Press.

Westermann, Diedrich. 1939. *The African Today and Tomorrow*. London: Oxford University Press.

White, John, ed. 1972. *The Highest State of Consciousness*. New York: Anchor Books.

Whitehouse, H. 2000. *Arguments and Icons: Divergent Modes of Religiosity*. Oxford: Oxford University Press.

Wright, Robert. 2009. *The Evolution of God*. New York: Back Bay Books.

Index

adualism *see* animistic mode of perception
Aeschylus 9, 12
agency detection 115–117, 120
Alexander, Eben 105–107
animism *see* animistic mode of perception
animistic mode of perception 85–86, 88–93, 120–123, 136–137, 154–155, 160–161, 164, 168, 192
anthropomorphism 88–90, 95
archetypes 168–169, 175–178
atheism 180–184, 191

Barrett, Justin 54–55, 57, 115
Batson, C.D. 53–54
Becket, Samuel 77
Bergson, Henri 199–200, 205, 214
Blake, William 58, 200
Buber, Martin 37, 93, 120, 154–155, 188, 195–199

Catholic Church 1, 25, 148–152, 157, 180
Charles Bonnet Syndrome 70
cognitive evolution *see* Donald, Merlin
cognitive unity *see* cognitive-perceptual unity
cognitive-perceptual unity 38, 42–52, 56, 58, 69, 71–110, 122–123, 166–167, 175, 187–188, 202, 213–217
Coles, Robert 89–90
critical period for spiritual development 94–97

D'Aquili, Eugene *see* Newberg, Andrew
Dawkins, Richard 2, 24–25, 90–91, 165
deafferentiation 76–77, 106–107
digital media 5, 15–18, 28–36, 42, 48, 72–78, 93–94, 99, 104–110, 153–158, 169, 174–178, 196–198, 202–214

DMT 107–109
Donald, Merlin 11–14, 15–18, 31–35, 39–46, 103–104, 111, 135
doubled consciousness 64–66, 74
dreams 6–7, 9–10, 18–23, 28–35, 43–45, 52, 90, 104–110, 121, 160–161, 164, 168–169, 171
Dyer, Sir Edward 114

eidetic memory 44–46, 70, 78
Einstein, Albert 3, 52, 55
electronic media 153
Eliade, Mircea 194–195
Eliot, T.S. 64

faith 2–4, 56, 187, 191
Farah, Mohammed 37–38, 43, 54, 72, 74, 77, 92
Fitzgerald, F. Scott 64
flatland 5
Frankl, Viktor 171
Freud, Anna 18
Freud, Sigmund 66–67, 82, 164–168
Fromm, Erich 19, 170–171
Fugelsang, Andreas 37–38, 44
fundamentalism 149–153

Geiger, John 65
Gopnik, Alison 83
Guthrie, Stewart 88–89

hallucinations 67–72, 161
Harrison, George 76, 156
hemispheric dominance 38–78
Hippolytus 73
Huxley, Aldous 92, 96
hyperactive agency detection *see* agency detection

245

iconoclasm 128–129, 140, 151–153
idols and idol worship 124–131, 140, 156–158
imaginary friends 90–92

James, William 92, 101, 103, 161–163
Jaynes, Julian 38, 52, 157
Jesus 35, 74–75, 77, 89, 131–132, 141–143, 157–158, 161, 169, 188, 200, 216
Jung, Carl 74, 101, 110, 168–169, 175, 185, 194

Kelemen, Deborah 85
Kurzweil, Ray 30, 109–110, 207, 211

language-based consciousness *see* oral language
Leary, Timothy 156
literacy 13–14, 31, 41–52, 93–97, 133–153, 178–187

MacLean, Paul 19
Marian apparition at knock 1–2
Maslow, Abraham 162, 172–174
mass media *see* electronic media
mathematics 132–133
May, Rollo 97, 99
McGilchrist, Iain 42, 47–48, 51, 214
McLuhan, Marshall 14–17, 35, 42–46, 49, 111, 185–186, 200–205, 216
Mohammed 77
money 131–133
monotheism 139–141, 167
Moore's Law 214
music 145
mystical experience 83–84, 161–163
mystical state of consciousness *see* mystical experience
Mzimu 37–38, 54, 77, 92

near death experience 105–110
neurotheology 6, 24–27, 105
Newberg, Andrew 25, 75, 105–107, 212
nirvana 80–81, 103–110
nominal realism 86–87
numbers *see* mathematics

oral language 13, 40–46, 86–90, 92–94, 96, 111–114, 120–123, 133, 135–146, 148
oral tradition *see* oral language
Otto, Rudolf 191–194

Paleolithic cave paintings 13, 33
paradoxicality 55–58, 99–103, 151–152, 208
Pascal, Blaise 181–182

peak experiences 172–178
perception 58–72
Persinger, Michael 24–26, 29, 74
phantom limbs 66–67
photographic memory *see* eidetic memory
Piaget, Jean 79–83, 85–95, 97–99
Pindar 81
Poe, Edgar Allan 27–28, 98
Pope, Alexander 113
print 147–153
Protestantism 143–153, 157

Qualia 4, 62–63

Ramachandran, V.S. 24–26, 48, 50, 62–63, 66–67, 71
Rank, Otto 81–82, 108
Rossetti, Stephen 84–85

Sacks, Oliver 22–23, 27, 58, 65–66, 68–69, 71, 77
Scriptural Age 141–147
scriptural experience *see* Scriptural Age
scriptures *see* Scriptural Age
Seaford, Richard 131
sexuality 210–214
Shakespeare, William 1, 62, 67, 118, 212
Shermer, Michael 65
singing and song *see* music
singularity 214–217
Sperry, Richard 46–47, 49
Spinoza, Baruch 182–183
spiritual unity *see* cognitive-perceptual unity
Strassman, Rick *see* DMT
synesthesia 63–4, 82–83, 106

technological secularity *see* singularity
temporal lobe epilepsy 25–27
Tennyson, Alfred 31
Theory of Mind 115–120
Thurber, James 70
Tillich, Paul 57, 89, 99, 157, 179, 190, 200–203
Tylor, E.B. 160–161

Unio Mystica 25, 32, 77, 216
Uroboros 103–105

Wallas, Graham 53–54
Whitehouse, H. 148
Wiltshire, Stephen 44
Wordsworth, William 94, 153
written tradition *see* literacy